MW01700328

The First Book of Quicken®

Includes Version 3.0

Gordon McComb

HOWARD W. SAMS & COMPANY
A Division of Macmillan, Inc.
11711 North College, Suite 141, Carmel, IN 46032 USA

FIRST EDITION
SECOND PRINTING—1990

International Standard Book Number: 0-672-27306-3
Library of Congress Catalog Number: 89-64235

Product Director: *Richard Swadley*
Manuscript Editor: *Sara Black*
Production Coordinator: *Becky Imel*
Cover Artist: *Held & Diedrich Design*
Production: *Brad Chinn, Sally Copenhaver, Tami Hughes, William Hurley, Dennis Sheehan, Mary Beth Wakefield*
Indexer: *Sherry Massey*
Technical Reviewer: *C. Herbert Feltner*

Printed in the United States of America

Contents

2 Getting Started with Quicken, 19

3 Setting Up Accounts, 47

6 Keeping Track of Transactions, 93

Introduction

Money. Bread. Cash. Dough. Booty. Moolah. Dollars. Whatever you want to call it, the world revolves around money. If you're like most people, you want to spend your productive hours *making* money, not figuring out where your money goes or how it's spent. With the advent of the personal computer, software publishers have developed programs to make money management easier. Though it was a good thought, the approach taken by these programs left a lot to be desired. They were difficult to use, offered little or no flexibility, and required in-depth knowledge of financial matters and accounting practices.

Quicken, from Intuit, offers something different. This one program for the IBM PC lets you track your checking account, savings, cash, credit cards, investments, rental property, business accounting, payroll, and much, much more. Yet it does this job with surprising simplicity. Quicken is designed to make child's play out of money matters—giving you the ability to track, print, and review all of your financial business.

This is a book on learning Quicken on the IBM PC. With the information contained in this book, you'll be able to use Quicken to create checkbook and savings account registers, print checks, manage cash and credit card accounts, track business accounts receivable and accounts payable, print financial reports, and lots more. *The First Book of Quicken* is a beginner's guide to get you started using Quicken for all your financial affairs.

Though Quicken is not an overly complex program, it does have many features and capabilities that can confuse first-time users. This book pares it all down to manageable size. You'll learn everything you need to know to use Quicken to track all types of finances, including checking and savings accounts, cash, investments, income rental property and even business payroll.

How to Use This Book

The chapters in *First Book of Quicken* are organized in the same manner that you are likely to use the Quicken program.

Chapter 1, "An Introduction to Quicken," is an overview of Quicken. It provides a quick summary of the program, how it works, and what it does.

In Chapter 2, "Getting Started with Quicken," you'll learn how to install the program on floppy or hard disks, how to set up the program to match your computer and printer, how to activate Quicken's commands and menus, and how to access on-line help.

Chapter 3 is "Setting Up Accounts." Here, you'll discover Quicken's five account types and what they're used for. You'll also learn how to start a new accounts, maintain accounts, and back up account data.

Chapter 4, "Writing Checks," explains the heart and soul of Quicken: how to prepare checks and record them as transactions in a check register.

"Maintaining the Check Register," Chapter 5, explains how to access the check register, edit transactions, find transactions using specific search criteria, and more.

Chapter 6 is "Keeping Track of Transactions." This chapter details some of the finer points of Quicken, writing memos in checks, splitting transactions, using categories and classes, and reconciling the checking account to the bank statement.

Chapter 7, "Transaction Shortcuts," highlights two of Quicken's time-savers: memorized transactions and transaction groups.

In Chapter 8, "Printing Checks," you'll learn how to print checks you've written with Quicken. You'll learn how to print all the checks that are waiting and how to select only those checks for printing that you want. You'll also learn how to make sure your printer is properly aligned for check printing and how to diagnose potential problems.

Chapter 9 is "Working with Other Quicken Accounts." Here, you'll discover the ins and outs of using Quicken's cash, credit card, other asset, and other liability account types and how they are used.

Chapter 10, "Creating and Printing Reports," tells you everything you need to know to produce printed reports with Quicken.

"Quicken Applications," in Chapter 11, describes some of the ways you can use Quicken in real-world situations, including monthly budgeting, tracking home improvements, and maintaining business accounts receivable and accounts payable ledgers.

An appendix lists the preset home and business income/expense categories provided with Quicken.

Although you don't have to read this book from cover to cover and in order, at the very least you should start by reading Chapters 1 and 2. These provide an overview of Quicken and how to access its features and capabilities.

Conventions Used in This Book

You need little advance information before you can dive head first into this book. We've used the following conventions to make your trip with Quicken more enjoyable and effective.

This is a beginner's quick start guide to Quicken, but it assumes you are familiar with the IBM PC and its disk operating system. If you are unfamiliar with DOS or how to use your computer, read the instruction manual that came with the computer, or consult one of the many fine books on using the PC and DOS. A good place to start is *Understanding MS-DOS*, published by Howard W. Sams & Company.

Many chapters include step-by-step "Quick Steps" that help you promptly master a particular command or function of Quicken. The Quick Steps outline only the most commonly used Quicken procedures. Refer to the inside front cover of this book for an alphabetical list of Quick Steps.

Trademark Acknowledgments

All terms mentioned in this book that are known to be trademarks or service marks are listed below. In addition, terms suspected of being trademarks or service marks have been appropriately capitalized. Howard W. Sams & Company cannot attest to the accuracy of this information. Use of a term in this book should not be regarded as affecting the validity of any trademark or service mark.

IBM, IBM PC, and IBM PC AT are registered trademarks of International Business Machines Corporation. IBM PC XT and PS/2 are trademarks of International Business Machines Corporation. Lotus 1-2-3 is a registered trademark of Lotus Development Corp. Microsoft Works is a trademark of Microsoft Corp.

Chapter 1

An Introduction to Quicken

1

In This Chapter

- *Using Quicken in home or business*
- *What Quicken will do for you*
- *A typical application of Quicken*
- *Computer hardware you'll need*
- *Terms you'll want to know*

Quicken. Even the name promises fast results. Speed and ease-of-use are the secrets behind Quicken, the number one best-selling home/business finance program for the IBM PC and compatibles. In one package, you get all the tools you need to keep track of money matters at home or in a small business. Quicken lets you juggle just about any number of checking and savings accounts, credit cards, and even cash and miscellaneous income and expenses.

While Quicken was designed so that you could install it in your computer and be crunching numbers in less than 15 minutes, its finer points are slightly more obscure. In this book, you'll learn everything you need to know about using Quicken in your day-to-day affairs, along with some tricks of the trade that will make you a Quicken pro.

This chapter introduces you to Quicken: what it does, how it does it, and what you can expect from it. You'll see how Quicken lets you set up flexible accounts for your income and expenses, how you can automate check-writing, and ways in which Quicken makes bank statement reconciliation child's play.

What Is Quicken?

2 Quicken is a home and business finance program that helps you keep track of expenses and income. No matter where you use Quicken, it has features of particular interest to both the home and the business user.

In the Home

On the home front, Quicken can be used to maintain your checking and savings accounts, track the checks you write (or withdrawals you make from savings), and balance that against your deposits.

Just as in real life, Quicken uses checks for paying out money and a check register to keep track of everything. The check-writing screen, shown in Figure 1-1, is one of Quicken's strong points. To pay a bill, you just fill in the check. Quicken automatically catalogs it in the register, which is illustrated in Figure 1-2.

Quicken can print your checks for you—using almost any dot matrix, ink jet, daisywheel, or laser printer on the market. You can order specially printed checks that are suitable for use with Quicken. Several styles are available, including wallet-size, standard (three checks per 8-1/2 by 11-inch sheet), and payroll/voucher.

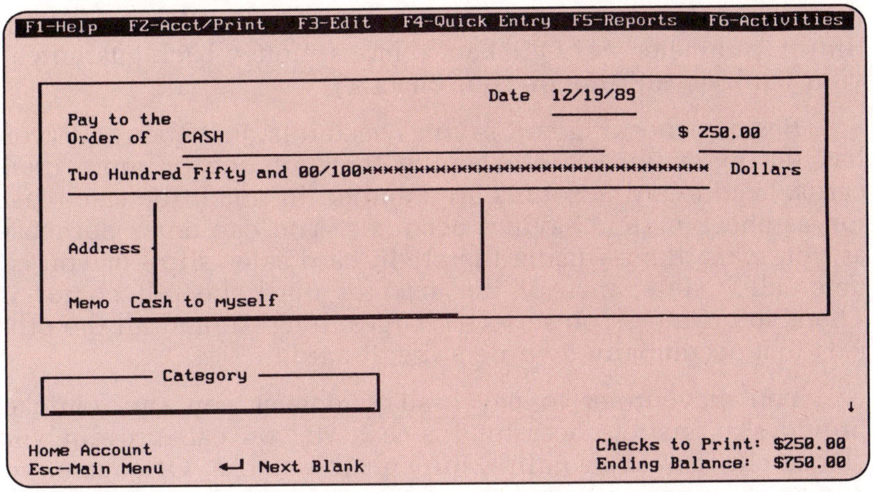

Figure 1-1. A sample of the check-writing screen.

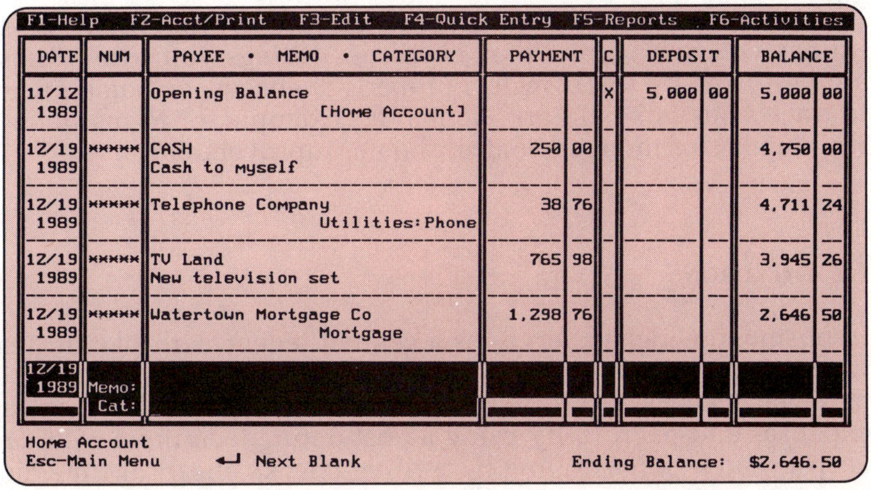

Figure 1-2. A sample of the check register screen.

Of course, you don't need to use Quicken to print the checks, but you'll find it makes bill-paying much easier. Quicken checks follow the rules and regulations of the North American banking community, so even though you don't order the checks from your bank, your bank will still honor them. (Intuit, publisher's of Quicken, offers a money-back guarantee if your bank doesn't honor your checks.)

Besides checking and savings accounts, just about everyone has the extra burden of keeping track of one or more credit cards. Credit card accounts are handled in much the same fashion as checking and savings accounts. You can enter purchases as you make them—using the credit card sales slip—or you can defer all maintenance of the account until the bill comes in. Then, you can tack on service charges, interest, and all the other fees that accompany owning a credit card.

You may prefer to pay cash whenever you can. Quicken provides a separate account for cash so you can prevent your "loose change" from falling through the cracks. Of course, you don't need to record every purchase you make (10 cents for the bubble gum machine will hardly make a difference). Quicken automatically accounts for miscellaneous expenses so the balance is always correct.

Quicken offers two additional account types: Other Assets (things you own) and Other Liabilities (things you owe). These are best used by the investor, property manager, or home owner to track sales of stocks and bonds, for example, or to maintain a running list of money spent on home improvements.

In Business

In business, Quicken serves as a general ledger with payroll features. You still use the checking account to monitor expenses, but you can easily differentiate between general operating expenses and payroll. By using a post-dating technique, you can keep a watch on cash flow by writing checks ahead of time and seeing what expenses you'll have throughout the month (you can even project several months in advance). When your bills are due—assuming you receive your money as you expect—you can mail the checks.

In addition to printing checks, Quicken prints a number of reports. These reports can be used by both the home and business user, but they really make a difference in a business environment. For example, you can quickly prepare a payroll expense report, an accounts receivable or accounts payable report, a cash flow report, or a breakdown of spending by job, client, department, property, or project. A sample business report (a profit and loss statement) is shown in Figure 1-3.

```
                              Sample P&L
                        1/ 1/89 Through 12/31/89
          Home Account
          12/19/89
                                                  1/ 1/89-
               Category Description               12/31/89
          ------------------------------------   ------------
          INCOME/EXPENSE
            EXPENSES
              Mortgage                                1,298.76
              Water, Gas, Electric:
                Phone                           38.76
                                             ---------
              Total Water, Gas, Electric                 38.76
              Expenses - Other                        1,015.98
                                                     ---------
            TOTAL EXPENSES                            2,353.50
                                                     ---------
          TOTAL INCOME/EXPENSE                       -2,353.50

Home Account
Esc-Create report              F1-Help                       F8-Print
```

Figure 1-3. This profit and loss report is just a few keystrokes away.

What Quicken Will Do for You

At its most basic level, Quicken is a glorified calculator, automatically tallying your income and expenses and providing an instant balance. Barring some freak glitch in your computer, you can be sure the balance will be correct. If you started with $100 in your checking account and wrote a check for $30, Quicken will display a balance of $70. It doesn't mistake $30 for $50 and report that you have only $50 left, nor does it press the wrong calculator buttons and arrive at some wild amount.

Quicken also allows you to know where your money is coming from and where it's going. Getting a handle on your money is more important today than it's ever been. With the average price of a car topping $20,000 and house prices skyrocketing more than $50,000 in one year, it makes good sense to watch where every penny goes. That's not easy when you work with pencil and paper, but Quicken does it for you almost automatically.

Quicken lets you set up income and expense categories. These *categories* help you identify where your money is coming from and where it's going. For example, let's say you receive your regular salary each week from your employer plus an extra $200 from a trust fund. You have two sources for income, so you create two income expenses: payroll and trust fund. With each deposit you make into your checking or savings account, you use the categories to identify where the money came from.

The same applies to expenses, although you're likely to have far more expense categories than income categories. For instance, you may have categories for rent, food, car payment, clothing, and entertainment. With each check you write, you record the category in the memo area of the check—rent, car payment, whatever.

At the end of the week, month, or year—or any other time frame for that matter—you can use Quicken to list expenses and income by category. The report, like the one in Figure 1-4, will include all the deposits you've made and all the checks you've written. Each category will be totaled for you, so you can quickly see how your money was spent.

Quicken lets you set up categories as you go. Even if you initially established just ten categories, you can expand it to dozens or even hundreds, if necessary.

In addition, you can create categories under other categories—*subcategories*—to keep track of similar but separate items. This is most helpful in a small business where you may want to separate the expense of, say, printing by the type of printing done. Here's an example:

Main Category	Subcategories
Printing	Postcards
	Envelopes
	Letterhead
	Business cards

Akin to categories are *classes*. These help you assign kinds of expenses to people, places, or times. You most often will use classes as individual entries under categories. For instance,

Sample Category
1/ 1/89 Through 12/31/89

Home Account   Page 1
12/19/89

Date	Num	Payee	Memo	Category	Clr	Amount
		INCOME/EXPENSE				
		EXPENSES				
		Mortgage				
12/19	*****	Watertown Mortgage		Mortgage		-1,298.76
		Total Mortgage				-1,298.76
		Water, Gas, Electric:				
		Phone				
12/19	*****	Telephone Company		Utilities:Phone		-38.76
		Total Phone				-38.76
		Total Water, Gas, Electric				-38.76
		Expenses - Other				
12/19	*****	CASH	Cash to myself			-250.00
12/19	*****	TV Land	New television			-765.98
		Total Expenses - Other				-1,015.98
		TOTAL EXPENSES				-2,353.50
		TOTAL INCOME/EXPENSE				-2,353.50
		BALANCE FORWARD				
		Home Account				
11/12		Opening Balance		[Home Account]	X	5,000.00
		Total Home Account				5,000.00
		TOTAL BALANCE FORWARD				5,000.00
		OVERALL TOTAL				2,646.50

Figure 1-4. Sample category report.

under the category of printing, you could assign the expenses to individual jobs (“people”). In that way, when you get ready to bill for the job, you can easily extract all the expenses for the particular job.

Main Category	Subclasses
Printing	Anderson Meat Packing
	Bill's Garage Door Opener Co.
	Uncle Walter's Newsstand

No matter how you decide to set up Quicken for your home or business, the end result of tracking your income and expenses is to make your money last longer. You may not be aware of how much money is spent each month on eating out, for example. Upon seeing the facts, you may have second thoughts the next time you don't see anything appetizing in the kitchen and suggest a quick bite to eat at the corner restaurant.

Or, you may find that you're not spending as much money on clothing or vacations as you could. With the figures in front of you, you can prepare a quick budget for redistributing your expenses among some of the items you didn't think you could afford.

Quicken can practically automate tax calculations, which is a feature that is as important as regular check-ups on your financial health. If you've indicated those items that are tax deductible and those that are not, Quicken will prepare a report that itemizes your income and expenses and lists how you can apply them to your tax forms. Quicken provides data-compatibility with the JK Lasser's Your Income Tax and TurboTax packages. Use of these ancillary programs is not covered in this book.

The Process of Using Quicken

The way you use Quicken depends on the kinds of accounts you're tracking with it. The most straightforward application of Quicken is to maintain a single checking account. To open the account:

1. Provide the opening balance.
2. Identify the income and expense categories (you can add or remove categories at any time).

You can now write one or more checks. Quicken automatically numbers and dates the checks, but you can change these if you like. To write a check, you enter the payee, the amount, and optionally an address and memo. If you're using Quicken to print checks, you can either print the check now or wait until you've written more and print them all at once.

The check register lets you make changes to checks you've written but not yet printed, void checks, write in deposits, include automated teller machine (ATM) withdrawals, add service charges, and perform all other regular check register duties. Quicken initially organizes the transactions (e.g., checks you've written and deposits you've made) in the order you entered them. When you print checks, the checks are re-ordered by number. Other transactions are re-ordered by date, so you can find them easily.

Use the list of transactions compiled by Quicken to make sure that your balance corresponds to the balance the bank says you have when you receive your bank statement. This entails subtracting deposits that have not yet shown up in the statement, adding checks that have not yet cleared, and making adjustments for any service fees. If the reports match, the balances agree. If Quicken and the bank disagree, the program tells you the amount of the error. You can then look for items you missed.

You can print reports that show how your money is coming and going at any time, but preferably after you're sure the Quicken check register accurately reflects the condition of your checking account. Quicken provides the following personal and business reports:

Personal
- Cash flow
- Monthly budget
- Itemized categories
- Tax summary
- Account balances

Business
- Profit and loss statement
- Cash flow
- Accounts payable, by vendor
- Accounts receivable, by customer
- Job/project
- Payroll
- Balance sheet

These reports are generated by Quicken using predesignated defaults. If you don't like the way Quicken prepares a report, you can design your own custom reports of transactions, summaries, budgets, and account balances. For example, as shown in Figure 1-5 for the Create Summary Report, you can restrict transactions between certain dates, control row and column headings, and indicate which accounts to include in the report.

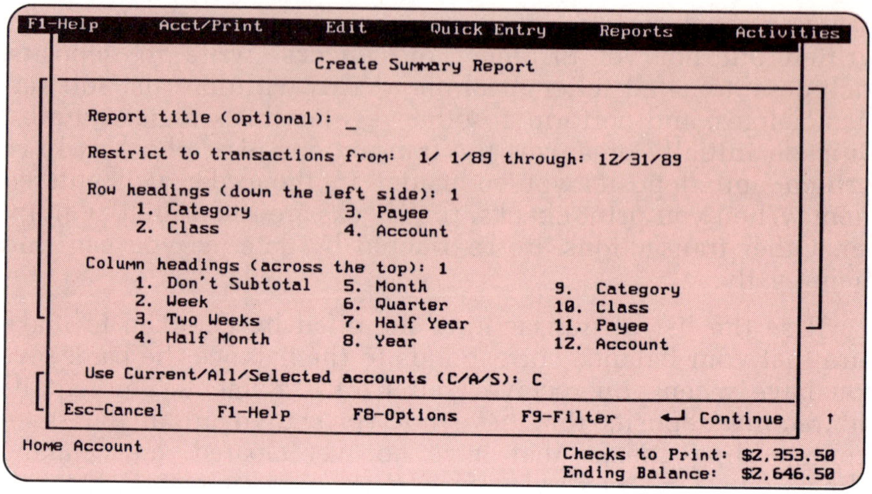

Figure 1-5. The Create Summary Report window.

The Quicken Way

Quicken is completely menu driven. Your available choices are shown on the screen. Quicken has two types of menus:

- Pop-up box
- Pull-down

The pop-up box menu, such as the one shown in Figure 1-6, presents a list of commands. Beside each option is a number or letter. You select the command by pressing the appropriate key on the keyboard. You can also select the command by moving the selector (a highlight or arrow) over the item and pressing the Enter key. Quicken uses pop-up box menus when it's not displaying anything else on the screen.

Pull-down menus, like the one in Figure 1-7, are used to select an option or command while writing checks or working an account register. You "pull" the menu into view only when you need it. Pull-down menus are activated by pressing one of

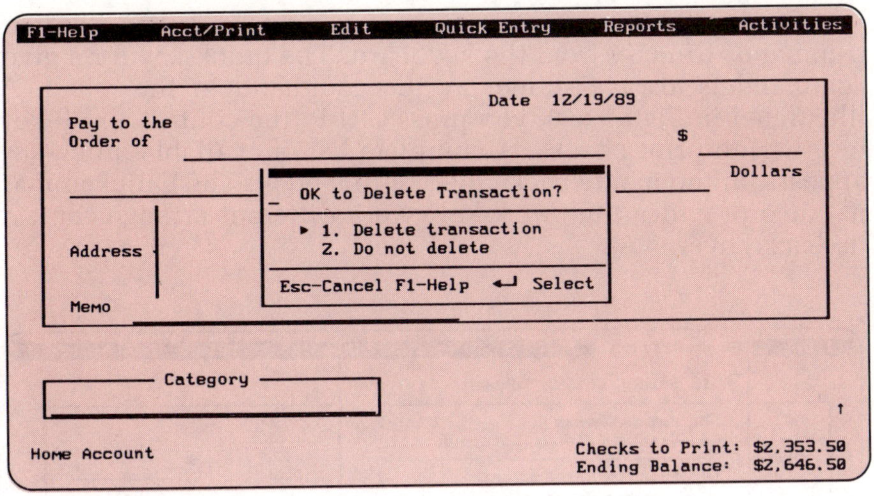

Figure 1-6. Sample pop-up box menu in Quicken.

the function keys on the keyboard. For example, to choose the Reports menu, press the F5 key when in the Write Checks or check register screen.

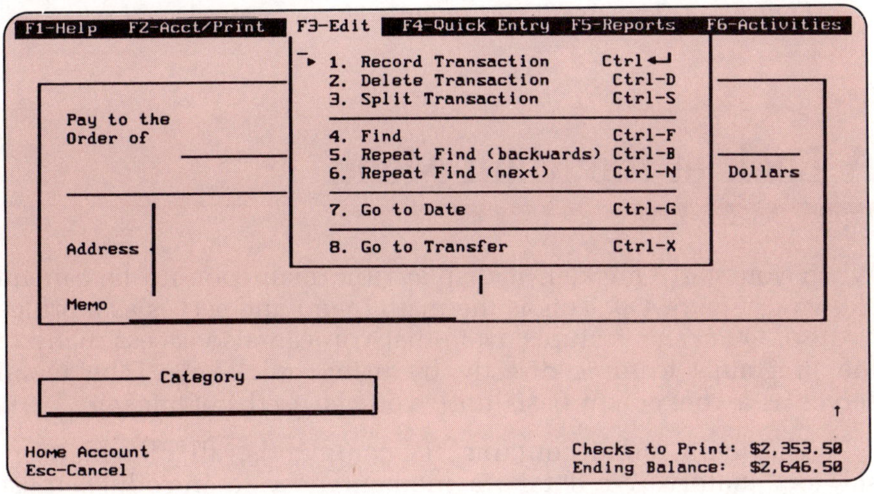

Figure 1-7. Sample Quicken pull-down menu.

Quicken uses numerous quick-keys to activate common commands directly from the keyboard. The quick-key for a given command is always shown by the command in the menu. As illustrated in Figure 1-8, you press Ctrl-P (the control and P keys together) to print checks. A complete list of available quick-keys appears on the inside back cover of this book. The Quicken manual also provides the quick-keys, in a different arrangement, on its back cover.

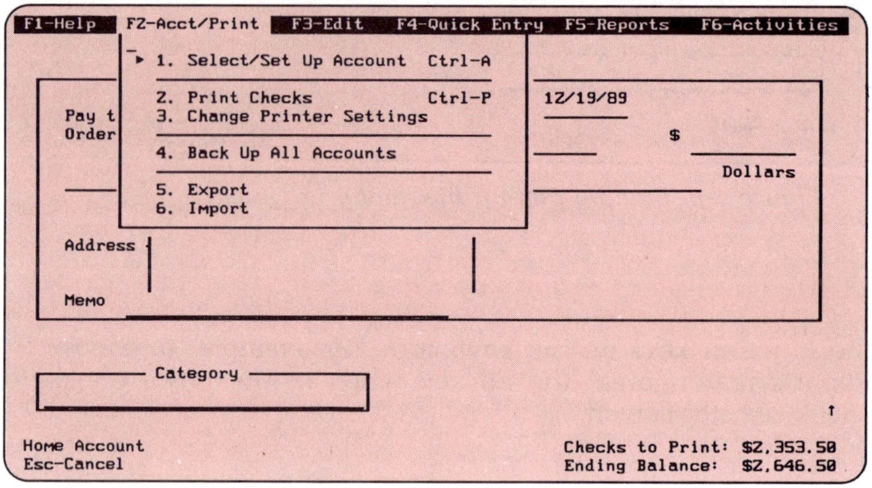

Figure 1-8. The Acct/Print menu.

A Look at the Main Menu

When you start Quicken, it displays the main pop-up box menu shown in Figure 1-9. This is the main menu and serves as a bridge to all of Quicken's features. Note that you can also access many of the program's features directly by using quick-keys. The menu serves as a convenient basis until you get used to Quicken.

The main menu contains six commands, all of which are self-explanatory. We'll take a moment now to introduce these commands and to note where to find more information about them in the remainder of this book.

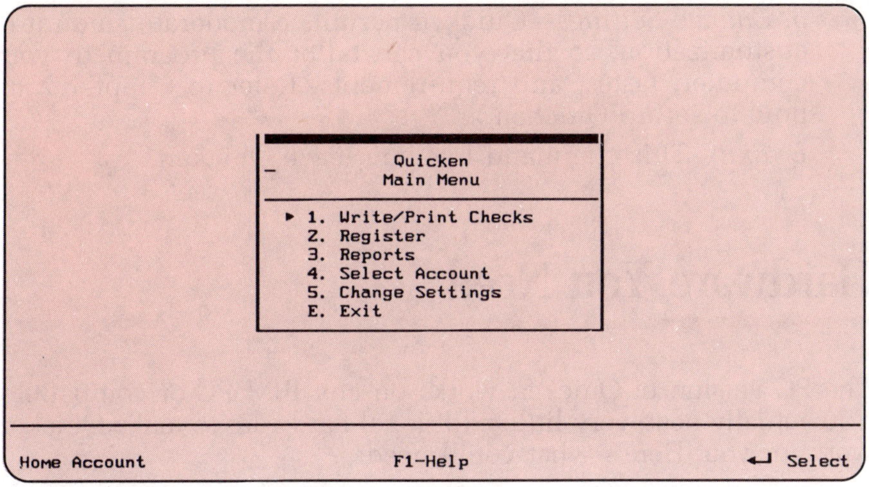

Figure 1-9. The Quicken main menu, the bridge between Quicken's functions.

1. *Write/Print Checks*—This command lets you write checks and optionally print them. When you write a check, it's automatically added to the register. See Chapters 4 and 8 on writing and printing checks, respectively.

2. *Register*—The register is where you maintain all checking account transactions. If you are using Quicken to maintain other account types, you record the transactions in their respective registers. For more information on registers see Chapter 5.

3. *Reports*—Reports provide a convenient summary of your account transactions. See Chapter 10 on how to prepare printed reports.

4. *Select Account*—You can maintain any number of accounts with Quicken. (You are limited to 255 accounts per account group, but you can have as many account groups as you want.) The Select Account command allows you to select a previously created account, or to start a new one. See Chapter 3 for information on setting up and changing accounts.

5. Change Settings—Quicken permits a moderate amount of customization, so that you can tailor the program to your computer, tastes, and requirements. Refer to Chapter 2 on how to set up Quicken.

E. Exit—This command lets you leave Quicken.

Hardware You Need

The PC version of Quicken works on any IBM PC or compatible. You actually need very little additional hardware to make Quicken work for you. Here's what you'll need:

IBM PC, XT, AT, PS/2 or a close compatible
At least 320 kilobytes of RAM
Monochrome or color monitor
DOS 2.0 or later (3.0 or later is recommended.)

Quicken will work from either floppy disks or a hard disk. Your work will go faster if you use a hard disk. The Quicken program and data files consume less than 1 megabyte of hard disk space. If you don't have a hard disk, you can still achieve good results using floppy disks. You'll need a minimum of two 5-1/4-inch drives or one 3-1/2-inch drive.

Quicken *does not* use a mouse or other alternate input device, nor does it need a graphics monitor and display adapter. The Write Checks and check register screens are produced using standard display characters. Of course, if you happen to have a mouse connected to your computer, you can leave it there; Quicken won't mind. You can also use a graphics display with Quicken. When you run Quicken, the display will switch to text mode automatically.

Quicken can be used as effectively with a color monitor as with a monochrome monitor. Note, however, that using a color display is a little easier on the eyes. Quicken allows you to select a color scheme, including light blue with dark blue, red with gray, shades of gray, and white with blue. If you have a color display you can experiment with each color palette to find the one you like best.

If you're planning to use Quicken to print checks or reports, you'll need some type of printer. An impact printer, such as a dot matrix or daisywheel, is recommended for printing checks, although you can also use ink jet and laser printers. Because laser printers print an entire page at a time, you need to order special "laser checks."

You *cannot* use a thermal printer to print checks, as the check stock is not made with thermal paper. You can, however, print with a thermal transfer printer. These produce an image by melting a waxy ink from a ribbon onto the paper. Keep in mind that both ink jet and thermal transfer printers work best with a smooth, polished paper. Nonimpact printers, which include laser, ink jet, and thermal transfer, cannot be used in multipart (NCR) type checks.

Some Useful Terms

Throughout this book we'll be using some basic financial terms. You probably know the meanings of some, if not all, of these terms, but if you don't, here's a quick review of the more common ones. Note that Quicken generally eschews the more exotic financial terms. We'll keep within that tradition, but we'll use some additional terms common in banking and financial affairs.

account Any one of several independent records of money or financial transactions. In Quicken, accounts are subdivided into type: Bank (checking and savings), Credit, Cash, Other Asset, and Other Liability deposited at a bank.

asset Something you own. These include cash, real estate, office furniture, and the clothes on your back. See also *liability.*

automated teller machine Also called an ATM. A machine that performs the duties of a bank teller, including accepting cash and checks for deposits and paying cash for withdrawals. It is often friendlier than its human counterpart.

balance The difference between the money that was originally in an account (called the starting balance) and the payments you made against that money. If you start out with $1,000 in the bank, and write $900 in checks, the balance is $100.

cash flow The amount of money you receive versus the amount of money you spend. If you receive more money in a given period of time than you spend, then you have a positive cash flow. If you spend more money than you receive, your cash flow is negative.

category A means of classifying income and expenses. As applied to income, a category indicates the source of the income; as applied to expenses, a category indicates what your money is being spent on.

class Another means of specifying how money is spent. Classes are generally limited to classifying by people, places, or times.

clear A check that is acknowledged by the bank and shows up as being paid on your statement. Cleared items also pertain to credit card purchases (when they show up on your bill).

credit Apart from the usual meaning, the term also means a transaction where you add money to your account. It's synonymous with *deposit.*

debit A transaction where you subtract money from your account. An example is a check or an ATM withdrawal.

deposit A transaction where you add money to your account.

ending balance The money you end up with after you've tallied up all credits and debits.

liability Things you owe. These include the things you haven't yet paid for in full, including real estate, office furniture, and the clothes on your back. See also *asset.*

overdrawn Also called an overdraft, trying to withdraw more funds from your account than you have. If you write a check and don't have funds to cover it, it "bounces" back from your bank as an overdraft.

payee Who you're writing the check to. It can be a person or a company.

payment A transaction subtracted from your account. A typical payment is a check you write.

post-date To provide some future date on a transaction. With Quicken, post-dating is most often used to maintain a positive cash flow. For example, you write all the checks for a given month but date the checks for the days they are due. This helps Quicken to know that you're not overdrawn, even if you don't currently have enough money in the bank to pay all the checks. As money that you're expecting comes in, you can mail the checks.

reconcile To compare the ending balance the bank says you have against the one you say you have. If the ending balances are the same, the account is reconciled. Differences often occur because of check charges, service fees, and other debits that you may not have included in your ending balance.

register A place to record the transactions in an account. In a checking account, the register contains the checks you write, your deposits, and additional debits and credits including ATM withdrawals, service fees, and check charges.

split Dividing a single transaction (such as a check) among several categories or classes.

statement A balance sheet provided by your bank or other financial institution that itemizes your deposits and withdrawals. The statement also shows a beginning and ending balance. A bill from a credit card company serves as a statement.

transaction Any payment from, or a deposit to, an account. A transaction is anything that affects the ending balance of your account, whether it's a $1,200 monthly mortgage payment or a five cent check charge.

transfer To withdraw money from one of your accounts and deposit it into another. You can readily transfer money from your savings to your checking account, for example. (The complete transfer is performed in one step, assuming Quicken is handling both accounts.)

withdrawal Removal of money from. It usually refers to a savings account.

What You Have Learned

This chapter introduced Quicken and its various capabilities. Here's what you should have learned:

- Quicken keeps track of five types of accounts: banking (checking and savings), cash, credit cards, miscellaneous assets, and miscellaneous liabilities.

- Quicken can print your checks using almost any printer.
- By using a post-dating technique, you can keep a watch on cash flow by writing checks ahead of time and seeing what expenses you'll have throughout the month. When your bills are due and you have the cash to cover them, you can mail the checks.
- An important use of Quicken is to keep track of where money is coming from and where it's going.
- Categories and classes let you catalog your money so you can more easily track its origin and destination.
- After setting up your checking account with Quicken, paying bills is a four-step process: write the check, print the check (optional), record any other transactions in the register, and reconcile the register when your statement comes in.
- Quicken provides the following personal reports: cash flow, monthly budget, itemized categories, tax summary, and account balances.
- Quicken provides profit and loss statements and balance sheets as well as the following business reports: cash flow, accounts payable, accounts receivable, job/project, and payroll.
- At a minimum, Quicken needs an IBM PC, XT, AT, PS/2 or compatible with DOS 2.0 or later, 320 kilobytes of RAM, a monochrome or color monitor, and two 5-1/4-inch floppy drives (or one 3-1/2-inch floppy drive).

Chapter 2

Getting Started with Quicken

In This Chapter

- *Installing Quicken*
- *Customizing the program*
- *Starting Quicken*
- *Accessing on-line help*
- *Moving around within Quicken*

Quicken is almost ready to use right out of the box. But if your computer is equipped with a hard disk drive, you'll want to install the Quicken files on the hard drive before using the program. Quicken also works with dual-floppy drive systems. If you're using floppy drives, you should make working copies of the Quicken distribution disks before proceeding.

This chapter tells you how to install Quicken on floppy or hard disks, how to set up and customize Quicken for your computer and printer, and how to use Quicken's basic operating conventions. You'll also get to know a little more about Quicken by creating a "trial" checking account and printing several sample checks.

Installation

Quicken comes on two distribution diskettes. Among the files included on the distribution diskettes is an installation program. This program, called INSTALL, automates the installation process for hard and floppy disk computer systems. INSTALL serves three functions:

- Copies the Quicken files to the appropriate drive and/or directory.
- Updates the CONFIG.SYS file (if any) on your hard disk to ensure that it contains the minimum settings for the FILES= and BUFFERS= commands.
- Optionally installs the Billminder program on your hard disk and adds a command line to your AUTOEXEC.BAT file to run BILLMINDER automatically each time your computer is started.

To use INSTALL, insert the Quicken Help disk into drive A and type

```
INSTALL
```

at the A> prompt. If you are installing Quicken on floppy disks, format one 3-1/2- or two 5-1/4-inch diskettes ahead of time. If you're using a hard disk, you don't need to create a Quicken subdirectory ahead of time. INSTALL will do that for you.

After starting INSTALL, it tells you what it will do before it happens, as shown in Figure 2-1. At any time you can cancel the installation by pressing the Escape key. To go on, press the Enter key.

Floppy Disk Installation

You can install the Quicken files onto a previously formatted disk in drive A or B. At the menu prompt shown in Figure 2-2, choose option 1 for drive A or option 2 for drive B. Press the Enter key when you're done. INSTALL will prompt you when to insert the disks into the appropriate drives during the installation process.

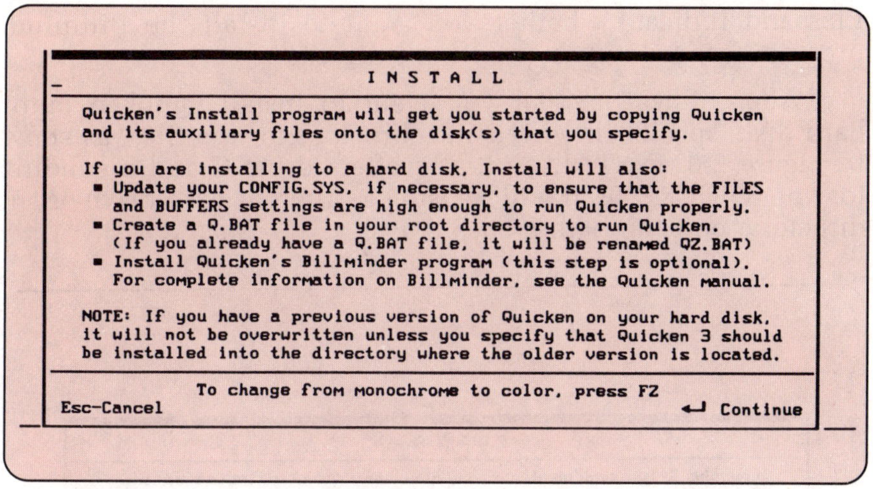

Figure 2-1. You see this opening screen when you first start Quicken.

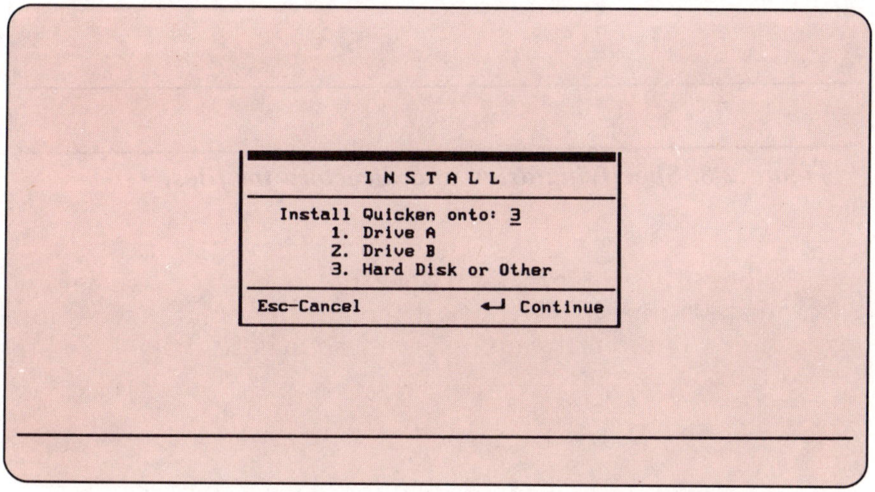

Figure 2-2. The floppy disk/hard disk installation menu.

Hard Disk Installation

Two extra steps are required when installing the Quicken files onto a hard disk: indicate the drive and subdirectory path for the files and indicate whether you want to install the Billminder program (see below) on your hard drive.

After indicating that you want to install Quicken onto a hard disk, specify the drive and directory for the files, as shown in Figure 2-3. INSTALL initially offers drive C and a subdirectory of \QUICKEN3. If you're using a different hard drive or subdirectory, edit the path as desired.

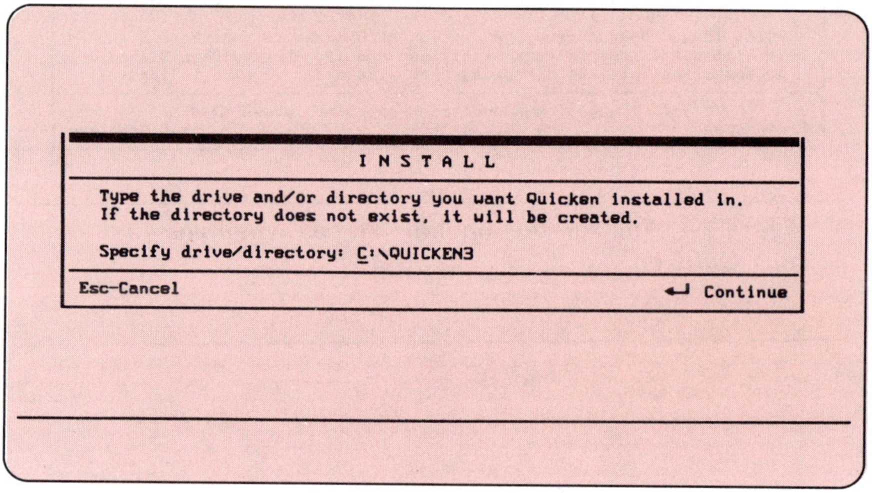

Figure 2-3. Specifying drive and directory for files.

Note: The subdirectory *does not* need to exist before installation. INSTALL will create the subdirectory for you if one doesn't already exist on your hard disk.

Installing Billminder

For hard disk drive users, one of the options during the installation process is whether to include the Billminder program. BILLMINDER is a small program that runs each time your computer is started. The program checks the current date (as set by the DOS clock) and locates recurring bills (like car and mortgage payments) in any of your Quicken registers. If a bill is due, you're prompted to run Quicken so that you can pay it.

You have the option, as shown in Figure 2-4, of either installing BILLMINDER on your hard disk or leaving it off. If you enter No, the Install program does nothing. If you enter Yes, INSTALL places the Billminder program (BILLMIND.EXE) in the root directory of your hard disk and adds a command line to your AUTOEXEC.BAT file. This command line, shown in the example in Figure 2-5, executes BILLMINDER each time you run your computer. (To view this file, type `AUTOEXEC.BAT` at the DOS prompt.)

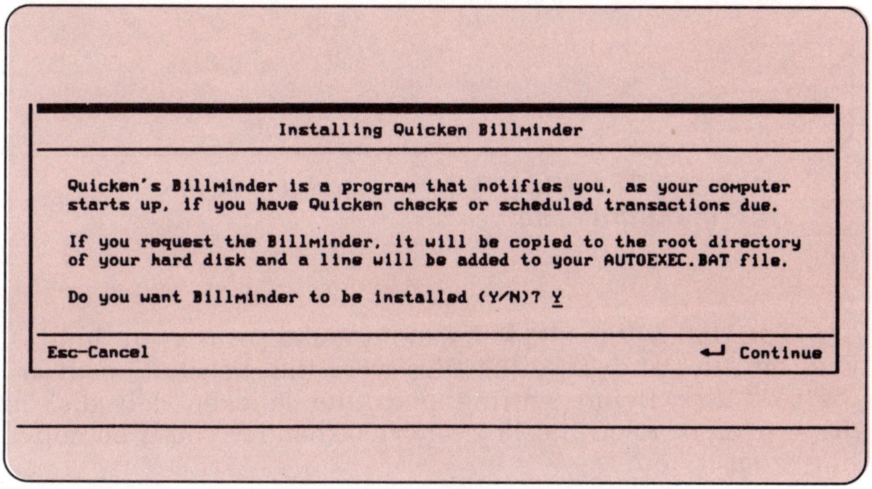

Figure 2-4. The Billminder program install option screen.

Depending on how you've structured your AUTOEXEC.BAT file, you may wish to omit the BILLMIND command line or to move it to another spot in the file. For example, if the last line of your AUTOEXEC.BAT file initiates a menu or starts a DOS shell program, you'll want to place the BILLMIND command line earlier in the AUTOEXEC.BAT file.

Manual Installation

If your computer is equipped with a hard disk drive, you can also manually install the Quicken files and by-pass the automated Install program. Manual installation takes a little less time.

```
C:\>type autoexec.bat
ECHO OFF
path C:\UTIL;C:\;C:\PCTOOLS;C:\DOS;
Mirror C:/TC
PC-CACHE /IA /IB /SIZEXP=512K
cd \batch
prompt $p$g
\ws4\wf
billmind

C:\>_
```

Figure 2-5. The BILLMIND command line in the AUTOEXEC.BAT file.

The following steps create a subdirectory to hold the Quicken files and copy the files from the distribution disks to the hard disk. Before starting, place the Quicken Help disk into drive A or B. Keep the Program disk handy; you'll be copying files from it, too.

Installing Quicken Manually

1. Type `CD \` and press Enter. — Moves to the root directory on your hard drive.
2. Type `MKDIR QUICKEN3` and press Enter. — Creates a subdirectory called QUICKEN3 to hold the Quicken files. (You can use a subdirectory of your own choosing if you wish.)
3. Type `CD \QUICKEN3` and press Enter. — Moves to the QUICKEN3 subdirectory, making it current.
4. Type `COPY A:*.*` and press Enter. (Substitute B for A if you're copying files from drive B.) — Copies all files from the disk in drive A.

After copying is complete, remove the Help disk from the drive, insert Program disk, and repeat step 4. If you want to use the Billminder program, add the following command line to your AUTOEXEC.BAT file:

```
C:\QUICKEN3\BILLMIND
```

This automatically runs BILLMINDER at startup.

Note: If you've placed the Quicken files in a subdirectory other than QUICKEN3, edit the AUTOEXEC.BAT command line as required.

About the Q.BAT File

If you're installing Quicken onto a hard disk drive, the Install program automatically adds a batch file to the root directory of the drive. The Q.BAT batch file starts Quicken quickly. The Q.BAT file works best when the AUTOEXEC.BAT file contains a PATH statement that includes the root directory. With the root included in the PATH statement, you can start Quicken from any subdirectory of your hard disk.

If the AUTOEXEC.BAT file on your hard disk lacks a PATH statement, you can add it easily enough. Using any word processor that can save files in standard DOS (plain text or ASCII format), open the AUTOEXEC.BAT file and, near the end of the file, add

```
PATH=C:\
```

This assumes that drive C is the hard drive you want to use. If it's not, substitute the appropriate drive letter.

If the AUTOEXEC.BAT file already contains a PATH statement, you can include the root directory as an alternate path. For example,

Before `PATH=C:\DOS`

After `PATH=C:\DOS;C:\`

As shown in the example, you can extend the PATH parameters by adding a semicolon, then entering the full DOS path—in this case simply `C:\`.

Customizing Quicken

Once installation is complete, you can immediately use Quicken to handle your financial affairs. But first, you'll probably want to alter some of its preset options to conform to your particular computer and printer. You change Quicken's setting directly inside the program. Although you can change the settings at any time, take a moment right now to familiarize yourself with the available options and how to modify Quicken to suit your needs. Among the settings you can alter are screen color, monitor speed, printer, and password. To make any changes to Quicken, you must first start the program, then choose the Change Settings command.

Q Changing Quicken Settings

1. Press Q then Enter. Alternatively, you can start Quicken by activating the QUICKEN subdirectory, typing `QUICKEN`, and pressing Enter.	Starts Quicken.
2. Press 5.	Chooses Change Settings command. The menu in Figure 2-6 appears. ☐

To select one of the subcommands in the Change Settings menu, type the corresponding number or press the up or down arrow keys to highlight the option you want, then press the Enter key.

Setting the Screen Color

Quicken offers a choice of five "palettes" for displaying its screens. Your choices are monochrome, navy/azure, white/navy,

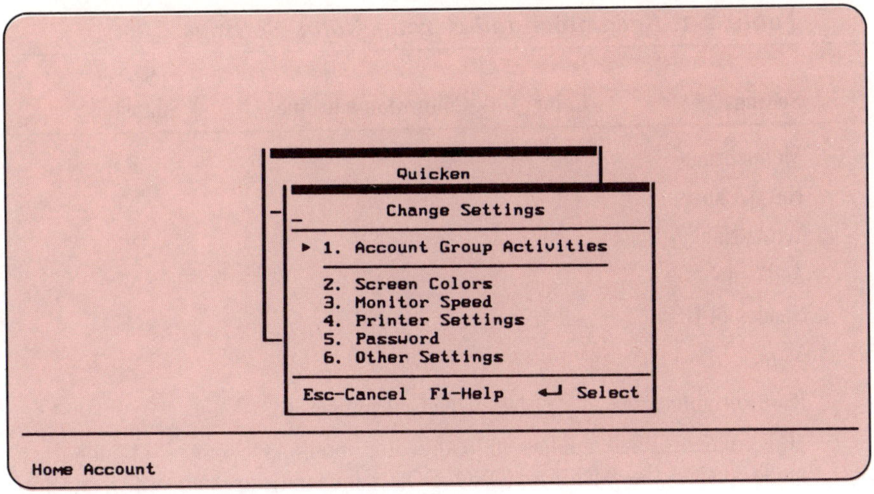

Figure 2-6. The Change Settings menu.

red/gray, and shades of gray. You can use any palette with any type of monitor—color or black & white. Even so, you should avoid using the color palettes if your computer is equipped with a monochrome monitor, or you are using a color monitor in monochrome mode. Table 2-1 shows recommended settings for different monitor types.

Quicken uses a patterned background (see Figure 2-7) when you select any but the Monochrome setting. If you don't want the background, choose Monochrome. Note that the screen shots throughout this book were made with the Monochrome setting—the pattern does not appear.

To change the screen color (from the Change Settings menu):

1. Press 2. This selects the Screen Colors option.
2. In the Screen Colors menu, press the number that corresponds to the screen color you want. For example, to choose Red/Gray, press 4.

Setting the Monitor Speed

If you're using a Color Graphics Adapter (CGA) monitor, you can select Fast or Slow monitor speed.

Table 2-1. Recommended Screen Color Settings.

Settings	Color	Color/Monochrome*	Screen Snapshot**
Monochrome	R	R	R
Navy/Azure	R	NR	NR
White/Navy	R	NR	NR
Red/Gray	R	NR	NR
Shades of Gray	R	NR	NR

Notes

R = Recommended NR = Not recommended

*Color/monochrome applies to both color monitors operated in monochrome mode (using the MODE=MONO DOS command) or standard monochrome monitors.

**Screen snapshot includes Hijaak, Hotshot, and many other screen memory programs that take a "snapshot" of the display and store it on disk or print it on a printer. Unless the image is saved in color, highlighted text within Quicken will not appear.

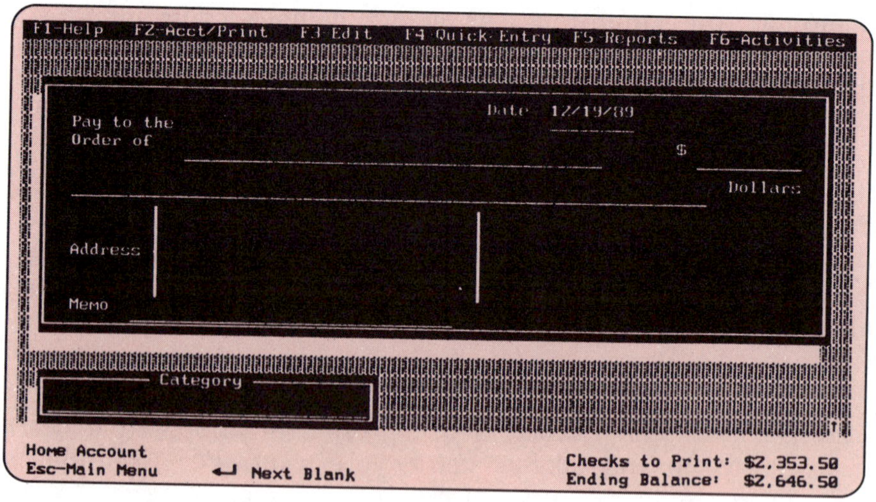

Figure 2-7. A sample of the patterned background provided by Quicken.

The Slow setting causes the display to write text somewhat slower than normal, but "snow" (caused by the flicker of the cursor as it scans across the screen) *does not* appear during text scrolling and changes.

The Fast setting causes the display to write text at the usual speed, but snow appears when scrolling or changing text.

The Fast and Slow settings make no difference if you're using a display adapter other than the CGA.

To change the monitor speed (from the Change Settings menu):

1. Press 4. This selects the Monitor Speed option.
2. You have two choices, Fast or Slow. Choose the speed you want from the Screen Update Speed window.

Setting Printer Functions

Quicken is designed to print checks and reports. You don't have to print anything with Quicken, if you don't want to, but you'll get the most from the program if you take advantage of its printing features. Before you can use Quicken to print checks or reports, however, you must indicate the type of printer you have and how it's connected to your computer.

You must furnish four main tidbits of information to Quicken about your printer:

- *Type of printer,* usually by make and model.
- *Printing style,* such as normal or compressed.
- *Interface port* used to connect the computer to the printer.
- *Settings for general printing,* including lines per page, margins, and standard print pitch (normally 10 characters per inch).

Follow these steps to select a printer from the Change Settings menu:

1. Press 3. This selects the Printer Settings option.
2. Choose a printer setting type, as shown in Figure 2-8. Quicken separates its printing functions into three discrete areas: check printing, report printing, and alternate printing. The remaining steps are the same no matter which printer setting type you select. However, if you plan on using

Quicken to print both checks and reports, you need to change the settings for both Check Printer and Report Printer.

3. From the list shown in Figure 2-9 (not all of the available printers are displayed at once), select the printer you wish to use. To select a printer, highlight it (with the cursor keys) and press the Enter key. See Table 2-2 for a directory of printers Quicken supports.

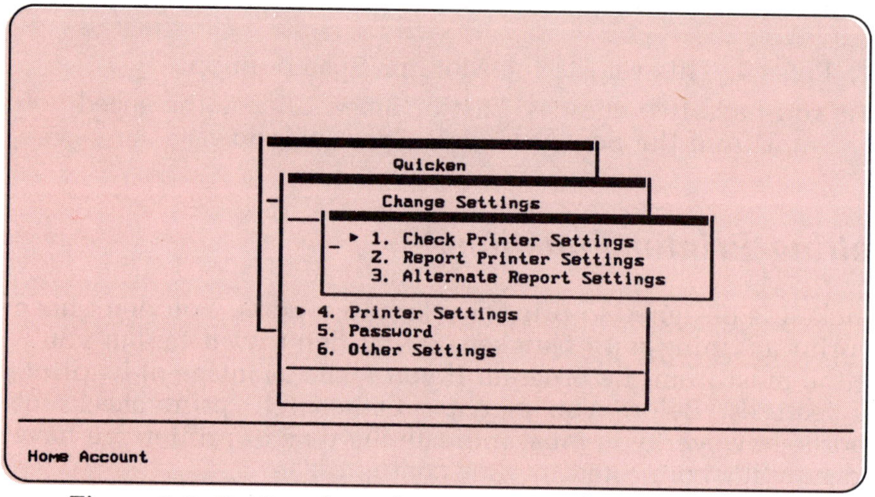

Figure 2-8. Setting the printer type.

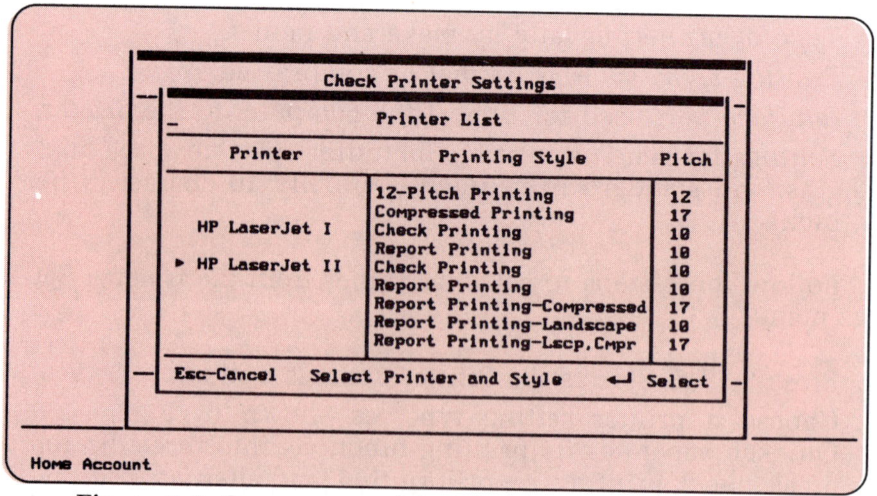

Figure 2-9. One screen of Quicken's printer list.

Table 2-2. Printers Supported by Quicken.

Brand	Model	Print Style	Pitch
IBM Compatible		Normal printing	10
		12-pitch printing	12
		Compressed printing	12
Hewlett-Packard	LaserJet I	Check printing	10
		Report printing	10
	LaserJet II	Check printing	10
		Report printing	10
		Report printing—compressed	17
		Report printing—landscape	10
		Report printing—lscp, cmpr	17
	DeskJet	Check printing	10
		Report printing	10
		Report/compressed	17
	ThinkJet	Normal printing	10
		Check printing	10
IBM	ProPrinter	Normal printing	10
		Compressed printing	17
		Near letter quality	10
	4216	Normal printing	10
		Check printing	10
Epson	FX, MX	Normal printing	10
		Near letter quality	10
		Compressed printing	17
NEC	3530	Normal printing	10
		Compressed printing	17
	8023A	Normal printing	10
		Compressed printing	17
Okidata	83,92,182, 192,292	Normal printing	10
		Compressed printing	17
	320	Normal printing	10
		Compressed printing	17
Star	All	Normal printing	10
		Near letter quality	10

Continued

***Table* 2-2.** *(continued)*

Brand	Model	Print Style	Pitch
Unlisted		Normal printing	10
		Wide carriage	10
Unlisted Laser		Normal printing	10
		Compressed printing	17

Notes

Quicken uses "pitch" to indicate the number of characters printed in 1 inch. A pitch of 10 means 10 characters per inch.

"Normal" printing is standard portrait orientation without print compression.

"Wide carriage" printing is landscape orientation.

"Compressed" printing is 17 pitch.

The printer list provides three "blanks" where you can use Quicken with your printer, even if your printer is not listed.

Use the *IBM Compatible* printer selection for any dot matrix or daisywheel printer that uses the standard IBM character set and IBM printer control codes (IBM ProPrinter compatible).

Use the *Unlisted* printer selection for any dot matrix, daisywheel, thermal transfer, or ink jet printer that is not listed and that is not compatible with the IBM ProPrinter.

Use the *Unlisted Laser* printer selection for any laser printer other than the LaserJet I or II. It's acceptable to use the LaserJet printer settings if your laser printer is HP LaserJet compatible, but be sure your printer is *truly* LaserJet compatible.

Once you've selected a printer (for checks or reports), you need to tell Quicken how it's set up and how your computer attaches to it. Press F8 at the Change Settings window to get in the Check Printer Settings window. It appears after you select a printer (see Figure 2-10), you set:

Name of the printer (optional).

Port connecting the computer to the printer.

Indent margin, if any.

Page size—Length is expressed as number of lines from top to bottom, and width is expressed as number of characters from left to right.

Print pitch, or the number of characters printed per inch (normally 10 or 12, but you may want to select a condensed or compressed pitch—15 or 17 pitch).

Whether you'd like the printing to *pause* between each page (if you're hand-feeding the paper into the printer, for instance).

Page orientation of the printer (e.g., a laser printer ejects no less than an entire page).

Whether the printer supports *IBM graphics characters.*

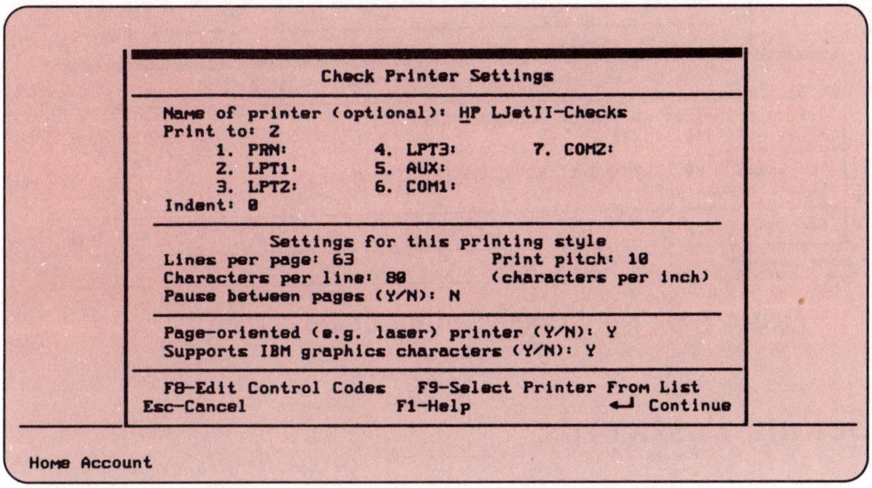

Figure 2-10. The Check Printer Settings screen.

To fill in the settings, place your entry at the appropriate *data field* (entry blank), and press the Enter key when you're done. If the setting is already the way you want it, just press Enter to confirm the default.

You can optionally edit the control codes Quicken sends to the printer prior to, during, and after check and report printing. Quicken already provides the necessary control codes to use with the printers listed in Table 2-2. If you need to change the codes—or need to enter codes for a printer not on the list—you should refer to your printer's manual on the codes that are necessary for each of the functions Quicken supports.

As shown in Figure 2-11, you can enter control codes that are sent before printing starts, after printing finishes (to reset the printer, for instance), and at the start of each page. If your printer is capable of *landscape* (sideways) printing, you can insert the control codes for that function in the appropriate blank.

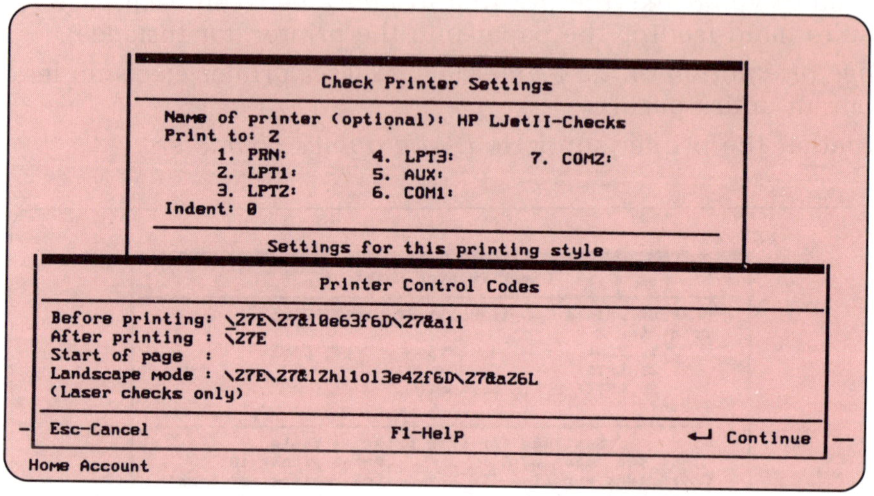

Figure 2-11. The Printer Control Codes screen.

Setting Passwords

Quicken lets you set passwords for accessing the program and for changing transactions. The use of a password is strictly optional. For most home and many business users, a password is unnecessary. You will want to use a password if you want to prevent unauthorized persons from accessing or changing the information in your Quicken accounts. Quicken offers two levels of password protection: main and transaction.

The *main password* allows access to all your accounts in the current Quicken account group. (An account group is a collection of all your accounts. You'll create additional account groups if you are tracking the finances of several different people, households, or businesses.)

The *transaction password* allows access to transaction records and enables you to make changes to those records even if the account period for those transactions has been "closed." With password protection on, no one else can make changes to transactions that are dated prior to the closing period.

Both passwords are set using the Password menu. Follow these steps to set the main password from the Change Settings menu:

1. Press 5. This selects the password option.
2. Press 1, for Main Password.
3. Enter a password. You can type any word or phrase, up to 16 characters. Check it carefully. Press the Enter key to record the password.

Follow the same general steps to set a transaction password at the Change Settings menu:

1. Press 5, for Password menu.
2. Press 2, for Transaction Password.
3. Enter a password (up to 16 characters).
4. Enter a closing date for transactions. Transactions prior to this date will be locked out from future changes, unless the transaction password is provided. Press the Enter key when done.

> **Tip:** Don't choose a password carelessly. If you forget your main password, you will not be able to access *any* of your accounts, and your Quicken files will be useless. Choose a password that others won't be able to guess easily (your first or last name is out, for instance) but that you won't forget. If necessary, write it down in an inconspicuous place—on the back of a picture you carry in your wallet or purse or as a "fake" name in your Rolodex file.

You can change or remove your main and transaction passwords at any time. You need the original password to do it, however. If you want to change your password, repeat steps 1 and 2 above (for either main or transaction password), and enter the current password into the Old Password slot. Enter a new password into the New Password slot. If you'd like to delete the password, leave New Password blank.

Additional Settings

As shown in Figure 2-12, Quicken allows you to select a number of other settings. To get to the Other Settings menu, enter 6 at the Change Settings menu. You can leave the settings as they are or change them. Their use is fairly self-explanatory, but here's a summary:

Beep when recording and memorizing—Sounds a beep when Quicken is recording and memorizing transactions. Set to Yes or No.

Request confirmation—Displays a yes/no query when Quicken is about to record or delete data. Set to Yes or No.

Require Category on transactions—Forces Quicken to ask for a category name for each transaction. Set to Yes or No.

Extra message line on check—Allows you to write and print an extra message line on the check; Quicken does not record the line in the register. Set to Yes or No.

Days in advance to remind of postdated checks and scheduled groups—Sets the number of days in advance Quicken will alert you to print checks you've entered into the check register. If you use your computer every day, you don't need to be reminded more than 1 or 2 days in advance. Set a number from 0 to 30.

Change date of checks to today's date when printed—Prints all checks with the current date, as set by DOS. It is used mostly when printing post-dated checks. Set to Yes or No.

MM/DD/YY or DD/MM/YY date format—Sets month/day/year format for checks and registers. Set to M (month first) or D (day first).

Billminder active—Tells Quicken that Billminder is active (for hard disk users only). Set to Yes or No.

Print categories on voucher checks—Prints category names (that you've typed in the Split Transaction window) on voucher checks. Quicken always prints text entered into the Description column of the Split Transactions window. Set to Yes or No.

43 line register/reports—Displays register and reports in 43 lines. For use only with EGA and VGA monitors that are supplied with appropriate 43-line display drivers. Set to Yes or No.

Show Memo/Category/Both—Determines the information displayed on the second line of the Payee-Memo-Category in the register (when the transaction is not selected). Set to M (for memo), C (for category), and B (for both memo and category).

In reports, use category Description/Name/Both—Determines how classes and categories are labeled in printed reports. Set to D (for description), N (for name), or B (for description and name).

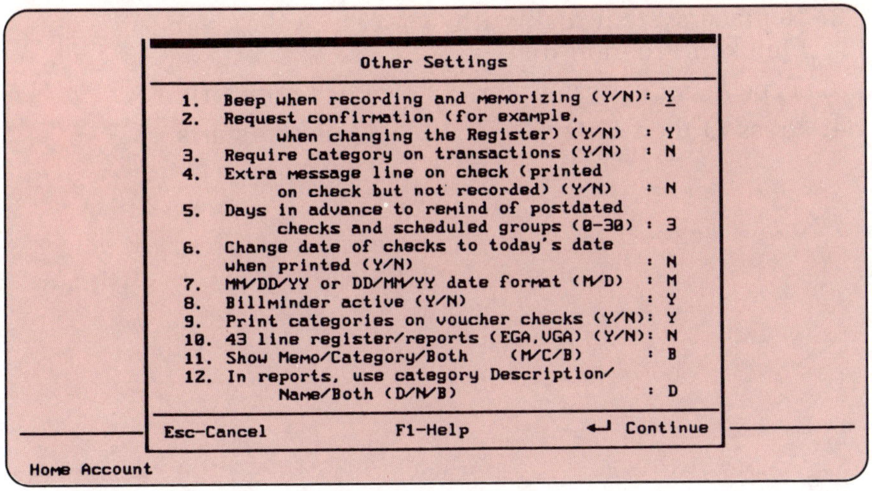

Figure 2-12. Make additional changes in Quicken at this screen.

Table 2-3 lists the miscellaneous option settings offered by Quicken. Shown are the default (factory) settings, as well as suggested settings for expert Quicken users. Of course, you should configure Quicken in the way you like best; use the suggestions in the table as a guide only.

Starting Quicken

The way you start Quicken depends on how you've installed the program: on a hard disk or on floppy disks.

Starting Quicken, Hard Disk Installation

1. Turn on your computer (if it's not already on).
2. Press Q then Enter. — Quicken starts. ☐

Starting Quicken, Floppy Disk Drive

1. Start computer with system disk (if it's not already on).

2. Replace system disk with Quicken Program disk.	
3. Type A: and press Enter.	Logs onto drive A.
4. Press Q then Enter.	Quicken starts.

▶ **Note:** The Q.BAT file must be in the current directory, or the PATH statement (in the AUTOEXEC.BAT file, as detailed earlier in this chapter) must include the root or other directory that contains the Q.BAT path file.

▶ **Note:** If your computer is equipped with two floppy drives, you should place the data disk in drive A.

Table 2-3. Default and Suggested Expert Miscellaneous Settings.

Option	Setting Original	Setting Expert
Beep when recording...	Y	N
Request confirmation	Y	N
Require Category on transactions	N	N
Extra message line on check	N	N
Days in advance to remind...	3	0
Change date of checks...	N	Y
MM/DD/YY or DD/MM/YY date format	M	M*
Billminder active	Y	N
Print categories on voucher checks	Y	Y
43 line register/reports	N	N**
Show Memo/Category/Both	B	B
Use category Description/Name/Both	D	B

Notes

*Depends on personal tastes and conventions used in your country.

**Depends on your personal tastes and the capabilities of your display adapter.

First Time Startup

If this is the first time you're using Quicken, the program asks if you have a color monitor. Press 1 (if color) or 2 (if monochrome).

> **Tip:** Quicken's settings are stored in a file called Q.CFG. If this file is ever lost, damaged, or erased, Quicken will revert to its original settings, and you'll have to select printer and screen options again. In addition, some programs on your computer may reset the DOS display mode to MONO, even if your machine is equipped with a color monitor. Should this happen, Quicken may load and display either a blank screen or a screen with only partial characters. You need to either reset your computer or change Quicken's display options. After Quicken loads (even if you can't see the main menu), type 5 2 1. This sets the monitor type to monochrome.

Date Set

Some computers—particularly the IBM PC and clones—lack a built-in clock/calendar. If the computer has a clock/calendar function, it is provided by an accessory card, which is optional. Without a clock/calendar card, DOS has no means to remember the date each time the computer is turned on or off. Unless you manually set the date when the computer is first turned on, DOS will think the date is January 1, 1980—the first day of DOS's time-keeping clock.

Quicken tracks financial data by date, and the setting of the current date is important. Quicken is designed to detect if the DOS clock is set to January 1, 1980; if it is, you're asked to provide the current date, as shown in Figure 2-13. The program initially provides the date of the last transaction. You can either type the date explicitly or use the + and − keys to set the date one day at a time.

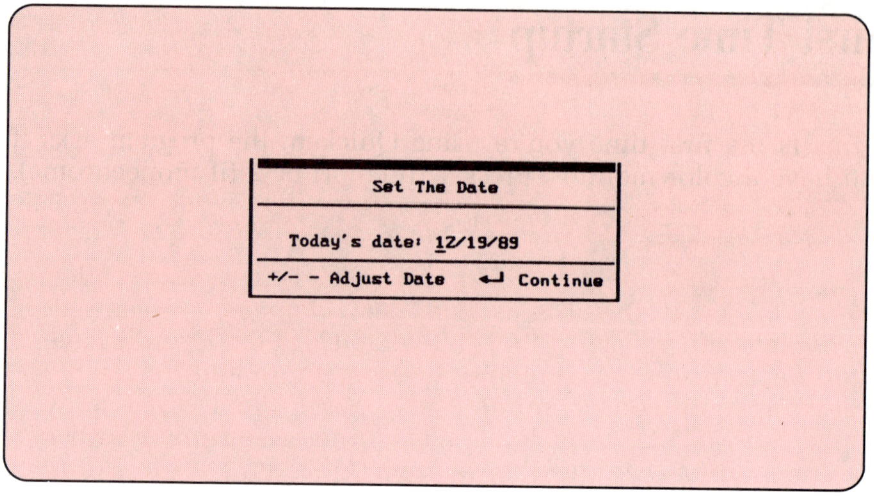

Figure 2-13. Quicken requests that you enter the current date if the clock in your computer is set to 1/1/80.

If your computer is equipped with a built-in clock/calendar, the battery used to retain the date and system information will eventually fail. When it does fail, the computer will lose the current date information. Each time you start your computer the clock/calendar will reset to January 1, 1980. Again, Quicken will recognize that the date is not valid and ask you to update it.

Accessing On-Line Help

Quicken provides an on-line, context-sensitive help feature for times when you need a little nudge to get you going in the right direction. At just about every screen and menu in Quicken, you can access help by pressing the F1 key. A help window, like the one in Figure 2-14, splashes on the screen. If the help message is too long to fit in one window, you can scroll to see the remainder of its contents with the Page Down key. Conversely, press the Page Up key to scroll back through the help window.

When you're done reading help, press the Escape key to return to Quicken.

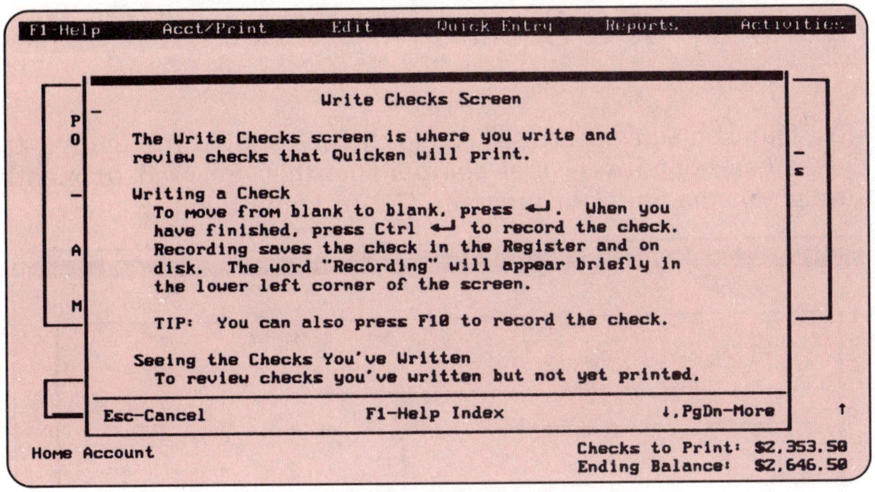

Figure 2-14. Sample of Quicken's on-line help.

Tip: Because Quicken's help feature is context-sensitive, it always displays a help message about the current screen, window, or menu. If you'd like to see an index of available help topics, press the F1 key again. Scroll through the help index, as illustrated in Figure 2-15, and press the Enter key when you find the topic you want. Quicken will then display the help window for that topic.

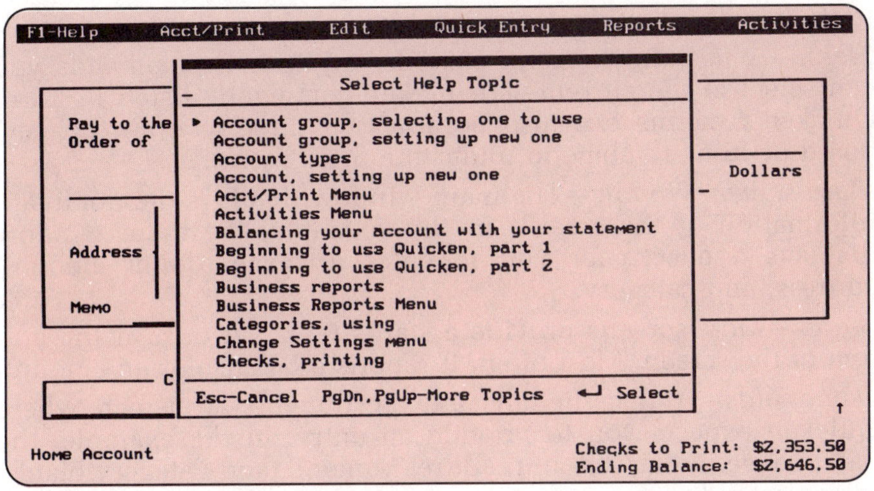

Figure 2-15. The help index.

Anatomy of a Screen

Most Quicken screens are similar to the one shown in Figure 2-16. The screen contains several components that are used frequently throughout the Quicken program. Get to know them.

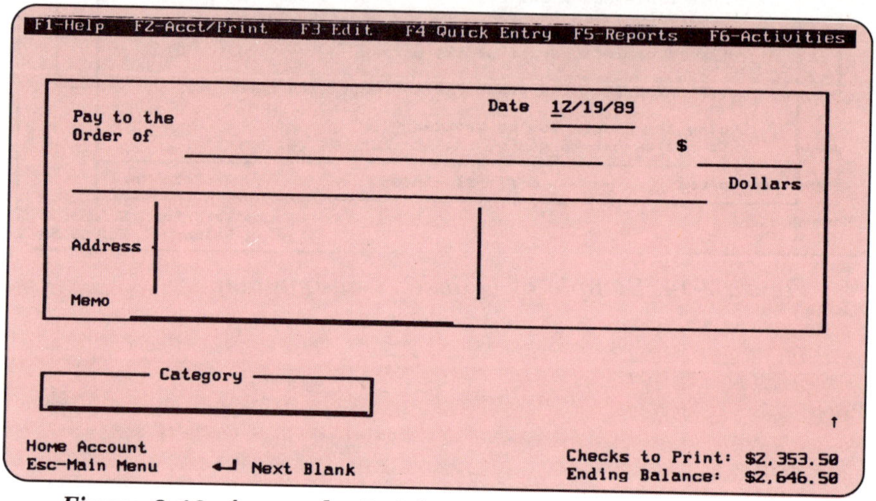

Figure 2-16. A sample Quicken screen.

Menu bar—The menu bar, which is displayed at the top of the screen, shows the menus currently available. To select a menu, press its corresponding function key.

Menu—A pull-down menu provides additional commands you can select at the current screen. The commands listed in all of Quicken's menus can also be accessed directly from the keyboard or from a submenu under the main menu.

Main screen window—The main window displays the dominant information of the screen. In this example, the main window displays a check, for you to enter a payee, dollar amount, address, and category.

Status—Most screens provide a status report at or near the bottom of the screen. Most often, it reports a balance or an amount.

Data fields—A data field is any portion of the screen where Quicken expects you to provide an entry. In the example, the date, payee, dollar amount, address, memo, and category blanks are data fields.

Moving Around Quicken

One of the strongest features of Quicken has nothing to do with money: it's the way you move around the program. Quicken employs an intuitive and consistent interface to help you maneuver from one screen and command to the next. Quicken uses the same keys for the same functions, no matter where you are in the program. Table 2-4 lists most of the functions within Quicken and the keys you'll press to activate those functions.

Table 2-4. Common Quicken Functions and Associated Keys.

Function	Keys
Help	F1
Help topics	F1, F1 (press F1 twice)
Access Account/Print menu	F2 (from selected screens only)
Access Edit menu	F3 (from selected screens only)
Access Quick Entry menu	F4 (from selected screens only)
Access Reports menu	F5 (from selected screens only)
Access Activities menu	F6 (from selected screens only)
To select a command in an item	Highlight the command or press the corresponding number
To move to the next data field	Tab or Enter
To move to the preceding data field	Shift-Tab
To select a command, complete an entry, or advance to next data field or screen	Enter
Delete character at cursor	Delete
Delete character to left of cursor	Backspace
Move to next word	Ctrl and right arrow keys
Move to previous word	Ctrl and left arrow keys
Delete all data from a field	Ctrl and Backspace
Cancel current screen and go back to previous screen or menu level	Esc
Confirm all data field entries on the screen	Ctrl and Enter

For a summary of Quicken keys and their uses, see the inside back cover of this book.

Leaving Quicken

When you're done with Quicken, press the Escape key to return to the main menu (if necessary), then press E to quit. Quicken automatically saves all of your data as you use the program and upon exiting, so you don't have to worry about doing it manually.

You can also make safety backups of your Quicken account files prior to leaving the program. To make a backup and remain in Quicken, press Ctrl-B at the main menu. To make a backup and leave Quicken (return to DOS), press Ctrl-E at the main menu.

For the backup, Quicken prompts you to insert a formatted data diskette. Be sure to have a formatted data diskette ready before requesting the backup. In addition to making quick backups using the Ctrl-E and Ctrl-B keys, you should make periodic backups of all Quicken program and data files, as detailed in Chapter 3, "Setting Up Accounts."

Do not leave Quicken by turning off or resetting your computer. Doing so may cause serious data loss.

What You Have Learned

This chapter examined the basics of getting started with Quicken. Here's what you should have learned:

- The Quicken Install program copies the Quicken files to your disks, updates your CONFIG.SYS file (if necessary), and optionally installs a command line to run the Billminder program whenever you start your computer.
- When using a hard disk drive, the Q.BAT file lets you quickly start Quicken without having to be in the Quicken directory.

- Quicken lets you set screen color, monitor speed, printer type and settings, and password to suit your needs and hardware requirements.
- To start Quicken from a hard disk, press Q then Enter.
- To start Quicken from a floppy disk, insert the Quicken program diskette in drive A, then log onto drive A. Press Q then Enter.
- Press the F1 key to access Quicken's on-line, context-sensitive help. Press the F1 key again when in the help window to view the available help topics.
- When you're ready to leave Quicken, press the Escape key to return to the main menu (if necessary), then press E to quit.

Chapter 3

Setting Up Accounts

In This Chapter

- *Setting up Quicken accounts*
- *Identifying account types*
- *Using account groups*
- *Maintaining account files*
- *Backing up account files*

Now that you've installed Quicken on your computer, you're ready to use it to keep track of your financial affairs. Quicken needs very little advance information about your finances, but it does need to be told the kind of accounts you want to track and the beginning balances.

This chapter shows you how to set up accounts in Quicken, how to maintain account records, and ways to keep backups to protect against data loss. You'll also learn about the types of accounts Quicken can handle, and the information you should have on hand when you actually enter new account data into Quicken.

Types of Accounts

Quicken lets you track your finances regardless of their form or content. While the program is ideally suited for tracking your checking account, you can also use it to maintain savings accounts, record assets and liabilities, provide budgetary projections, handle payroll accounts, and much more. Quicken is designed to work with five specific types of financial accounts, although you are free to use any of these account types for other purposes. The five account types directly supported by Quicken are:

- Checking or savings account (called "Bank Account" by Quicken)
- Credit Card
- Cash
- Other Asset
- Other Liability

The first time you start Quicken, it asks you the type of account you'll be using, either business or personal, as shown in Figure 3-1. This helps Quicken set up standard categories for you. Choose

1 to use Quicken's standard home categories.
2 to use Quicken's standard business categories.
3 to use standard home AND business categories.
4 to omit all standard categories.

If you're just starting out with Quicken, choose option 3, both account types. Appendix A lists the categories Quicken automatically provides for home and business use. Remember

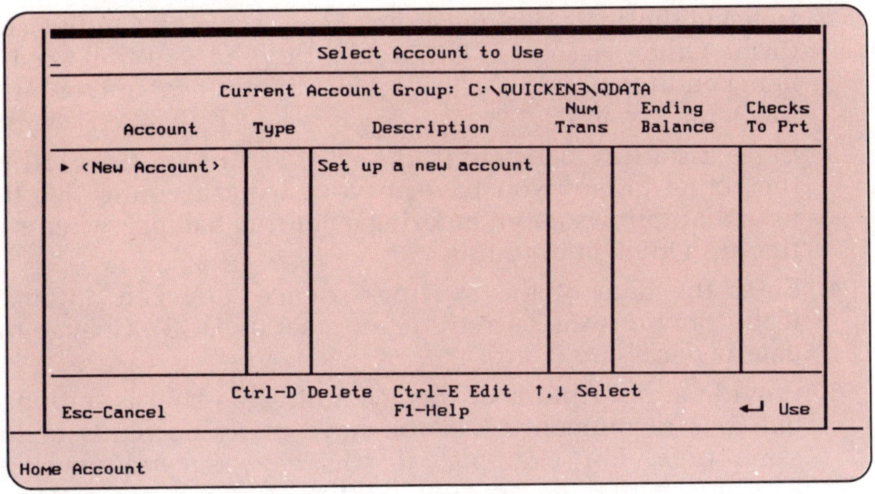

Figure 3-1. Screen shown on first time setup.

that you can always delete categories you don't want and add new categories. For now, you don't need to worry about categories.

In this same screen, Quicken asks where the data files are located. If you're computer is equipped with:

Two floppy drives (any capacity), specify drive B (which should contain the data disk).

One high-capacity drive, specify drive A.

Hard disk, specify the drive letter (usually either C or D) and the full path, normally \QUICKEN3\.

Press Enter to go on to the next step. The Set Up New Account screen, shown in Figure 3-2, appears. Follow these steps to complete the entries in this screen. With the exception of selecting the account type, press the Enter key after providing the necessary information.

1. Provide a name for the account. Account names can have up to 15 characters, and can use any characters except [ ] / :. The brackets are used by Quicken to denote transfers between categories; the slash is used to enter main categories, subcategories, and class names; and the colon is used to separate category names from class names.

2. Indicate the account type, either Bank Account, Credit Card, Cash, Other Asset, or Other Liability. If you'll be using Quicken to maintain a checking or savings account, enter 1, for Bank Account.
3. Enter a starting balance, if known. Most often, this will be the actual money you have in your bank account. See the note that follows about entering a starting balance when setting up Quicken accounts.
4. Enter the date of the starting balance. Quicken automatically provides the current date (as set by DOS). Change the date if necessary.
5. Provide a description of the account. This step is optional, but it is recommended if you have many accounts of the same type. For example, if you have several checking accounts, enter the account number or bank name (if the accounts are at different banks).

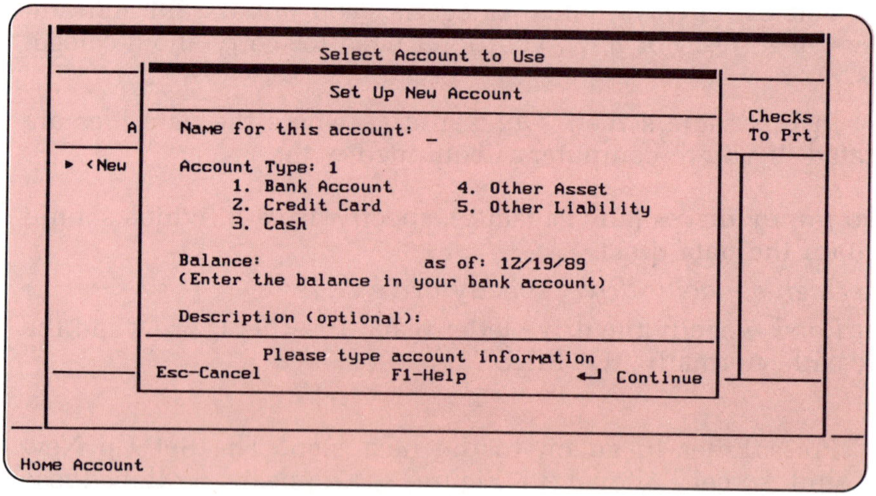

Figure 3-2. Set Up New Accounts screen.

When you're done filling in the new account information, press the Enter key one more time. Quicken then takes you to the Write Checks screen, where you can immediately use your new account. We'll save actually using the account for the next chapter.

Setting Up a Starting Balance

Although it seems a trivial matter, setting the starting balance for a new account can be a tough proposition. Normally, when dealing with checking and savings accounts, the starting balance is the amount of money you currently have in the bank. But the amount your bank says you have, and the amount indicated in your checkbook or savings passbook, may be wildly different.

If you are charged a monthly checking fee or are charged for each check you write during the month, your bank may have a slightly different balance than the one reflected in your check register. If your checking account is interest-bearing (and the same applies to savings accounts, which always accrue interest), your check register won't reflect the actual balance held by your bank's computer.

The best time to set up a new Quicken account is right after you've received the checking or savings account statement from the bank. Reconcile it against your own register, to make sure there are no errors, and enter the remaining balance into the starting balance data field in the Set Up New Account screen.

You will then need to enter into Quicken all those transactions that are listed in your paper register, but that have not yet shown up in the bank statements. For instance, if you've written five checks that are listed in your old register but aren't shown as being cleared at the bank, you'll need to enter them into Quicken to keep your account straight. Do the same for deposits and other transactions, including over-the-phone transfers and automated teller machine withdrawals.

Another approach is to enter the amount shown in the last entry in your checking account register. This entry doesn't include service charges or interest, and it may be in error (due to mistakes in computing your balance, for example), but it's a good rough estimate of what you have in the bank. Then, when the statement comes in, you can make adjustments within Quicken to amend for fees, interest, and corrections.

A final approach is to enter 0.00 in the standard balance entry field. Quicken will accept that as a temporary balance but will still let you track checks and deposits, and even write checks. At a later date, when you receive the bank statement in the mail, you can change the starting balance to reflect the amount you really have.

Selecting the Right Account Type

Quicken offers only five account types, which at first may appear to be very limited. What if you want to track your IRA account or maintain records on a money market fund? Or what if you want one general savings account, but then separate the accounts in your own records into compartments—one for travel, one for clothing, one for home improvement, and so forth?

Quicken doesn't really care what the account is. As long as the account deals with money—how and when it's spent and received—Quicken can handle it. While Quicken is not a full-fledged accounting package that can be used by Fortune 500 companies for their budgetary, payroll, and expense accounts, it is perfectly suited to personal and small business use.

Although you are free to try different approaches, here are some real-world financial records and the Quicken account types you may want to use when maintaining them:

Account	Quicken Account Type
Checking	Bank Account
Savings	Bank Account
Money market fund	Bank Account
Certificate of deposit	Bank Account, Other Asset
Real estate holdings	Other Asset
Spending cash	Cash
Petty cash (as used in business)	Cash, Bank Account
Personal belongings (antiques, jewlry, etc.)	Other Asset
Business property	Other Asset
Payroll	Bank Account
Income (regular income, plus income from alimony, royalties, trust funds, sponsorships, grants, etc.)	Bank Account, Other Asset
Revolving credit accounts (department store cards, Visa, MasterCard, etc.)	Credit Card

Account (cont.)	Quicken Account Type
Closed-end accounts (credit cards, car loan, boat loan, personal line of credit)	Other Liability, Credit Card
House/property mortgage	Other Liability
Leases (you pay on)	Other Liability
Leases (you get paid)	Other Asset
Stock/bond portfolio	Other Asset
Personal debts (you pay on)	Other Liability
Personal debts (you get paid)	Other Asset

Here are some general guidelines to help you select the best Quicken accounts to take care of your financial matters:

An *asset* is something you own.

A *liability* is something you owe.

If the money is in a bank and you can write checks or make regular withdrawals to get it out, it's a *Bank Account.*

Other Assets are money that belongs to you or property (real or personal) you own. You can, with varying degrees of difficulty, withdraw the money or sell the property and receive the money for it.

Other Liabilities are money you've borrowed or property you are still paying for. If you sell the property, some or all of the money you get may have to be paid back to the lender.

Cash is usually considered *liquid* (easy to get at) money. This money is not in a bank account but rather can be readily found, say, in your wallet or under your mattress. Quicken is designed to treat the money in a Cash account as dispensable—you can spend some and just list it under "miscellaneous."

If the money is in a bank but you are restricted from withdrawing it, it's an *Other Asset.*

Your income (like your paycheck) can be applied to almost any account, depending on where it goes. Income can be applied to a Bank Account (the most frequently used), Credit Card, Cash, or Other Asset. If you get special income you want to track (e.g., grants, royalties for best-selling books, or scholarships), you can record it as an Other Asset.

About Account Groups

You can define any number of accounts in Quicken, limited only by disk space and your willingness to spend endless hours behind a computer. However, Quicken can handle accounts only when they are in groups. Most likely, you'll be using just one account group to hold all the accounts you create in Quicken.

You may, however, want to create separate account groups if you handle financial matters for others. As you learned in Chapter 2, "Getting Started with Quicken," Quicken lets you select a password to prohibit access to account information. You can give each account group its own password, for protection purposes.

Quicken *is limited* to holding no more than 255 accounts in any single account group. As even 255 accounts is far beyond the needs of the average Quicken user, this limitation is of no consequence.

Keeping Double Books

The first tenant of "computerizing the books" is to maintain the old-fashioned paper ledger while you enter the same transaction information into the computer. The same is true when starting out with Quicken. While it's not Quicken's style to record data incorrectly or to miscalculate balances, your newness to the program can cause an occasional slip-up or two.

For at least the first few weeks of using Quicken, record your transactions in your checkbook and savings passbook registers, as you've always done. Then, when you feel comfortable that you've gotten the hang of using Quicken, you can store the registers in a safe place (you'll want to keep them at least until the bank statement comes) and use Quicken to record all your financial transactions.

Maintaining Account Files

The accounts you create in Quicken are recorded as files on your data disk or hard disk. Quicken is designed so that you never have to copy, rename, or delete these files manually; you can do it all within the program using menu commands.

When you initially use Quicken and make your first account, it is stored in an account group named QDATA. Most likely, this is the only account group name you'll work with, but you can create a new account group, edit an account group file you no longer need, and more.

Making a New Account Group

You need to create a new account group before you can stash accounts in it. From the main menu:

1. Choose 5 for Change Settings.
2. Choose 1 for Account Group Activities.
3. Choose 1 for Select/Set Up Account Group.
4. Select Setup New Group in the window that appears, and press the Enter key.

The Create An Account Group screen is displayed, as shown in Figure 3-3. Note that this screen is almost the same as the First Time Setup window that is displayed when you initially install Quicken. The only addition is that you can provide a unique DOS name for the account group. Provide a name, using up to eight characters, following standard DOS file name practices. Do not provide an extension.

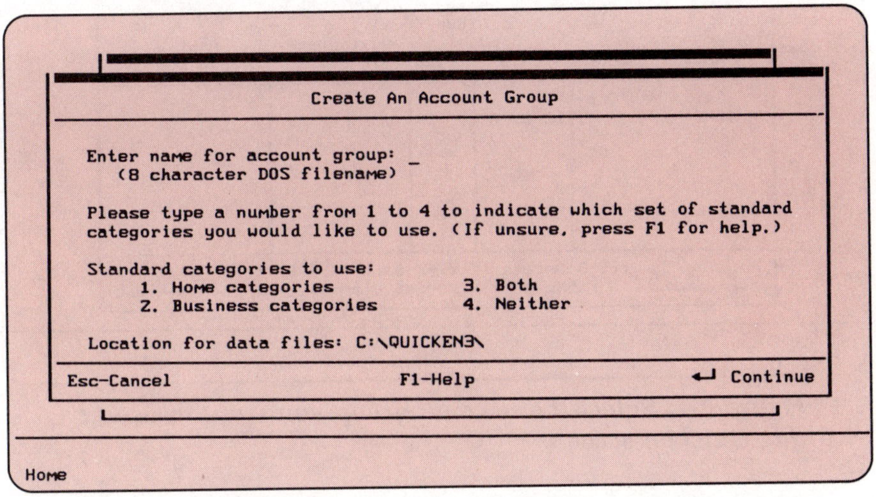

Figure 3-3. Fill in this blank to create an account group.

Selecting an Account Group

If you have more than one account group stored on your data disk or hard disk, you can easily switch between them. Quicken allows you to use only one account group at a time. You can't access a checking account in account group A at the same time that you access a savings account in group B.

To select an account group, start at the main menu, then:

1. Choose 5 for Change Settings.
2. Choose 1 for Account Group Activities.
3. Choose 1 for Select/Set Up Account Group.

The window shown in Figure 3-4 appears. All of the account group files currently on your disk are shown. Use the up and down arrow keys to select the account group you want to use, and press the Enter key. If there's more than one account in the group, Quicken also asks you to select the specific account you want to access.

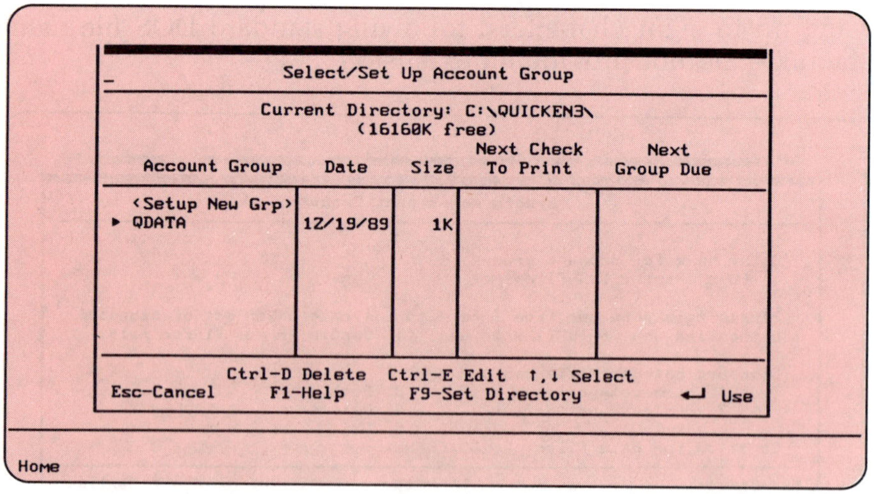

Figure 3-4. Select the account group you want to use at this Quicken screen.

Tip: If you don't see the account group you want in the list, and you have other Quicken data files stored in another directory or disk, press the F9 key and indicate the directory/disk you want to view.

Other Account Group Activities

At the Select/Set Up Account Group window, Quicken also allows you to rename and delete account groups. To delete an account group, highlight it at the Select/Set Up Account Group window, then press Ctrl-D. Answer Yes to the prompt. To rename an account group, highlight it, and press Ctrl-E. Enter a new name (up to eight characters, following all standard DOS file name restrictions). Press the Enter key when you're done.

Backing Up Account Information

As with all the data stored on your floppy disks and hard disk, you should periodically make backup or archival copies, in case something should ever happen to the original files. This is especially critical with Quicken files, because they represent your or your company's financial position.

The easiest way to make backups of your account data is to use the Ctrl-E and Ctrl-B quick backup shortcut keys. To make a backup and remain in Quicken, press Ctrl-B at the main menu. To make a backup and leave Quicken (return to DOS), press Ctrl-E at the main menu.

For the backup, Quicken prompts you to insert a formatted data diskette. Be sure to have a formatted data diskette ready before requesting the backup.

In addition, you can make backup copies of Quicken data manually. Use DOS to copy the data files to a floppy disk. Or, if you use floppy drives, simply make a copy of the entire data disk (use the DISKCOPY command). Hard disk users should use a reliable hard disk backup program, such as Fastback Plus or PC Tools Deluxe.

How often should you back up your Quicken data? An ideal backup plan for hard disk users is to archive all the files on the hard disk once a week and to archive just the files that have been created or modified once a day. All of the commercial hard disk backup programs for the PC allow selective archives in this manner. If you are a floppy disk user, you should make a copy of the Quicken data (or the complete data disk) every time you use the program and enter transactions.

While all this may seem like a lot of work, sooner or later it will pay off. By keeping vigilant watch over the data on your disks, you'll never lose more than a day or two of work. And should your entire computer go on the fritz, you can use the backup to re-install your data on a different computer. You can continue to use Quicken (as well as all your other programs) while your computer is in the shop.

What You Have Learned

This chapter examined how to set up accounts and maintain files in Quicken. Here's what you should have learned:

- Quicken can handle any financial account, but it is specifically built to maintain checking, savings, and cash accounts, as well as general asset and liability accounts (e.g., home loan and real estate).
- The starting balance indicates the amount you have in an account when you begin using Quicken. You can alter the starting balance at a later date, should it be necessary.
- You can define any number of accounts in Quicken, limited only by disk space.
- Quicken can handle accounts only when they are in groups. An account group can hold up to 255 separate accounts.
- When first starting with Quicken, maintain a separate paper ledger of your accounts. This helps prevent errors while you learn to use the program.
- You should periodically back up your Quicken account file. Quicken provides a quick method of making backups (press Ctrl-E or Ctrl-B at the main menu).

Chapter 4

Writing Checks

In This Chapter

- *Selecting the account to use*
- *Writing checks*
- *Check-entering shortcuts*
- *Reviewing, editing, recording checks*

What better way to pay bills with your computer than filling out and printing an "electronic" check. Quicken's check-writing screen is as easy to use as your checkbook, and you don't have to worry about remembering to enter the transaction in the register. Quicken does all the bookkeeping for you.

In this chapter, you'll learn how to select the account you want to use, write checks, provide memo and category information, and more.

Check-Writing Procedure

Writing a check with Quicken is almost as easy as writing a check in your checkbook. You must follow these five steps to write a check:

1. Select the account to use. Once you have selected the account, you can write a series of checks.
2. Access the Write Checks screen.
3. Fill out the check by providing a dollar amount, payee, payee's address, and other information.
4. Review the check for errors or omissions, and correct any mistakes.
5. Record the check in the Quicken register.

Selecting the Account to Use

Quicken can maintain an unlimited number of different accounts; your checking account may be just one of many. You may also have more than one checking account and want to use Quicken to track each one.

However you use Quicken, you need to select an account to use before you can write checks. Once you have selected this account, Quicken remembers it for subsequent checks you write. (If you've just created one account, Quicken automatically assumes it's the one you want to use; if you have only one account, you can skip this section and proceed directly to the section below entitled "Writing the Check.") Quicken even recalls the account each time you start the program. Once you've selected an account, Quicken assumes you want to keep using it, until you tell it otherwise.

If you have not yet set up any accounts with Quicken, you need to refer to Chapter 3, "Setting Up Accounts." There you'll learn how Quicken handles accounts, how you can create accounts for almost any financial need, and how to maintain accounts in discrete account groups. The following quick step assumes you are at Quicken's main menu.

Selecting an Account

1. Press 4. — Chooses Select Account command, and displays the Select Accounts screen, as shown in Figure 4-1.
2. Press up or down arrow keys to select an account to use.
3. Press Enter. — Selects the highlighted account, and makes it current. Quicken remembers your choice until you explicitly change it again. Quicken immediately takes you to the check register screen.
4. Press Esc. — Exits the check register screen, and returns to the main menu. □

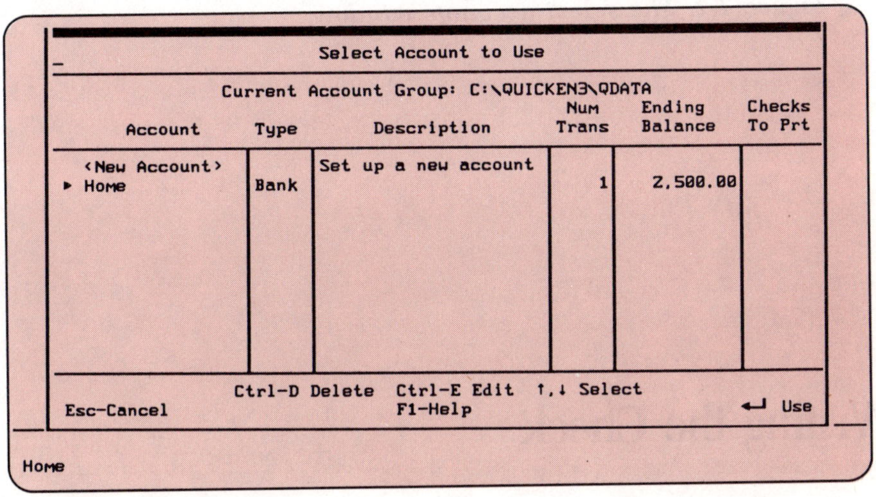

Figure 4-1. The Select Accounts to Use screen. Use this screen whenever you want to create or change accounts.

While in the Select Accounts screen, you can also either delete accounts or edit them. To delete an account you no longer need, highlight it and press Ctrl-D. Answer Yes to the prompt that appears. To edit an account, highlight it and press Ctrl-E. The editing screen, as shown in Figure 4-2, appears. Here, you may change the name and description of the account.

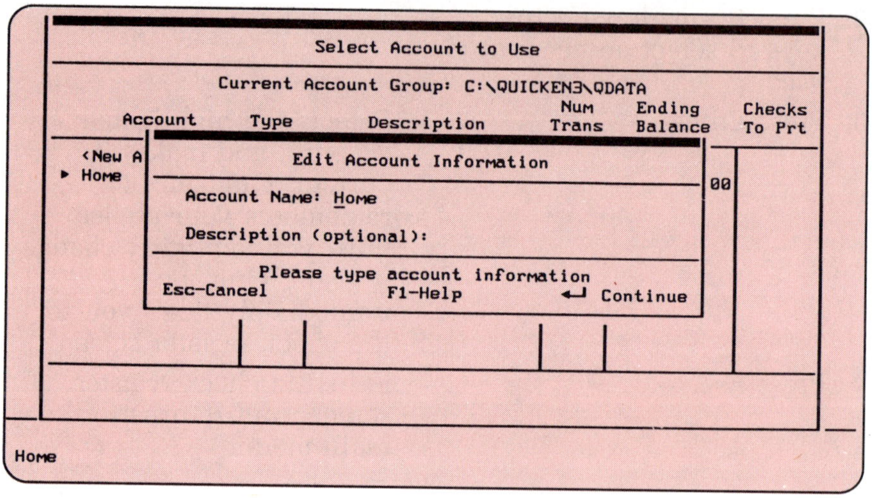

Figure 4-2. The select accounts window.

> **Tip:** To access the Change Accounts screen from anywhere within Quicken, press Ctrl-A. After you select the account you want to use, you will be returned to the spot where you left off.

Writing the Check

With the proper account selected, you are now ready to write checks. At Quicken's main menu, press 1 to select the Write/Print Checks command. Quicken presents the checking-writing screen shown in Figure 4-3. You may now fill in the check as desired.

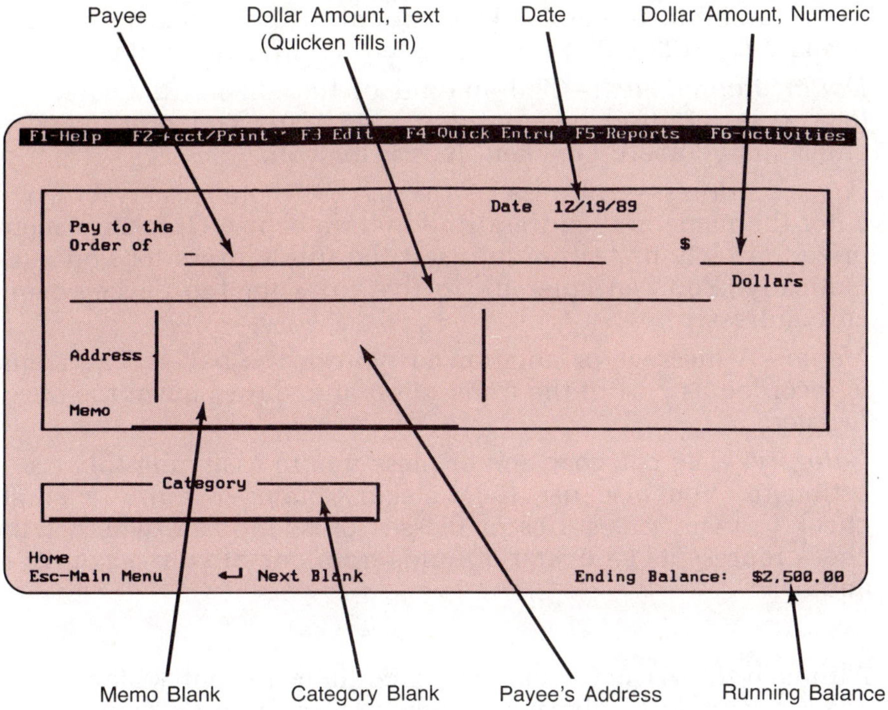

Figure 4-3. The Write Checks screen, with important points identified.

> **Tip:** You can immediately transfer to the Write Checks screen from almost anywhere in Quicken by pressing Ctrl-W.

The Write Checks screen contains six entry blanks. Here's what you enter into each of the blanks.

Date—The current date or, optionally, some date in the future. Quicken automatically enters the current date here, but you can post-date the check so you can write the check ahead of time, but not actually include it in your current transactions.

Payee—Who you're writing the check to.

Dollar amount, numeric—The amount of the check, in numeric format (e.g., 123.45). You don't need to enter the dollar sign.

Dollar amount, text—The amount of the check, in text format (e.g., One hundred twenty-three & 45/100). You *don't* need to enter this yourself; Quicken does it for you.

Payee's address—Address of the payee, if necessary. You can enter the name and address line by line or use Quicken's memorize transactions feature to insert the full address for you automatically. You can enter up to five lines for the payee's name and address.

Memo—A message or notation for you or the payee. The memo is recorded as part of the transaction and shows up in the check register.

Category—The category and/or class you're assigning this transaction to. You also use the Category blank to apply a single check to many categories or classes or to indicate whether the check represents a transfer of funds from one of your accounts to another.

Although the Write Checks screen contains six entry blanks, you need to complete only two of them. At a minimum, you need to enter the dollar amount (as a number) and the payee's name. Quicken automatically sets the current date; the payee's address, memo, and category information is completely optional.

Follow these steps to write a check. In all cases, press the Enter or Tab key when you are finished filling out a data field.

Writing a Check

1. Type date. If you don't use the current date, enter a new date. Or, press the + or − keys to go forward or back one day at a time. To accept the date that Quicken provides, press Enter.	Enters the desired date.
2. Type payee's name.	Enters the payee's name—either one or more individuals or a company.

3. Type the dollar amount in numerals.	Enters dollar amount, in numeric format.
4. Type address of payee. This step is optional.	Provides address of payee.
5. Type memo. This step is optional.	Adds memo when check is printed.
6. Type the category. This step is optional (but highly recommended).	Assigns the check to one or more categories or classes.
7. Press Ctrl-Enter. You can also choose the Record Transaction command under the Edit menu (press the F3 key then 1).	Records the check.

> **Tip:** If you're entering a whole dollar amount in the Dollar Amount data field—such as 100.00 or 1000.00, you can omit the decimal point and the two zeros to the right. Likewise, you don't need to enter commas when writing checks larger than "three figures." For example, to enter 1,005.00, just type 1005. Quicken will add the commas, decimal point, and trailing zeros automatically. The largest dollar amount Quicken can handle is 9,999,999.99.

A sample of a filled-out check is shown in Figure 4-4. Table 4-1 provides the maximum length (in characters) for each data field in the Write Checks screen.

Table 4-1. Maximum Length of Data Fields in Write Checks Screen.

Field	Maximum Length (in characters)
Date	8
Payee	40
Dollars	10 (up to 9,999,999.99)
Address	Five lines of 30 characters each (total: 150)
Memo	31
Category	31

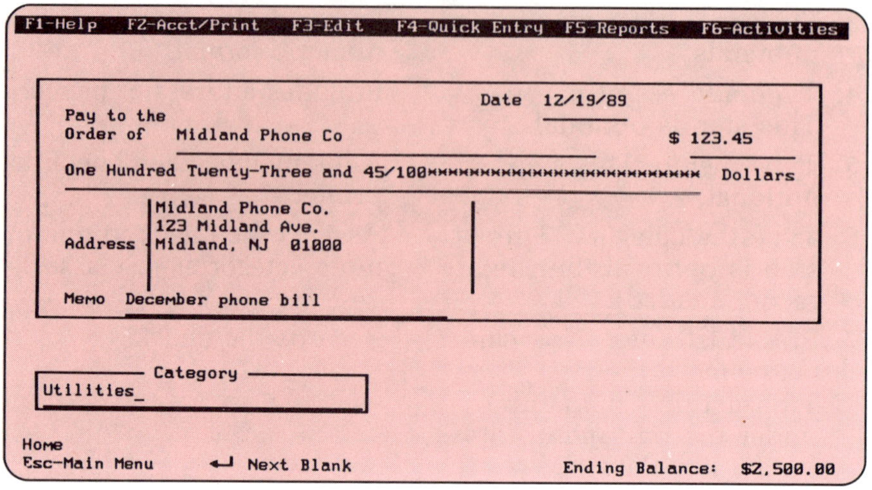

Figure 4-4. A sample of a filled-out check.

Setting the Date

Quicken automatically inserts the date into each check it writes. Initially, the date shown is the current date, as set by DOS. If your computer lacks a battery backup clock/calendar, or you don't manually set the time and date every time you start your computer, Quicken will display 1/1/80 on each check it prepares. Obviously, you can't write a check that's more than 10 years old, so you'll have to change it.

You may also wish to back-date or post-date a check you write with Quicken. *Back-dating* is selecting a date before today. You may wish to back-date a check for bill-paying purposes or when you're entering a check into Quicken that you wrote out of your pocket checkbook a few days before. *Post-dating* is selecting a date after today. Post-dating is helpful in Quicken when you want to write checks for all your bills at once, even though you don't have money to cover them all.

As shown in Figure 4-5, Quicken will display your current balance, which reflects checks you've written and printed that are not post-dated. These are the checks that you must have sufficient funds for. Quicken also displays the amount of checks yet to print. These are checks that have been post-dated. If you use post-dating, you can also use Quicken to keep tabs on accounts payable and cash flow.

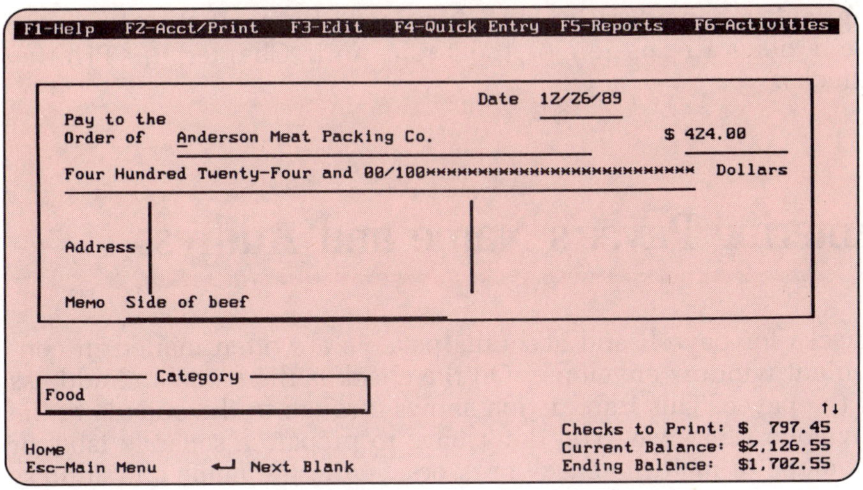

Figure 4-5. Quicken displays the current balance with each check you write.

Another use of post-dating has been to write someone a check, with the clear understanding that it should not (and theoretically could not) be cashed before a certain date. While you can always use Quicken's post-dating feature for this, most banks no longer recognize post-dating as a means to restrict honoring a check.

You can set the check date in either of two ways: by typing the date explicitly in the Date field (you can selectively change the month, day, or year) or by incrementing/decrementing the date by pressing the + and − keys. You can press the + and − keys that are located along the top row of the keyboard or the keys in the numeric keypad.

About Checking Numbering

Checks aren't given numbers until they are printed. That way, you don't "waste a check" because you made a mistake. Most banks require that check numbers be preprinted on each check. Others allow you to provide your own check numbering, as long as you are careful not to duplicate the numbers. Check numbering isn't a consideration until you actually print the checks, so we'll defer discussion of the topic until Chapter 8, "Printing Checks."

Entering Payee's Name and Address

Checks for payroll and accounts payable are often mailed in convenient window envelopes. On the check is the name and address of the payee. This information shows through to the outside of the envelope. That way, you don't have to prepare a separate label or envelope to mail the check or, worse, write the name and address by hand.

All of the preprinted checks you can purchase from Intuit for Quicken have a space for the name and address (window envelopes are available separately), including the personal wallet-size checks, although you probably won't bother with the payee's address for routine home bill paying.

To enter data in the Address data field, move there using the Enter, Tab, or cursor keys and start typing. You are limited to no more than five lines, which should be sufficient for most instances. You can include a personal name or company, a department, suite number or apartment, street address, city, state, ZIP, and country. You may need to combine information on some lines if the address takes up more than five lines. For example, you can combine

```
555 Mill Road
Suite 1098
```

on just one line:

```
555 Mill Road, Suite 1098
```

> ▶ **Tip:** If the name in the first line of the Address data field is the same as the name in the Payee data field, you can use a handy Quicken shortcut to copy the payee's name into the address. In the first line of the Address field, type a double-quote character ("). Quicken automatically copies the entry in the Payee field and pastes it into the Address field. Press the Enter key to move down one line and enter the rest of the address.

If you send checks to the same payee on a regular basis and you need to provide the full mailing address, use the memorize transaction feature of Quicken to fill in the required data automatically. See Chapter 7, "Transaction Shortcuts," for more details on memorized transactions.

Including a Memo

Almost all checks—personal and business—provide a blank line for a memo. You can use the memo to provide an account number when paying a bill or to remind you what the check is for (e.g., "radiator, car repair" for a check written to Bill's Garage). Quicken lets you include a memo of up to 31 characters. The memo is printed along the bottom of the check and is also recorded in the check register, so you can refer to it later.

Quicken allows you to search for a specific character, word, or phrase while in the check register (more about this in Chapter 5, "Maintaining the Check Register"), so the information you write in the memo blank can be located quickly, even if the register contains thousands of old check transactions.

Note that you should not use check memos to categorize or classify checks. Save that task for Quicken's category/class feature.

About Categories

As you write checks with Quicken, you'll want to include a notation of where the money is going. This helps you view the "big picture" on how you spend your money. It also helps at tax time to separate those items that are tax deductible from those that aren't.

Quicken lets you assign any check you write to one or more categories. As listed in Appendix A, Quicken comes with several dozen categories for business and home use. You can assign any check to one of Quicken's ready-made categories, or you can create a new category of your choosing.

Entering a Category

1. Move to the Category blank.	Readies Quicken for a category entry.
2. Enter a category. OR If the category does not already exist, choose an option from the window that appears (see Figure 4-6).	Enters a category.

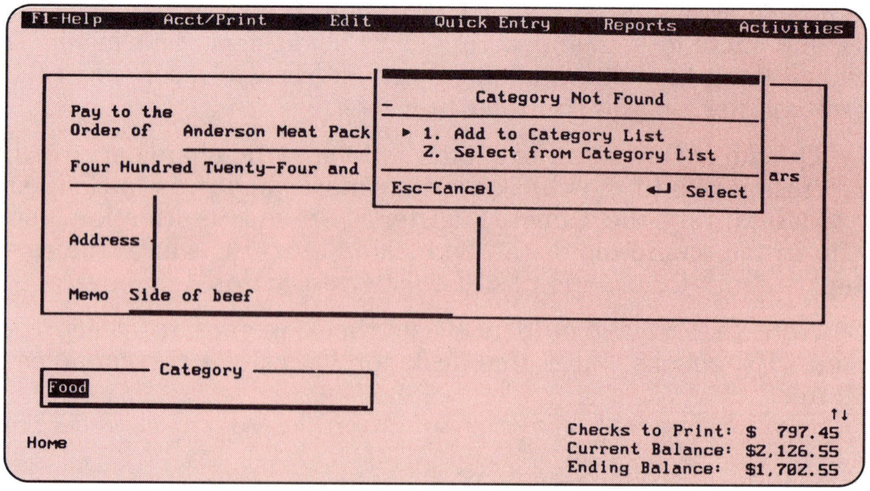

Figure 4-6. Quicken displays this window when the category you have provided can't be found.

If you choose the Add Category to List command, the category name you entered into the data field will be included in Quicken's category list. The next time you enter the category name, Quicken will recognize it, and the Category Not Found window will not appear.

If you choose the Select from Category List command, Quicken will display the Category and Transfer List window, as shown in Figure 4-7. The program automatically selects the category name that's closest to the one you entered. Use the cursor keys to select another category. Press Enter when you find the category you want. It will be inserted automatically in the Category blank in the current check.

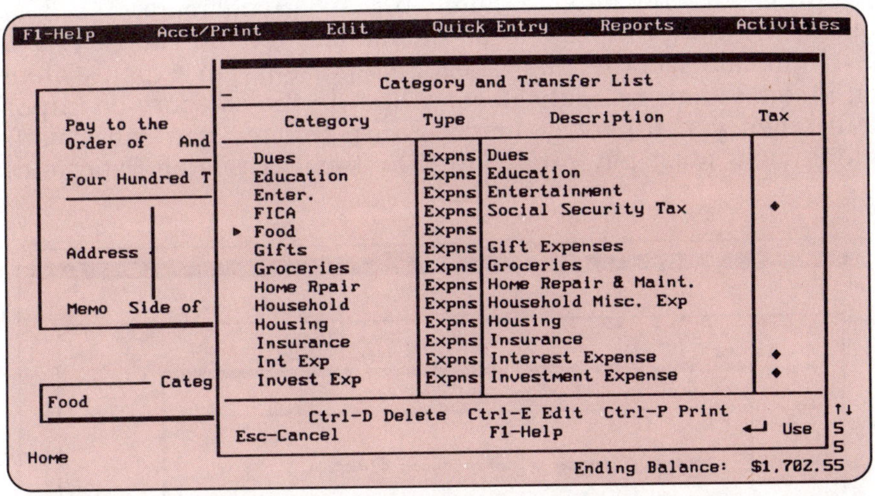

Figure 4-7. The Category and Transfer List window.

> **Tip:** You can use the Select from Category List command to help you locate and enter categories. When filling out the check, type the first two or three letters of the category you want to use. Press Enter then press 2 to choose the Select from Category List command. OR, press Ctrl-C to access the Category and Transfer List window directly.

Before creating a new category, see if it exists already, under a slightly different name (whether the category was provided by Quicken originally or is one you created). The reason: You'll want to apply categories to checks as consistently as possible.

For example, let's say that one month you apply the *Rent* category to your monthly rent check. In another month, you forget you've used the Rent category, and you assign the check to a new category called *Apartment Rent*. When you prepare reports with Quicken, the categories will be separate, and the total for each won't accurately represent the money you've paid on rent. When running Quicken, you may want to keep handy a notebook of the categories you use.

If you're creating one of your own categories, Quicken presents the window shown in Figure 4-8. The Set Up Category window lets you enter a name (up to 15 characters) and an optional description (up to 25 characters) for the category. You also indicate whether the category represents an expense item, an income item, or a subcategory. Should the category be important when you fill out your tax return (money you can save or money you must pay), indicate Y by the Tax-related data field.

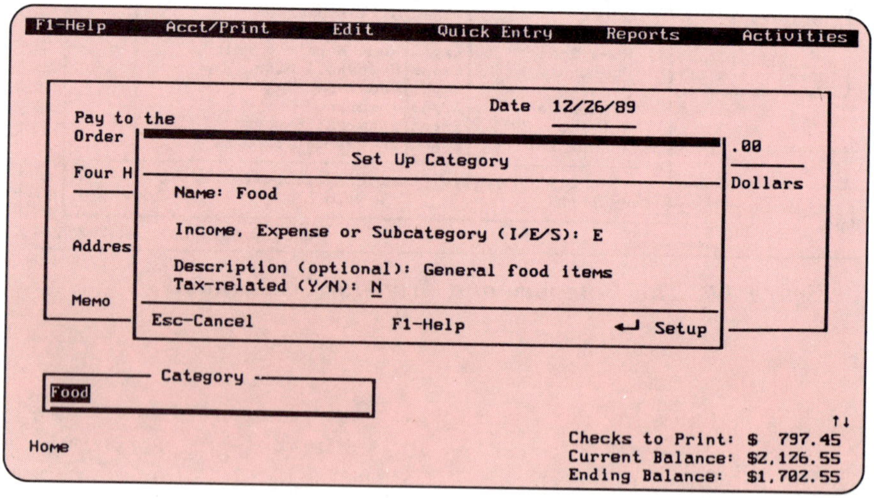

Figure 4-8. The Set Up Category window.

The topic of categories is an involved one and is central to getting the most out of Quicken. Chapter 6, "Keeping Track of Transactions," leads you through the maze of categories and also explains the use of subcategories and classes, as well how to split a check into several categories and to use categories to transfer funds from one of your accounts to another.

Reviewing the Check

Once you've filled out the check, take a few moments to check the data and be sure you've entered everything correctly. Check the following items:

Is the date set correctly? Most often it will be today's date.

Is the payee name's entered properly? Check the spelling.

Have you entered the dollar amount correctly? There's nothing like adding a zero to the dollar entry and writing a check for $5,000 instead of $500. Suffice to say, it leads to some surprises come check statement day.

If you've provided a name and address or a memo, double-check that the entry is satisfactory. Verify the address so the check finds its way to the payee.

Be sure that the check is applied to the appropriate category or class. (This is an optional step.)

To edit the check, use the cursor keys to move from one entry blank to another. Quicken provides a number of shortcut keys you can use to maneuver quickly around the check-writing screen, as detailed in Table 4-2.

Table 4-2. Moving Within the Write Checks Window.

Press	To
Ctrl-Right	Move one word or blank to the right
Ctrl-Left	Move one word or blank to the left
Enter	Move to the next blank
Tab	Move to the next blank
Shift-Tab	Move to the preceding blank
Ctrl-Backspace	Erase all text in the current blank

Recording the Check

With the check written and verified, you can now record it. There are three methods:

- Press the Enter key after providing a category name. (You can leave the Category data field blank, if you wish.) Quicken will automatically ask if you are ready to record the check. Unless you've turned off Quicken's confirm feature (with the Other Settings window under the Change Settings command), the program will ask if it's OK to record. Press 1 (or Enter) to record; press 2 (or Esc) to go back to filling out the check.
- Press Ctrl-Enter. This is the fast-record method and can be used when the cursor is in any data field in the Write Checks screen. You are not asked to confirm check-recording.
- Choose the Record Transaction command in the Edit menu. Press the F3 key then 1. This is the same as pressing the Ctrl-Enter keys. You are not asked to confirm check-recording.

Reviewing All Checks in Current Session

Most likely, you'll use Quicken to write several checks in one sitting. Table 4-3 provides a list of the quick-keys you can use if you'd like to review the other checks you've written. You can review all the checks you've written in the current session, as well as all other checks that are stored in the check register.

Table 4-3. Review Checks Quick-Keys.

Press	To
Page Up	See the previous check
Page Down	See the next check
Home	See the first check
End	See the last check

When you make changes to a check, be sure to re-save the alterations. Press Ctrl-Enter (or use one of the other check-recording methods detailed in the previous section) before viewing another check.

Deleting and Voiding a Check

Suppose you wrote a check in Quicken, then realized you already paid the bill. If you were using your regular checkbook, that would mean a wasted check and a mess in the check register. With Quicken, you can delete any check up until the time it is printed. (After it is printed you should void it.)

To delete a check:

1. Display the check you want to delete in the Write Checks screen. (You can also delete checks from the check register.)
2. Press Ctrl-D, or choose the Delete Transaction command from the Edit menu.
3. Quicken checks to make sure you really want to delete the check. Answer yes (press 1) at the prompt.

The check is no longer part of your checking account and is deleted from the check register. The ending balance shown in the lower right-hand corner of the Write Checks screen is updated.

If you've printed the check, or you've had one of your checks returned to you uncashed, you should mark it void in the register. The transaction will remain, but the ending balance will be updated to reflect the return of the money to your account. Also void a check if you've stopped payment on it or if it's been lost in the mail and never recovered. You can void a check only within the check register.

To void a check:

1. Press Ctrl-R to switch to the check register. (We'll talk about the check register more in the next chapter.)
2. Press the up or down arrow keys to highlight the check you want to void.

3. Choose the Void Transaction command from the Edit menu.
4. Press Ctrl-W to return to the Write Checks screen.

Quicken marks the check as void by placing a VOID in the payee's name.

What You Have Learned

This chapter explored check-writing procedures in Quicken. Here's what you should have learned:

- The check-writing procedure has five steps: selecting the account to use, accessing the Write Checks screen, filling out the check, reviewing the check, and recording the check.
- Once you select an account, remember the account name for subsequent sessions.
- At a minimum, for each check you write you must provide the payee's name and the amount of the check.
- Optionally, you can set a different date for the check than the one provided by Quicken. You can also enter the payee's address, a memo, and the category/class information.
- To set another date quickly, move the cursor to the date blank and press the + or − key to go forward or back one day at a time.
- The memo blank lets you write a short notation about the check to yourself or to the payee.
- The category blank lets you assign checks to specific account categories, to help you review your expenditures and draw up budgets.
- After writing a check, you should always review it to make sure the information is correct.
- To record the check (enter it into the check register so it can be printed), press Ctrl-Enter. You can also choose the Record Transaction command under the Edit menu.

Chapter 5

Maintaining the Check Register

In This Chapter

- *Accessing the check register*
- *Examining the contents of the check register screen*
- *Adding, editing, and deleting transactions*
- *Using Quicken find*

The Quicken check register automatically records the checks you write and tabulates the balance for you. While you can write all your checks using the Quicken Write Checks screen, you'll enter deposits, adjustments, ATM withdrawals, and other transactions directly in the register. To make it as easy as possible to use, the Quicken register functions like the paper checkbook register you're used to.

In this chapter, you'll learn how to use the register to enter all transaction types. The methods outlined here for managing the check register apply also to other Quicken account types, including Credit Card, Cash, Other Assets, and Other Liabilities.

Accessing the Check Register

The check register is never far away. You can access it directly with a keyboard shortcut or from the main menu.

Keyboard shortcut—Press Ctrl-R from almost any screen.
Main menu—Press 2, for Register.

The check register appears, as shown in Figure 5-1. The actual contents of the register will differ, depending on the transactions it contains.

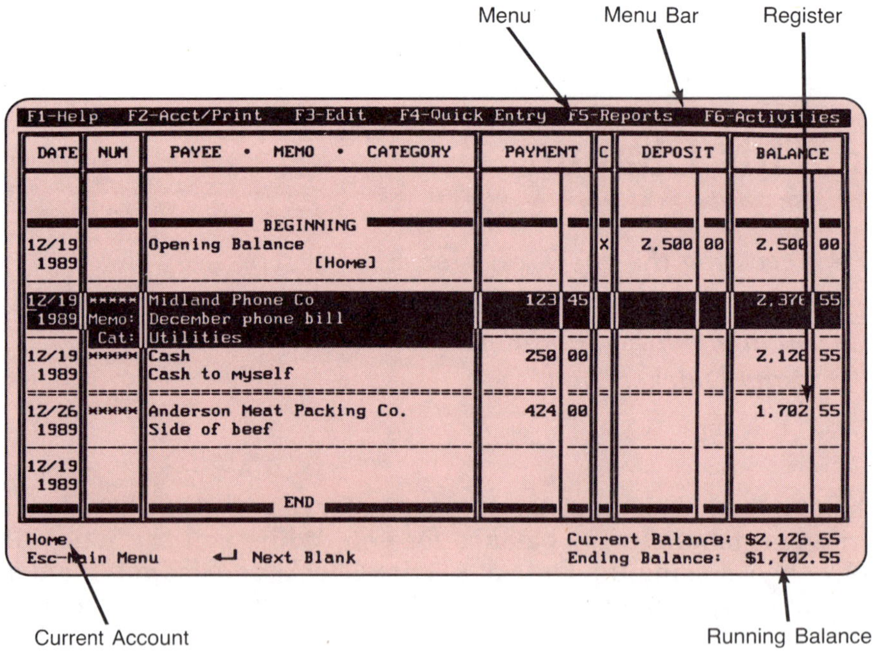

Figure 5-1. A sample check register, with important points identified.

The check register screen is divided into three major parts:

- *Menu bar*, where you can access the Quicken pull-down menus. (These menus are the same as those available during check-writing.)

- *Transaction columns*, listing important information about the check or other transaction type.
- *Status*, located at the bottom of the screen, showing the account currently in use, the current balance, and the ending balance. The current balance shows the amount you have in the bank before deducting any post-dated checks. The ending balance includes *all* transactions listed in the register, including post-dated checks.

Use the cursor keys to move around the check register screen. Table 5-1 lists those keys you can use to maneuver within the register and what they do. As you press the cursor keys, you move two types of cursors:

- The *highlight bar* indicates the current transaction you're working on.
- The *blinking cursor* indicates where the next character you type will be entered.

Table 5-1. Check Register Keys.

Key	What It Does
Up arrow	Previous transaction
Down arrow	Next transaction
Right arrow	Right one character or column
Left arrow	Left one character or column
Ctrl-Right arrow	Right one word
Ctrl-Left arrow	Left one word
Enter	Accept entry; go to next transaction
Tab	Go to next column
Shift-Tab	Go back one column
Home	Move to top of register
End	Move to end of register
Page Up	Move up one screen
Page Down	Move down one screen
Ctrl-Page Up	Go to start of previous month
Ctrl-Page Down	Go to start of next month

The *dotted horizontal lines* in the check register indicate separate transactions. While checks will be the most common transaction, you'll also include deposits, transfers, adjustments, ATM withdrawals, and so forth. A *double-dotted line* indicates that transactions listed below it are post-dated. You can have both post-dated debits (checks, fees, etc.) and credits. Each will be shown under the double-dotted line, as shown in Figure 5-2.

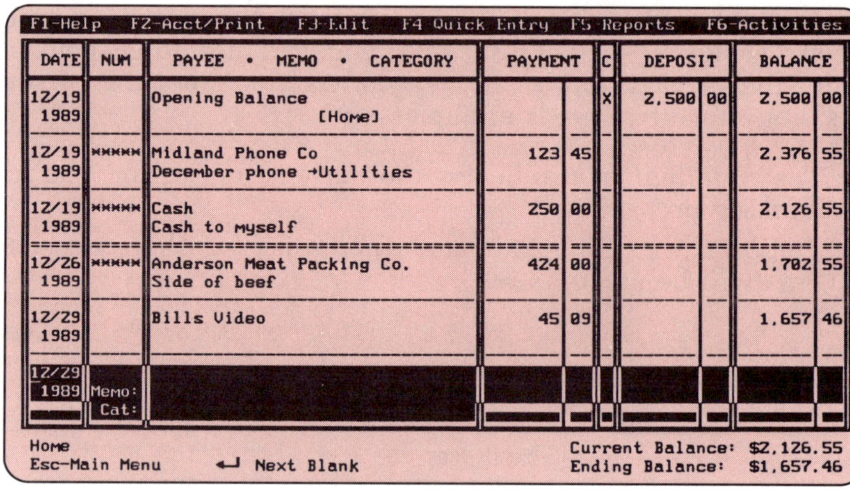

Figure 5-2. Register transactions are divided by double- and single-dotted lines; the double-dotted lines mean post-dated checks appear below.

Items in the Register

The check register records nine important tidbits about your checks or other transactions. These are date, number, payee, memo, category, payment, clear, deposit, and balance. This information is provided in the columns of the check register. The memo and category information is optional and is shown in the second line of the Payee column.

Date

The date is the date of the transaction. When writing checks, the date is normally the date you wrote the check. You can always change the date—to an earlier or later day. All other transactions in a checking account also occur on a specific date, so these each will include an entry in the date column as well.

For example, on a particular day you make a cash withdrawal from an automated teller machine. You enter the date of that withdrawal in the register. Similarly, adjustments to your checking account, including check fees and interest are usually dated as taking place on the last day of the account period. You enter that date as appropriate.

As in the Write Checks screen, you can change the date by writing a new one from the keyboard or by pressing the + or − key. Each press of the + or − adds or subtracts a day, respectively.

Number

Checks aren't given numbers until they are printed. In the check register, checks that have been printed are shown with a number in the NUM column. Checks that haven't been printed are shown with a ***** in the NUM column. When you print a check, Quicken asks for the check number. That number is inserted automatically in the NUM column for that check.

When you write a check by hand (it's hard to carry your computer and printer with you to the supermarket), you can manually enter its number by typing it from the keyboard. If the transaction is not a check (e.g., an ATM withdrawal, service fee, or counter check), press the Enter key to move the cursor to the next column.

> **Tip:** Use the + and − key shortcuts to select a check number quickly. With the cursor in the NUM column, press the + key; Quicken automatically looks up the number of the last check, adds 1 to it, and inserts that number in the current NUM column. Keep pressing the + key to advance the number. Press the − key to decrement the number.

Payee

The payee is the first line in the PAYEE/MEMO/CATEGORY column. It lists who you wrote the check to. Or, if the transaction is a deposit, ATM withdrawal, service charge, or the like, the Payee column will include a description of that transaction. Figure 5-3 shows some examples. For clarity, the illustration does not include entries for the memo or category.

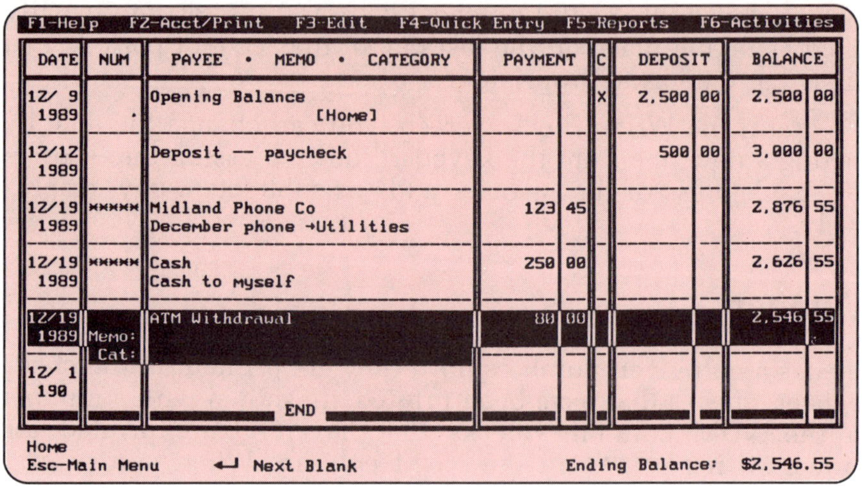

Figure 5-3. Some examples of payee entries.

> **Note:** You can alter the contents of the PAYEE/MEMO/CATEGORY column with the Other Settings window, located under the Change Settings menu. Specifically, you can show the memo, the category, or both on the second line. We will assume that you're using Quicken with the standard default of displaying both memo and category.

Memo

The memo message is optional. When you write a memo in a check, it appears on the second line of the PAYEE/MEMO/CATEGORY column. Memos aren't just limited to checks. You can also include a memo for a deposit, ATM withdrawal, or correction. Write a memo to help you remember the nature of the transaction or to have Quicken automatically select transactions to print in its reports.

Category

The category message is optional. If you've indicated a category for a transaction, that category is shown in the PAYEE/MEMO/CATEGORY column. If you've used subcategories and classes, these too are displayed, up to the first 14 characters of the category/class name. If the transaction has been split among several categories, you must select the transaction in the register and press Ctrl-S to see all the components of the split.

Payment

If the transaction is a debit (e.g., a check, a service fee, or ATM withdrawal), then the amount is shown in the PAYMENT column. A heavy line separates the dollar and cents. If you're entering the payment directly into the register, you can type it with or without dollar signs and commas. Quicken formats the entry with commas, but leaves out the dollar sign.

Clear

Unless you haven't written any checks or made a deposit in a while, your check register will always be ahead of the bank's statement of your account. You may have checks, deposits, and other transactions that the bank doesn't know about yet. And, as checking account statements come only once a month, they are rarely up to date with the actual status of your account.

The C (for CLEAR) column indicates those transactions that the bank has acknowledged in its monthly statement. Some transactions are posted by the bank almost immediately after you make them: ATM withdrawals, check charges, fees, and most deposits. Every month, when you receive your statement and compare it against the entries in the Quicken register, you mark the transactions that appear as cleared in your register. This helps you determine which credits and debits the bank is aware of and assists you in reconciling your register.

Quicken offers a nearly automated system for reconciling accounts, where you can clear checks, deposits, and other transactions quickly. But you can also clear individual transactions by moving the cursor to the CLEAR column and pressing C to enter an asterisk.

Deposit

Money you put in the bank is listed in the DEPOSIT column. Other forms of transactions are also entered in the DEPOSIT column, including interest, wire transfers, and corrections where your register shows a lower balance than the bank statement says you have in your account.

Balance

Quicken automatically enters the running balance for you. You don't need to do it. Whenever you add, remove, or alter transactions, Quicken automatically updates the balance for you.

Adding a Transaction

You can add any type of transaction in the register at any time.

Q Adding a Transaction to the Register

1. Display the register (if it isn't already displayed).	
2. Press Esc.	The transaction highlight bar moves to the very end of the register.
3. Enter the new transaction. Press the Enter or Tab keys to move to the next column. You can also use the left and right arrow keys to move back and forth between the columns.	Enters the new transaction information, as desired.
4. Review entry. Be sure the transaction information is correct.	
5. Press Ctrl-Enter.	Records the transaction. □

You can enter transactions into the register in any order. Quicken will rearrange the transactions in date order automatically. If you've written several checks on the same day, then those check transactions will be organized by number within that date. Checks that have not yet been printed, and therefore lack a check number, are kept with the other transactions you made on a particular day.

Editing a Transaction

Nobody's perfect. And when it comes to financial matters, you don't want mistakes to be left uncorrected. Quicken allows you to update and correct information easily at any time. (Note that you can lock out your accounts to prevent certain transactions from being changed by anybody except you; see Chapter 2, "Getting Started with Quicken," for details on the password option.)

Q Editing a Transaction in the Register

1. Display the register (if it isn't already displayed).	
2. Use the cursor keys to move the transaction highlight bar to the transaction you want to edit.	Moves to the transaction.
3. Edit the transaction information, as desired. Press the Enter or Tab keys to move to the next column. You can also use the left and right arrow keys to move back and forth between the columns.	Edits the transaction.
4. Review entry. Be sure the transaction information is correct.	
5. Press Ctrl-Enter.	Records the transaction.

> **Tip:** Normally, you'll use the Delete and Backspace keys to remove from a transaction characters you don't want. You can also replace characters as you type new data by pressing the Insert key once. With insert off, the characters you type replace existing text in the register. Press the Insert key again, and insert mode is turned back on.

If you alter the date of the transaction, Quicken will relocate it to maintain chronological order within the register.

> **Note:** The only information in the register you can't change is the balance in the BALANCE column. Quicken does that for you automatically.

Deleting a Transaction

You may have occasion to delete a transaction. For example, you may have entered an ATM withdrawal twice or written a check to someone who returned it to you. To delete a transaction, follow the same basic steps outlined above for editing a transaction. With the transaction you want to delete highlighted, press Ctrl-D (or choose the Delete Transaction command in the Edit menu). Answer Yes to the "OK to Delete Transaction" prompt. If you decide you don't want to delete the transaction, simply press the Esc key to cancel out of the delete process.

Similarly, you can void a transaction (usually a check) by highlighting the transaction, then pressing Ctrl-V (or choose the Void Transaction command in the Edit menu). Quicken doesn't double-check that you really want to void the check, so use this command carefully.

Using Find

The Quicken check register contains many shortcuts you can use to your advantage. Many of these shortcuts, including categories, classes, and split transactions, are detailed in Chapter 6, "Keeping Track of Transactions." Another helpful shortcut feature of the check register is find. With it, you can locate a specific transaction quickly, without having to scroll through the register manually and look for it.

To use the find feature, choose the Find command from the Edit menu or press Ctrl-F to access the Find command immediately. A find window like the one in Figure 5-4 appears on the screen.

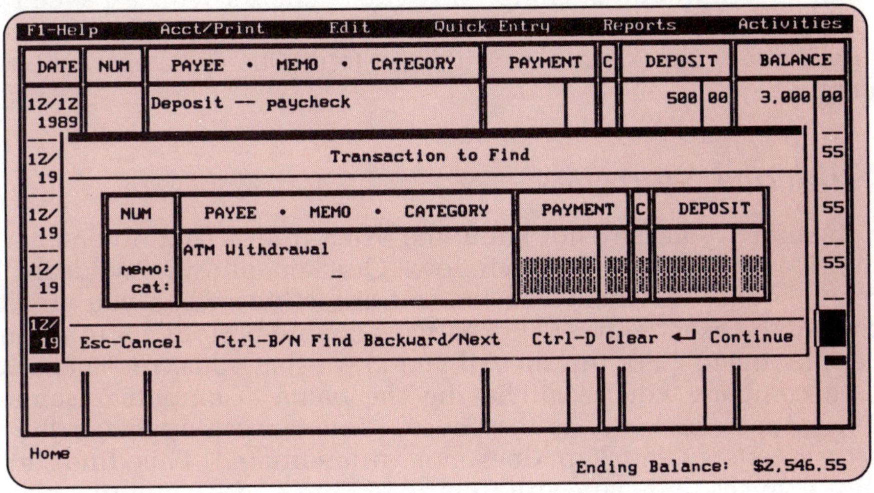

Figure 5-4. The Transaction to Find window.

In the columns provided, enter a word, number, phrase, or other text that matches the part of the transaction you want to locate. For example, if you want to find a check you wrote to "John Doe," type John Doe in the PAYEE/MEMO/CATEGORY column. If you think the transaction you want to find occurs *after* the current transaction in the register, press Ctrl-N. If you think the transaction you want to find occurs *before* the current transaction in the register, press Ctrl-B.

Tip: For the sake of simplicity and thoroughness, you may find it easier to locate transactions with the find feature by first moving to the start of the register (press the Home key), then using Ctrl-N for a forward search.

Your register may contain several transactions that match the criteria you've entered. After Quicken locates the first transaction, press Ctrl-N or Ctrl-B again to find the next one. If you want to locate a transaction using different criteria, clear the Transaction to Find window by pressing Ctrl-D.

You can look for more than one piece of information at one time. If you've written several checks to John Doe, but only want to find the ones that you entered into the Rent category, type `John Doe` as the payee and `Rent` as the category. Quicken will find only those transactions that meet all of the criteria you've entered. Using the example, only those checks with a payee of John Doe and a category of Rent are located, even if you have hundreds of checks either written to John Doe or categorized as Rent.

Wildcard Searches

Sometimes, you may not know the exact information to enter in the Transaction to Find window. Quicken allows "wildcard" searches that will help you locate transactions when you aren't sure of the exact entry. Quicken uses double periods (..) to mean "approximate." For instance, if you know that you wrote a check to a company you recall having the name "Computer" something, type `computer ..` as the payee. (You can use upper- or lowercase letters; Quicken does not differentiate.) This finds all those payees that start with Computer, and end in anything else, such as:

Computer Depot
Computer Specialists International
Computers R Us

Entering the periods before the word to search

```
(.. Computer
```

finds all those transactions where the payee name starts with any text and ends with Computer, as in:

Inland Computer
Basic Computer
Obsolete Computer

And using double-periods on each side of the word to find locates any entry where "Computer" is merely a part:

Touchstone Computer Center
Your Neighborhood Computerstore
Instant Computers, Inc.

Quicken also uses other characters as search wildcards:

Wildcard	**Meaning**
~	Search for everything except...
?	Replace question mark with any single character

You can combine wildcards characters to build complex search criteria. You can use these wildcards in the check register for finding transactions or when printing customized reports. For more information, see Chapter 10, "Creating and Printing Reports."

Go to Date

Similar to the find feature is Go to Date, where you can move to a specific date in the register instantaneously.

Q Moving to a Specific Date in the Register

1. Press Ctrl-G. OR Choose the Go to Date command from the Edit pull-down menu).	Activates Go to Date command. The window box in Figure 5-5 appears.
2. Enter date.	
3. Press Enter.	

Quicken takes you to the first transaction in the register with the indicated date. If no transaction was recorded on the date you specified, Quicken goes to the next nearest date.

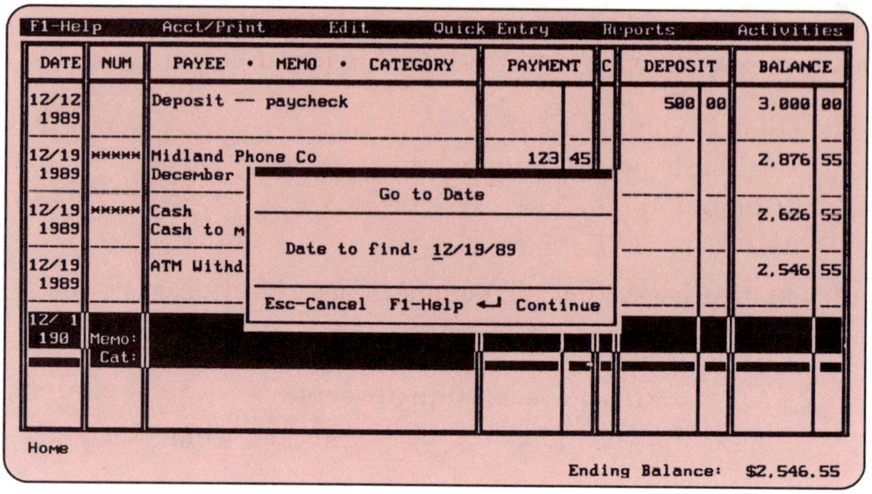

Figure 5-5. The Go to Date window.

What You Have Learned

This chapter examined the check register screen and discussed how to manipulate data within it. Here's what you should have learned:

- You can access the Quicken check register in either of two ways: press Ctrl-R from almost any screen or press 2 from the main Quicken menu.
- The check register uses columns to display the following items of interest: date, check number, payee/memo/category (all in one column), payment, clear, deposit, and balance.
- Checks aren't numbered until they are printed. Checks that have been written but not yet printed are shown with a ***** in the NUM column.
- The PAYEE column lists who the check is written to. If the transaction is not a check, it indicates whether it is a deposit, ATM withdrawal, service charge, or other transaction.
- The C (for CLEAR) column shows those checks and other transactions that have been acknowledged in the bank's monthly statement to you.

- Quicken automatically enters the running balance; you don't need to calculate the balance yourself.
- Within the check register, you can add, edit, and delete transactions. You can also void checks.
- Press Ctrl-Enter to record a transaction or the changes you've made in a transaction.
- The find feature helps you locate a specific transaction, without having to scroll through the register manually and look for it.

Chapter 6

Keeping Track of Transactions

In This Chapter

- *Writing memos*
- *Using transaction categories and classes*
- *Splitting transactions*
- *Entering transfers*
- *Reconciling your account*

Quicken provides many shortcuts to keep tabs on your financial matters. By using categories and classes, you can departmentalize your income and expenses so you know—at all times—your entire financial picture. You can also write memos directly onto checks (which are recorded in the check register) and use them as notes to yourself. You will not need to scribble in the margins of your paper register. With Quicken's flexible find feature, you can search for these notes quickly and easily. This can be handy, for example, when you need to verify that you've mailed out a check.

In this chapter, you'll learn how to use categories and classes to your best advantage. You'll discover the basics of setting up categories and classes and how to apply transactions to them. We'll examine categories and classes as they relate to checkbook transactions, but the fundamentals apply to all Quicken account types.

You'll also learn the ins and outs of *transaction reconciliation*—the process of making sure you and the bank agree on the ending balance. Few people enjoy reconciling their checking accounts, but Quicken makes the process about as painless as it can possibly be.

Writing Memos in Checks

Check memos let you jot down a note to yourself or to the payee. They are written and printed in the lower left-hand corner of the check. One application of the memo blank is to enter an account number when paying your Visa or car insurance bill. The memo is for the benefit of the payee rather than you—unless you have several Visa and car insurance accounts and need the numbers for your own benefit as well.

Another use for the memo blank, as shown in Figure 6-1, is to write notes to yourself. For example, you might enter "Loan to Uncle Joey," to indicate a check you wrote to Uncle Joey (step brother on your mother's sister's side) as a personal loan. Not only will the memo help you to remember what the check was for, it can help at tax time or when settling your estate.

When (and if) Uncle Joey pays you back, his checks might appear as income to the Internal Revenue Service. You will need your original check—with the "Loan to Uncle Joey" memo on it—to prove that his checks to you were repayments. Should something happen to you—you die or become hospitalized and can't manage your financial affairs—your family or executor will be able to track the Uncle Joey loan and determine whether you've been paid back.

In time, your check register will become full with checks, deposits, corrections, and other transactions, and finding the one

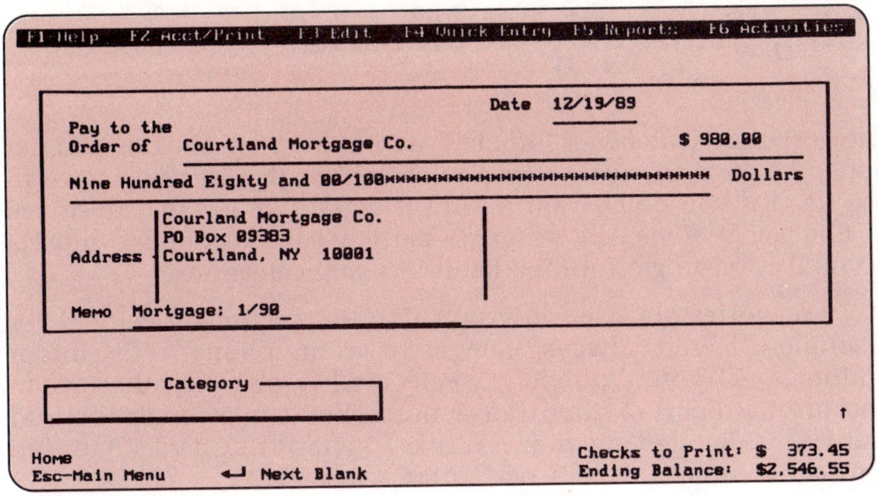

Figure 6-1. Filling in the memo blank.

check you write to Uncle Joey may become burdensome. You can use Quicken's find feature to locate it quickly. To use find, choose the Find command from the Edit menu (or press Ctrl-F). Type `Uncle Joey` in the memo blank. If you think Uncle Joey's loan check is above the current transaction in the register, press Ctrl-B (for backwards search). If you think the check is below, press Ctrl-N (for next). Quicken finds the first check that lists Uncle Joey in the memo blank.

Note that you can also find transactions based on other criteria: check number, date, category, and so forth. The find feature was more completely discussed in Chapter 5, "Maintaining the Check Register." Refer to that chapter for more information.

You can write a memo at the Write Checks screen or check register screen. Merely position the cursor within the memo blank and type. Press the Enter key when you are done. Because Quicken allows you to make changes to transactions even after the check has been printed, you can write memos to yourself that won't show on the check. In the case of Uncle Joey's loan, you might write "Irrecoverable loan to Uncle Joey...."

Using Transaction Categories

Categories are Quicken's "official" way of keeping track of transactions. As with memos, categories are optional: you don't have to use them if you don't want to. But if you'd like to take advantage of Quicken's advanced features—particularly customized reports—you'll want to get into the habit of using categories.

Categories are used to group like transactions together. For example, if you always categorize your phone bills under "phone," all your "phone" checks will appear together when you print a report of your transactions. You can also use the find feature (as detailed above in "Writing Memos in Checks") to find transactions that match a particular transaction.

Quicken comes with several dozen preset categories. These are divided between home and business use. When you first create a new account, you have your choice of indicating whether the account is for business or home use. Your choice determines the preset categories that are automatically applied to your account. You can also select neither (all preset categories are omitted) or both (you get all categories for home and business). Appendix A lists the preset categories for home and business.

By no means are you limited to the preset categories Quicken offers. You can add and delete categories at will. You can add categories in two ways:

- Directly in the Category List window.
- While writing checks (in the Write Checks screen or check register).

Each account you create with Quicken has its own unique set of categories. Your checking account may have different categories than your savings account. If you also use Quicken to manage your cash, credit cards, assets, and liabilities, these, too, can have their own unique set of categories.

Before you create any new categories, take a moment to jot down where your money comes from and where it goes. Leaf through the last two or three months of bank statements and note whom you wrote checks to. Make a list of recurring payments made to companies or individuals—rent, mortgage, utilities, school tuition, and so forth.

Other checks may have been written to a variety of payees, but reflect common purchases, such as clothes, gasoline, entertainment, or business supplies. If you're using Quicken to track your credit cards, go through the card statements and note your recent purchases.

Adding Categories in the Category List Window

The most direct way of adding categories is to enter them in the Category and Transfer List window. You can access the Category and Transfer List window in two ways:

- At the Quicken main menu, choose the Write/Print Checks or Register commands. In the Write Checks or check register screen, choose the Categorize/Transfer command from the Quick Entry menu.
- At the Write Checks or check register screen, press Ctrl-C.

The Category and Transfer List window appears, as shown in Figure 6-2. The actual contents of the window you see will be different, depending on the categories already assigned to your account.

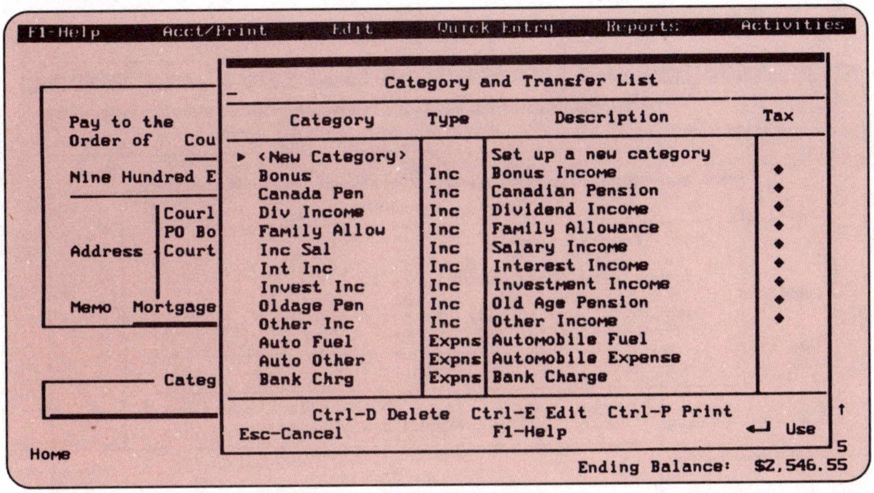

Figure 6-2. The Category and Transfer List window.

Flip through the category list with the cursor keys. Press Home or End to move to the beginning or end of the list; press Page Up or Page Down to scroll through the list one page at a time. Select a specific category to use by highlighting it with the up and down arrow keys.

Adding a New Category to the Category and Transfer List Window

1. Highlight <New Category>.	
2. Press Enter.	Quicken displays the Set Up Category window, as shown in Figure 6-3.
3. Enter category name and press Enter.	
4. Enter E for Expense, (default), I for Income, or S for Subcategory.	Defines type of category.
5. Enter a description and press Enter. Descriptions are optional, but recommended.	
6. Indicate if the category is tax-related.	

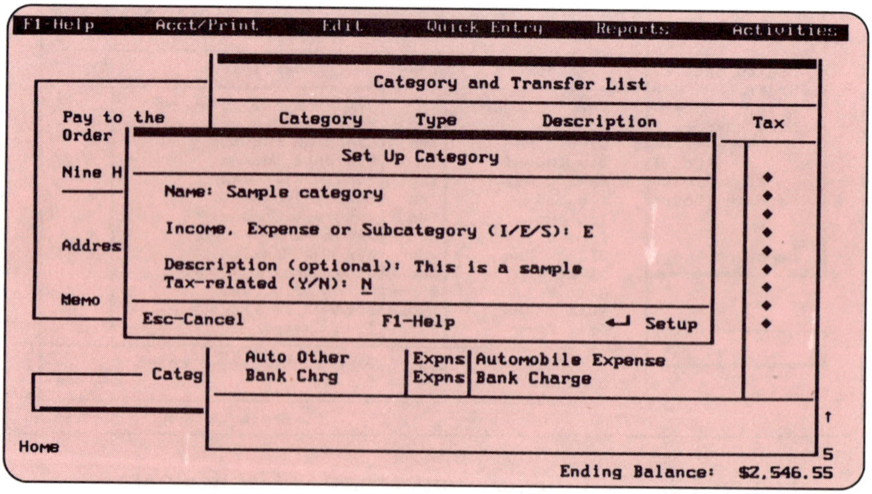

Figure 6-3. Set up categories in this window.

Tip: Categories (as well as classes, detailed below) consume memory. Although Quicken doesn't impose a limit on the number of categories you can create, the amount of memory available in your computer will determine the maximum number of categories you can create for any one account. On a computer with 320 kilobytes of RAM (and using no terminate-and-stay resident programs), you can create approximately 150 categories and classes. A computer with 640 kilobytes of RAM can accommodate over 1,000 categories/classes. The actual number of categories you can create depends in part on the length of names you use to identify the categories. Using shorter names helps conserve some (but not a lot) of memory. Get into the habit of choosing short names for your categories, but don't make them so short that you can't decrypt their function.

Repeat the procedure for each new category you wish to create. If you make a mistake (misspell the category name, for example), you can either edit or delete categories, as detailed below.

Note that other accounts you have created also appear in the category list. You can see them by scrolling to the end of the list. These categories are there to allow you to transfer funds from one account to another. See the section entitled "Splitting Transactions," later in this chapter.

When you are done entering transactions, press the Escape key to return to the Write Checks or check register screen.

Adding Categories While Writing Checks

You can create categories "on-the-fly" while you enter checks and other transactions in the Write Checks and check register screens. Enter a new category name in the Category blank in the check register. Quicken will prompt you that it can't find the category, as shown in Figure 6-4. You have two choices:

- Ask Quicken to add the category name to the category list. The name, exactly as it appears in the Category blank, is appended to the Category and Transfer List window and will appear there (in proper alphabetical order) the next time you access the window.

- ▶ Ask Quicken to display the category list so you can select another category. Use the cursor keys to select the category you want, then press the Enter key. The category you selected is inserted into the Category blank automatically.

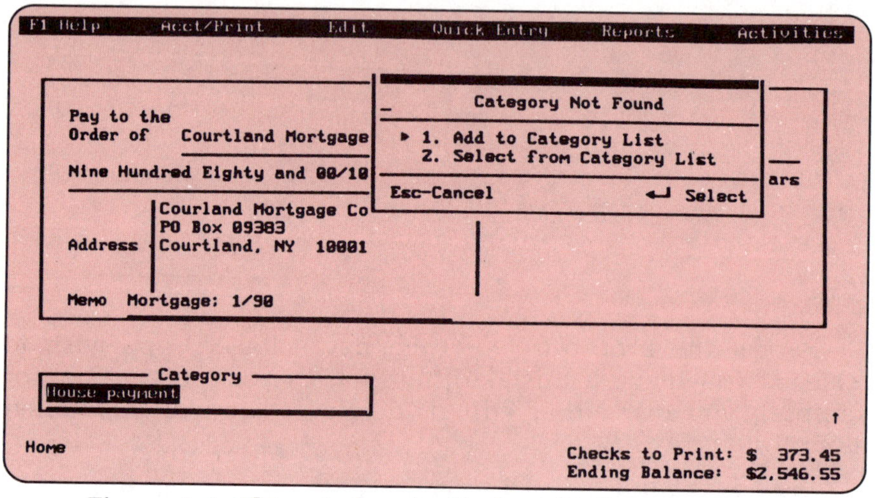

Figure 6-4. This window is displayed when Quicken can't find the category you've indicated.

You can also cancel the message and re-enter the category name. Press the Escape key to return to the Write Checks or check register screen.

The procedure for naming and describing the category is the same as it is when adding categories directly in the category list.

Proper Category Names

You can give any category just about any name you wish. Categories can include letters, numbers, spaces, and most other printable characters with four exceptions. The following keys are NOT allowed in category names:

```
[ ] / :
```

Quicken reserves these characters for special uses. The brackets are used to denote a transfer; the colon means you want to use a subcategory; and the slash means you want to use a class.

Editing and Deleting Categories

Let's say you no longer need a category or that you want to free up memory space and delete some of the extraneous preset categories Quicken offers. You can readily delete categories you don't want. You can also edit existing categories and change their names, descriptions, and other specifics. The following Quick Steps assume you are currently in the Write Checks or check register screen.

Q Deleting a Category

1. Press Ctrl-C.	Accesses Category and Transfer List window.
2. Scroll to category you want to delete.	
3. Press Ctrl-D. Quicken checks that you really want to remove the category permanently. Answer accordingly.	

The category notation for transactions that was linked to this category (if any) is blanked out. For example, if you had a category called Rent and deleted it, the category blank for all rent checks would be cleared. The rest of the check remains unaffected.

Q Editing a Category

1. Press Ctrl-C.	Accesses Category List window.
2. Scroll to category you want to edit.	

3. Press Ctrl-E. Displays the Set Up Category window, where you can edit the name and description, or change the category type (expense, category, or subcategory). □

The category notation for transactions that was linked to this category (if any) is updated to reflected your edits. For example, if you had a category called Rent and edited it to read "Rent—Main St.," the category blank for all rent checks would now read "Rent—Main St."

Using Categories

With categories in place, you can use them in your checks and other transactions. To use a transaction, type it in the Category blank of the Write Checks or check register screen. Don't worry about case—Quicken doesn't care if you use upper- or lowercase letters.

You can change category information for any transaction. Move the cursor to the category data, edit it in the normal fashion, and re-record the transaction. Quicken automatically updates all affected transactions.

You can use this approach to add categories later. Let's say that you're in a hurry and just want to write and print out a stack of checks before you go on a vacation to Hawaii. Write the checks without categories and print them. When you get back, go through the register and write in the categories, as desired. Now, when you print a transaction report, the checks are shown with the added category information.

▶ **Tip:** You don't need to type the entire category name when you enter it in the Category blank. Quicken can figure out what category you want when you type the first few characters of the name and press Ctrl-C. You need to enter enough characters to distinguish the category you want from others that begin with the same characters. For instance, to recall the "Housing" category, type `Ho` and press Ctrl-C. Unless you have other categories that also start with "Ho," Quicken will fill in the rest of the blank with the full name.

About Subcategories

Suppose you have several sources of income: from your regular job, from your spouse's regular job, and from a week-end job where you make wood name signs with your router and sell them. While you could create a different category for each source of income, a more beneficial approach is to use subcategories. Each of your sources of income comes under the main category of "Income," but each is differentiated with the use of subcategories. In the category list as well as most transaction reports, all your sources of income will be grouped together, making it easier for you to track.

Quicken understands that you want to use subcategories when you add a colon (:) after the main category name. For example,

Income:Joan's Pay
Income:Joe's Pay
Income:Wood Signs

These entries are shown in the category list in Figure 6-5.

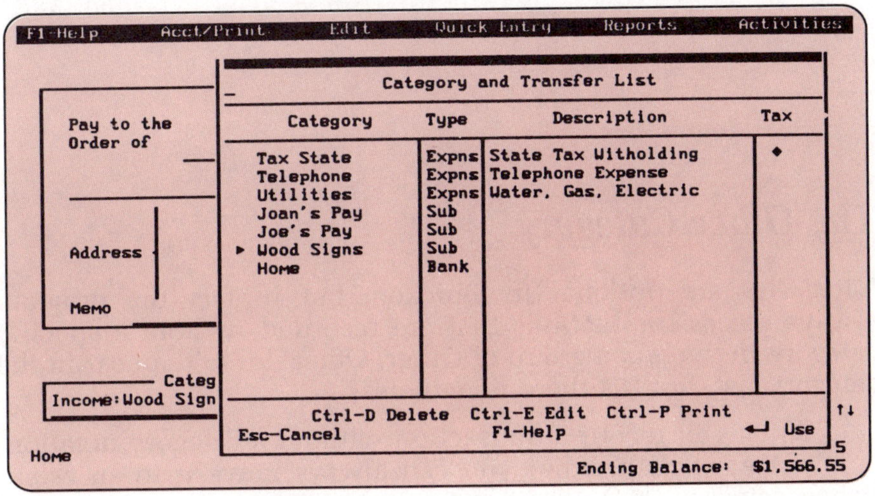

Figure 6-5. A sample of three incomes in the category list.

You create and use subcategories the same as you do main categories. To use a particular subcategory, enter the name of the main category, a colon, then the name of the subcategory. You can theoretically add additional subcategories under other subcategories, such as:

one level of subcategories	Utilities:Phone Mortgage:Interest Computer:Supplies
two levels of subcategories	Utilities:Phone:Business Mortgage:2nd TD:Interest Computer:Supplies:Diskettes

You should limit yourself to no more than two levels of subcategories, however. Any more and you're bound to make errors.

> ▶ **Tip:** When creating subcategories, always put the general category first. Utilities:Phone makes sense, but Phone:Utilities does not. Although you'll be guided by common sense to create subcategories in the proper fashion, some applications require forethought. For instance, do you enter "Alimony:First Husband" or "First Husband:Alimony"? You can always change it afterward, of course, but getting it right the first times makes you job that much easier.

The Other Category

Categories are optional in Quicken, but in fact the program always places transactions that are recorded without a specific category in the broad group of Other. Other doesn't appear in the category list, but it's there nonetheless.

When you record a transaction without a category notation, it is placed in Other, but you can always move it to an established category later on. Likewise, a transaction that you previously assigned a category to can be abandoned under Other.

Printing the Category List

You'll want to keep a crib sheet of the categories you have available to you. Quicken lets you make a quick printout of the category list.

1. Press Ctrl-C to access the category list.
2. Press Ctrl-P. The Print Category List window appears.
3. Indicate the printer you are using and press Enter or Ctrl-Enter to print the list.

Splitting Transactions

Unless you're in the habit of writing a separate check for every small item you buy, you're bound to pay for goods with one check that should be applied to any number of different categories. If you're buying office supplies, for instance, you may need to keep separate tabs on where the supplies are going and what they are for. This is especially true if you've created categories for different departments in your company.

Quicken lets you split a transaction many ways. The split is like an itemized list of categories. A good application of a split transaction is separating the monthly combined house payment into separate categories for principal, interest, taxes, and insurance. When tax times comes, you'll know exactly how much went to the principal (which is not tax deductible), interest (which is tax deductible), taxes, and insurance. You can split a transaction up to 30 ways.

Q Splitting a Transaction

1. Move to the Category blank (Write Checks or check register screen).
2. Press Ctrl-S. — The Split Transaction window appears, as shown in Figure 6-6.

3. Enter the splits; each on one line.
4. Press the F9 key to calculate the running total.
5. Press Ctrl-Enter when done.

   Returns you to the Write Checks or check register screen. □

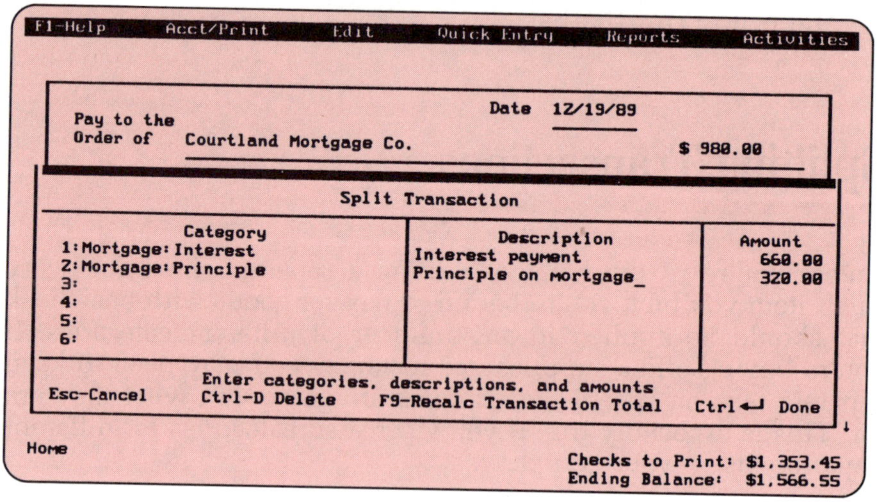

Figure 6-6. The Split Transaction window.

You need to provide three pieces of information for each tine of the split:

- The category name (including subcategory, if needed).
- A description (optional, but highly recommended).
- The dollar amount of the split.

In most instances, all of the splits will equal the face value of the transaction. (You can split checks, deposits, ATM withdrawals, and so forth.) You may not care to categorize all the splits, however. In that case, just enter the remainder in the next line and leave the category blank. If you've already entered the dollar amount for the transaction in the Write Checks or check register screen, Quicken keeps a running balance for you in the last line of the Split Transactions window. You can always tell when you have an outstanding balance if the amount is not $0.

In the Write Checks and check register screens, the Category blank says SPLIT when the transaction has been split up. This does not appear when the check is printed.

> **Tip:** Quicken offers a handy shortcut when in the Split Transactions window. Press a quotation mark (") in the Category blank, and Quicken will automatically copy the category information from the previous line. This is especially helpful for setting up split transactions because one check is often used to purchase items for one major category. Use the " method to copy the main category name quickly, then type in the subcategory.

Splits Printed on Voucher Checks

The first 15 lines of split transactions are printed on the stub of voucher checks. You can use this feature not only to keep track of your accounts payable but also to assist the payee in knowing what the check is for. You can enter account numbers, voucher numbers, invoice numbers, and so forth in the Split Transaction window, and they will appear on the voucher stub.

You'll probably want to print just the description of the split in the voucher. You can force Quicken to omit the category with the Other Settings menu, shown in Figure 6-7. Turn categories off by entering N for option 9. To access the Other Settings menu, select Change Settings at the main menu, then choose Other Settings. Refer to Chapter 2, "Getting Started with Quicken," for more information.

Making Changes to Split Transactions

At any time you can alter the information in the Split Transaction window. To edit a split, or even delete it altogether, select

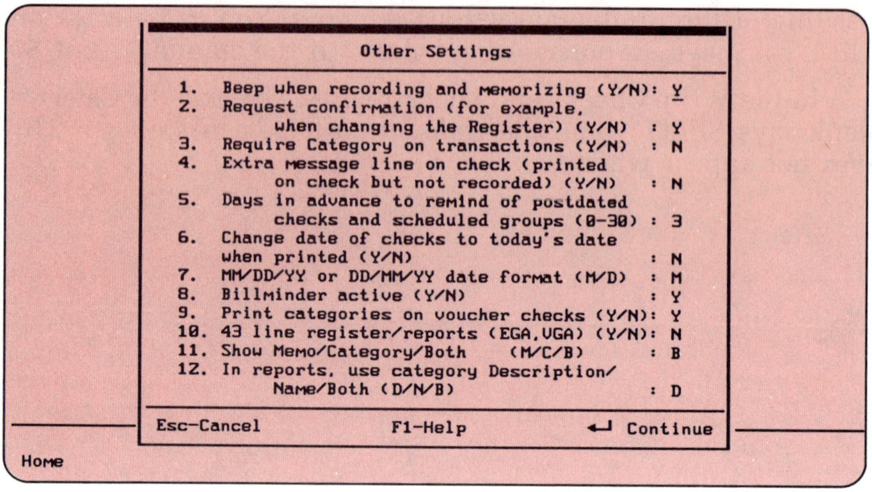

Figure 6-7. The Other Settings menu.

the transaction and press Ctrl-S to access the Split Transaction window. Move the cursor to the field you want to edit, and make your changes. When you're done, press Ctrl-Enter.

To delete one or more splits in the Split Transaction window, position the cursor on the line you want to remove and press Ctrl-D. Quicken asks you if you really want to delete the line. Answer yes or no accordingly. To delete the entire split transaction, remove each line then press Ctrl-Enter. The word SPLIT disappears from the Category blank. The transaction is no longer split.

Entering Transfers

A *transfer* is taking money from one Quicken account and putting it into another. For example, you can write a check to your savings account or take a cash advance from your Visa (which you monitor in a credit card account) and deposit it into your checking account. You need only record the first half of the transaction;

Quicken automatically records the second. That saves you time and reduces the chance of error.

To enter a transfer, merely type the name of the teamed account in the Category blank. If you're depositing money from your checking account into your savings account, for instance, enter the actual name of your savings account (Savings, My Savings Account, Money Market, or whatever) into the Category blank.

Before you can record a transfer to another account, that account must already exist. Unlike categories, which Quicken can create for you on-the-fly, you must specifically create new accounts ahead of time.

Accounts are always listed at the very end of the Category and Transfer List window. To see them, press Ctrl-C from the Write Checks or register screen, then press End to view the bottom of the list, as shown in Figure 6-8.

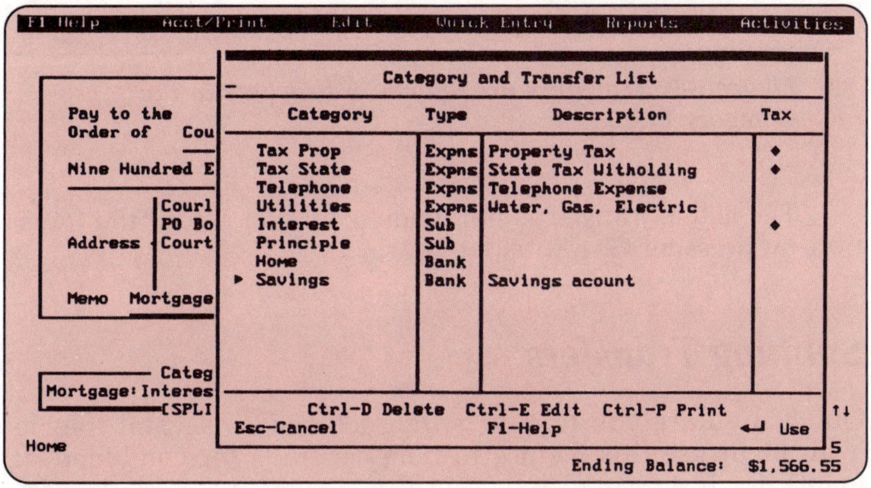

Figure 6-8. Sample accounts in the category list.

You use transfers just like categories. In the Category blank, type the name of the account you want to use. After you type the name and press the Enter key, Quicken will enclose the name in brackets, as shown in Figure 6-9. You don't have to type the brackets yourself. If you're not sure of the account name, enter a left bracket ([) in the Category blank, then press Ctrl-C. Quicken will display the account names at the bottom of the category list automatically. Scroll to the account you want to use and press Enter.

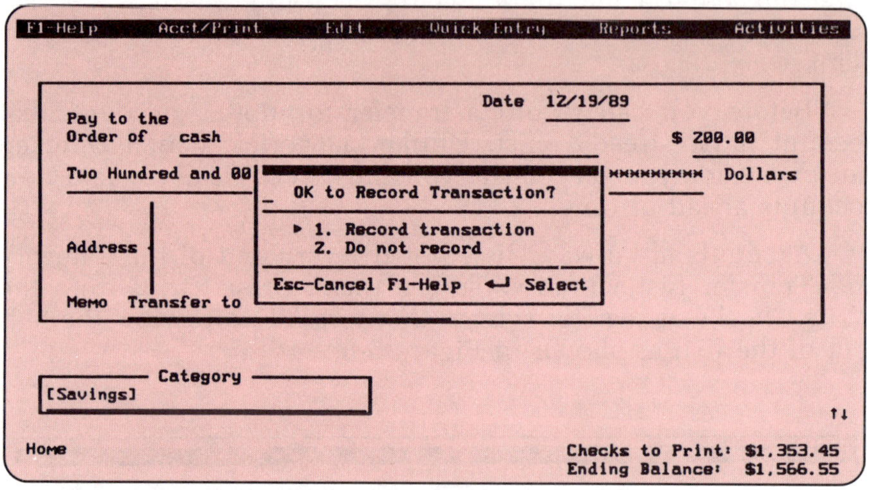

Figure 6-9. Transfers are shown in brackets in the Category blank.

The actual transfer is not made until you record the transaction by pressing Ctrl-Enter.

Splitting Transfers

Quicken allows you to split a transaction into several transfers. You might use this feature to note accounts for combined payments, for instance, or when writing a check where only part of the money is deposited into another account (when you've asked for money back when depositing a check at the bank, for instance).

To split a transaction into one or more transfers, use the Split Transaction window, as detailed earlier in this chapter. The technique is the same as splitting a transaction into several categories. You can split a single transaction into one or more categories as well as one or more transfers.

Going to a Transfer Transaction

Assume you're the Doubting Thomas of the family and you want to be sure that Quicken transfers your money between accounts properly. The program provides a quick and easy way of toggling between transfers.

After Quicken has recorded the transfer and while still in the Write Checks or check register screen, choose the Go to Transfer command from the Edit menu. Quicken immediately hauls you to the other half of the transfer transaction. While there, you can review the transaction or enter the notation as you desire. Use the Go to Transfer command again to return to your original location.

Altering Transfers

Just as Quicken automatically tracks transfers when you first create them, the link between the transactions remains in place. If you delete one of the transactions in the transfer, the opposite transaction is also deleted (e.g., you void a deposit into your savings). Changes in the amounts and account names are similarly updated automatically.

Using Classes

Classes add an extra dimension to Quicken's categories. Although you can use Quicken in any way you wish, a good application of classes is to track transactions by person, place, or time. Using the old journalistic axiom of who, what, when, where, and how, you can use categories to track the *what* and *how* and classes to track the *who*, *where*, and *when*.

Classes are created and used just like categories. Unlike categories, though, Quicken doesn't come with a preset list of classes. Classes are specific to the individual (like people's names, dates, and places), so you need to add all of them yourself.

Creating Classes

You can create a class when you're writing a check (or other transaction) or with the Class List window. To access the Class List window from either the Write Checks or check register screen, press Ctrl-L. The window in Figure 6-10 appears. Follow the same procedure outlined above under "Using Categories" to create a new class.

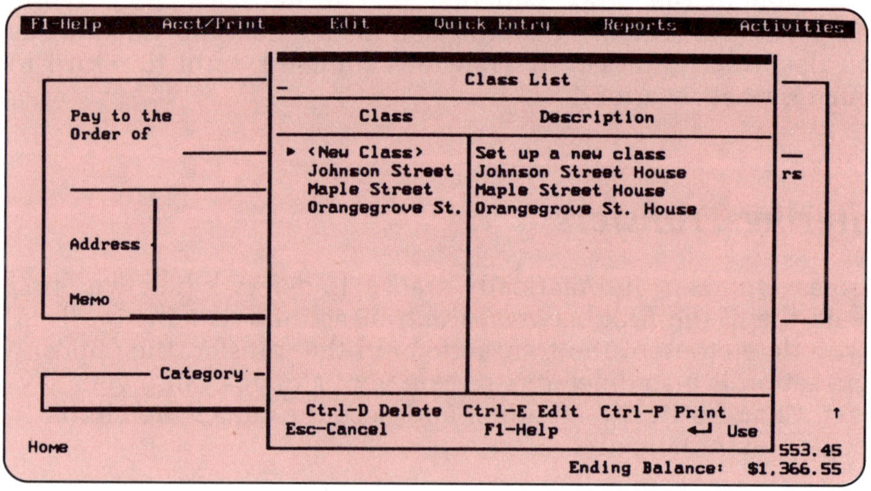

Figure 6-10. The Class List window.

Using Classes

Quicken understands that you want to use a class when you enter a slash (/) in the Category blank within the Write Checks or check register screen. You can enter just a class, or a category and a class, as in

Class only	/Maple St. House
Category and class	Mortgage/Maple St. House

If you enter a class name that has not yet been defined, Quicken asks you if you want to create it or choose from among the existing class names.

Using Subclasses

As with categories, you can assign subclasses to transactions. The more subclasses you provide, the more specific the nature of the transaction. For instance,

Mortgage/Maple St. House:April '92

indicates that the transaction is listed under the broad category of mortgage and is assigned to the Maple St. House main class. The April '92 notation indicates when the mortgage payment was made.

Modifying the Class List

At any time you can modify the entries in the Class List window. To edit a class, select it and press Ctrl-E. Make the desired changes, and press Ctrl-Enter. To delete a class, select it and press Ctrl-D. Verify that you want to erase the class.

Printing the Class List

Make a print of the class list so you can refer to it when you are entering transactions.

1. Press Ctrl-L to access the class list.
2. Press Ctrl-P. The Print Class List window appears.
3. Indicate the printer you are using, and press Enter or Ctrl-Enter to print the list..

Reconciling Your Transactions

Reconciling a checkbook ranks up there with having root canal work and visiting the in-laws for the holidays. Even with Quicken, the process of making sure you and the bank agree on the ending balance is not entirely without its frustrations. But Quicken does make the task more efficient, and because it reconciles your account on a semiautomated–automated basis, you're not prone to make as many mistakes or overlook steps.

Follow this procedure when reconciling your Quicken checking accounts:

1. Choose the Reconcile command from the Activities menu.
2. Fill in the balance, service charge, and interest information, as requested by Quicken.
3. Mark those transactions in Quicken that have cleared the bank (listed in this month's statement).
4. Compare the ending balance as displayed Quicken and the ending balance as reported by the bank. If they agree, the task is done. If they don't, you'll need to find the error(s) or adjust for the difference.

Starting Reconciliation

To start the reconciliation process, go to either the Write Checks or check register screen. Choose the Reconcile command from the Activities menu. As shown in Figure 6-11, the Reconcile Register with Bank Statement window appears. In the entry blanks provided, enter:

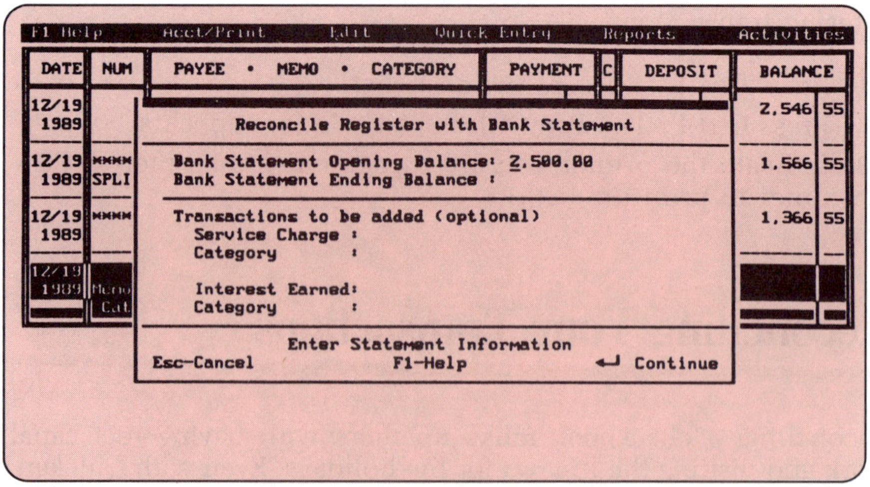

Figure 6-11. This window appears when you choose to reconcile the check register.

The opening balance, as shown on your bank statement—This amount should be displayed already and is either the opening balance you entered when you first started using Quicken or the ending balance of the preceding month. If the amount is different from what's shown in your bank statement, you may not have provided an accurate opening balance when you opened the Quicken account. You may wish to go back and check your earlier records or, if the difference is small, update the opening balance to match the bank's records.

The ending balance, as shown on your bank statement.

Service charges (combine all charges, including check charges, returned item fees, and so forth).

Interest earned, if any.

Press the Enter key when done, and continue to the next step. If you changed the opening balance, Quicken displays an information window to assist you in matching your old opening balance with that of the bank. You may now mark those transactions that have cleared the bank.

Marking Cleared Items

Items that have been posted in your bank statement are cleared: the bank has acknowledged them and has either added money to your account or paid money from your account. The major step of statement reconciliation is marking cleared items.

After entering opening and ending balances, Quicken automatically displays the cleared item screen, shown in Figure 6-12. This screen is a simplified version of the check register. Find those checks that are listed on the bank register as cleared and press the Spacebar. An asterisk appears in the C (for CLEAR) column. You can mark a range of checks by pressing the F8 key and entering the starting and ending check numbers.

> **Tip:** Use the Mark Range shortcut to mark as cleared all the checks you've written in a given month. Then, go back to those checks (and other transactions) that are not posted on the bank statement, and press the Spacebar to erase the asterisk.

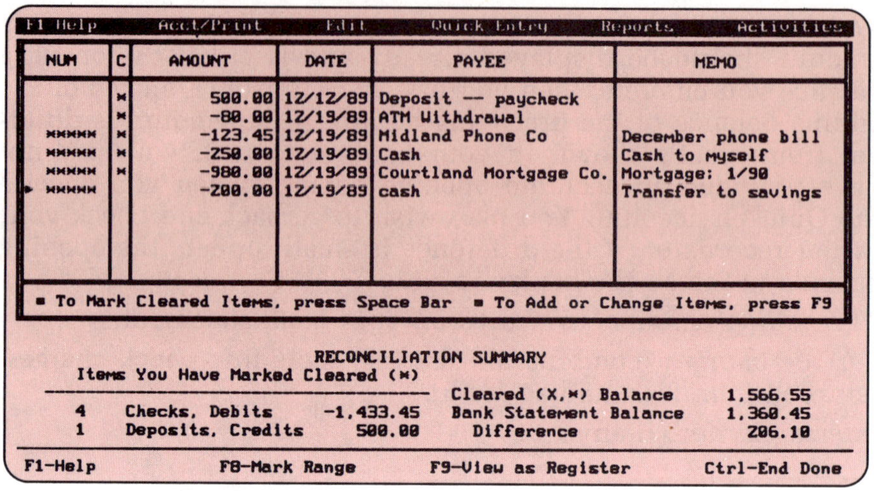

Figure 6-12. The cleared item screen.

It often happens: when reviewing your bank statement you spot a transaction that you forgot to enter into Quicken. It may be a deposit or perhaps an ATM withdrawal. It could also be an unexpected service charge or perhaps a voided check that you forgot to update in your register. While clearing items, you can make changes to the register to update your records to match the bank's. Press the F9 key to switch to register view. In the register, you can add transactions, edit those transactions that are incorrect, and make other changes as necessary. When you're done, press the F9 key once again, and you're back in the cleared item window.

Comparing Balances

While clearing items, Quicken provides you with a running tally. It shows the amount of checks and other debits you have marked as cleared, as well as the total for deposits and other credits. Quicken calculates the bank statement balance against the items you've marked as clear and indicates the difference.

Theoretically, when you've marked all the posted items from the register as cleared, the difference should be zero. If it is, then your job is done. Press Ctrl-Enter to go on to the next step. If the difference is some positive or negative value, it means either that the bank is in error or that you've missed some item and it's not reflected in your Quicken register. Take a moment to double-check your records.

If the difference is small—say under $20 one way or the other—you may want to call it quits and accept that somewhere there's a mistake. You should make every attempt to look for possible errors in your bank statement or register, but there comes a time when the difference isn't worth the effort. You can ask Quicken to make the adjustment for you, or you can enter a "correction" transaction yourself.

To adjust the difference automatically, press Ctrl-End, and answer Yes to the prompt that asks if you want to have Quicken adjust the ending balance (see Figure 6-13). The program will add an adjustment transaction for you, indicating whether the adjustment is a credit or a debit.

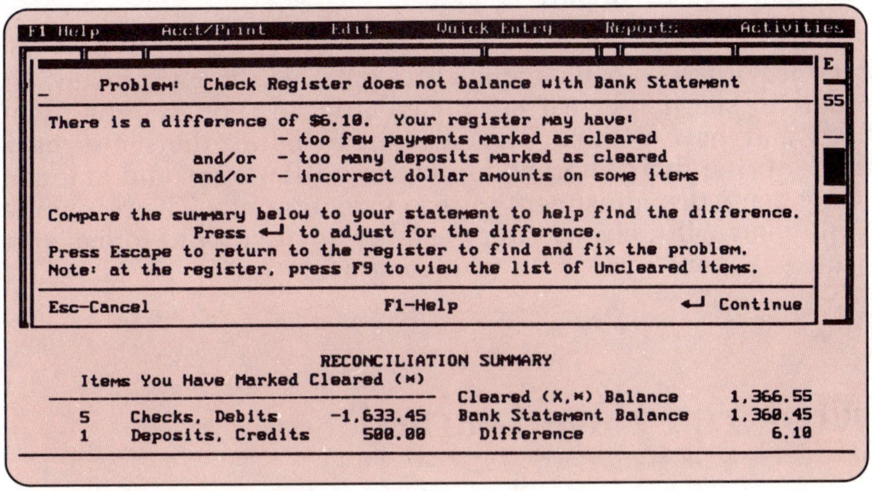

Figure 6-13. Quicken can automatically adjust for differences between your register and the bank statement.

To adjust the difference manually, switch to the register (press the F9 key), and enter a special transaction. If the difference is in the bank's favor (they say you have less money than your records show), enter the adjustment as a debit. If the difference is in your favor, enter the adjustment as a credit. Return to the cleared items list (press the F9 key) again, and mark the adjustment as cleared. Press Ctrl-End to finish reconciling.

Obviously, you'll want to exercise extreme care when making adjustments to your account. Just because you're using Quicken doesn't mean that errors can't occur. You may enter the wrong amount for a deposit or record an ATM withdrawal as $80 instead of $180. Or, the fault could be on the side of the banks. If the amount is considerable, you may want to examine the statement and your returned checks carefully to make sure that only your checks are listed and that the dollar amount on the checks is the amount the bank debited from your account.

Printing the Reconciliation Report

After reconciliation, Quicken asks if you want a detailed report. If the reconciliation went smoothly with no adjustments, you may not need the report.

But if an adjustment was necessary, print the report and keep it with your bank statement. Come next month, review the report to see if the real error has surfaced. For example, your bank may have debited your account twice for the same check, then, during their internal audits, found the error and automatically made the adjustment in the current month. The reconciliation report will help you to remember what you did to make the bank statement agree with your records.

What You Have Learned

This chapter detailed how to keep better track of your Quicken transactions. Here's what you should have learned:

- You can use memos as notes to yourself or to the payee.
- Categories help you separate transactions into logical groups. You can also use categories to find a particular transaction.

- Quicken's preset home and business categories are optional. You can use them as you like, remove those you don't want, and add your own.
- The easiest way to create new categories is to enter them in the Category blank in the Write Checks or check register screen. Quicken asks if you want to add the category to your list.
- Transactions that fill many categories can be split. You decide how much of the transaction goes toward each category.
- A transfer is taking money from one Quicken account and placing it into another. Quicken automatically establishes the link between the accounts so that if you later change one side of the transfer, the other is immediately updated.
- Classes provide an extra dimension to Quicken's categories, letting you catalog your transactions by people, places, and times.
- Quicken greatly automates the process of reconciling your checking account statement. When necessary, Quicken can make adjustments automatically.

Chapter 7

Transaction Shortcuts

In This Chapter

- *Using memorized transactions*
- *Manipulating transaction groups*
- *Using Billminder*

Quicken's forte is saving you time. The program offers a number of time-saving shortcuts you can use with your checkbook account, as well as any other account maintained by Quicken. If you find yourself entering the same transactions week after week, or month after month, you'll find relief in two Quicken shortcuts: memorized transactions and transaction groups. With these two features, you can reduce repetitive bill-paying chores to an efficient science.

With transaction groups, not only can you instruct Quicken to remind you when to pay a certain bill, you can also have the program automatically prepare the check for you. And with memorized transactions, you can record the data in a check or other register entry and recall it any time in the future, just by pressing a few keys.

For home users, you can use these features (either together or separately) to write regular checks for such payments as mortgage, insurance, rent, and school tuition.

For business users, you can use memorized transactions and transaction groups to simplify payroll and accounts payable. Even if some of the payable information changes from month to month, you can still automatically insert the name and address of the payee, category information, and other time-consuming tasks.

In this chapter, you'll learn all about memorized transactions and transaction groups. You'll learn how to record transactions for later recall, and you'll learn how to program Quicken so that it will prepare your regular recurring payments and deposits automatically.

Memorized Transactions

The best way to explain the concept of memorized transactions is by example. Suppose you mail out a mortgage check each month to your bank. The check is the same dollar amount month after month and is addressed to the same bank. Because the one payment includes principal, interest, tax, and insurance, you have set a split transaction where the $1,200 per month house payment is divided among four different categories.

This would be a time-consuming check to fill out each month. You'd be required to enter, for a total of 360 times (assuming a 30-year loan) the following repetitive information:

Payee
Dollar amount
Payee's address (you use the address in a window envelope)
Memo
Four-way split transaction information

Instead of going through this hassle, Quicken can take a "snapshot" of one of the mortgage payment checks you've filled out and record it as a memorized transaction. Next month, you pick the mortgage payment transaction from a list, press the Enter key, and all of the information (except the date) is re-entered. Press Ctrl-Enter to record the new check, and you're ready to print it.

Recording a Memorized Transaction

You can fill out the entire check for a memorized transaction or just part of it. The mortgage payment scenario is a good example of a check you'd fill out completely, with dollar amount, address, memo, and category.

Q Recording a Memorized Transaction

1. Press Ctrl-M.	Highlights the data it will record and displays the memorize transaction window, as shown in Figure 7-1.
2. Press Enter.	The data in the check is memorized and added to the Memorized Transactions List (more about this later).

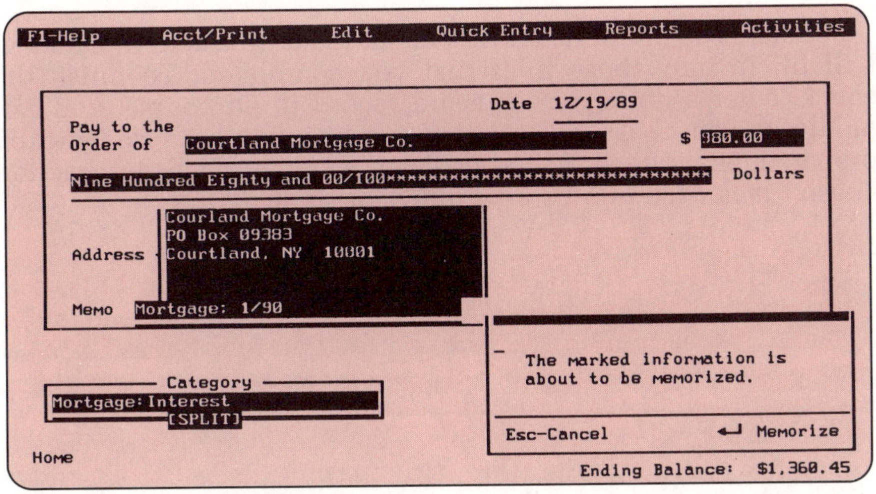

Figure 7-1. The highlighted areas of this check are about to be memorized.

Other checks don't require you to fill in all the blanks. For example, your phone bill changes every month, so you'd create a memorized transaction that contains the name of the phone company, its address (if you're not using a preprinted addressed envelope), and optionally entries in the memo and category blanks. Now, when you press Ctrl-M, as shown in Figure 7-2, Quicken highlights only those items that you filled in.

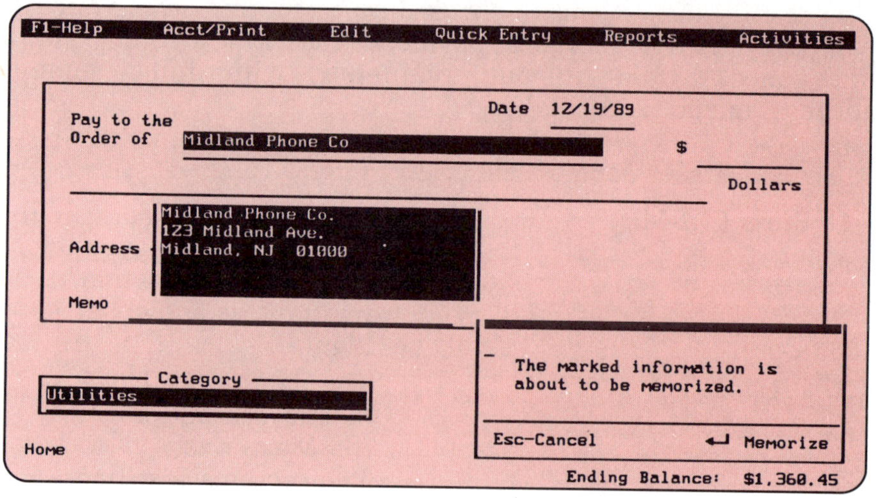

Figure 7-2. Only part of this check is filled in, so only part will be memorized.

Later, when you recall this memorized transaction, Quicken will fill in only those lines that you completed. To finish the check, enter a dollar amount and record it. Of course, you can modify the check in any way that you like. Just because Quicken prepared the check for you from a memorized transaction doesn't mean the entries are etched in stone.

Tip: If you'd like to record several memorized transactions, but not actually prepare the checks, fill out the data as needed, memorize the transaction, then press Ctrl-D for delete. This deletes the entries in the check and lets you start all over again. If you accidentally record a check, go to the register or bring the check back into view (press Page Up until the check you want is displayed). Press Ctrl-D, and confirm that you want to delete the transaction.

Quicken stores all memorized transactions in the same pool, regardless of the account you are using. This lets you share memorized transactions between accounts—you can use the same memorized transaction for your savings and checking account, for example.

Quicken can store only a set number of memorized transactions, depending on the available memory in your computer. The more memory you have at your disposal, the more memorized transactions you can hoard. If you try to memorize a transaction, and Quicken reports an out-of-memory error, you should:

Remove some of the *categories* and *classes* you no longer need. (These also take up memory space.)

Remove some of the *memorized transactions* you no longer need.

Quicken stores the memorized transaction by payee's name. At the very least, you should fill in the payee's name. All other entry blanks can be empty. You should avoid entering two memorized transactions with the same or similar names for the payee. While Quicken will let you record two or more identical memorized transactions, the practice makes it harder for you to use the system.

Recalling Memorized Transactions

Recalling a memorized transaction is simple.

Q Recalling a Memorized Transaction

1. In a blank check, move to the payee blank.
2. Type the first few letters of the payee's name for the memorized transaction you want to use.
3. Press Ctrl-T. — Displays the Memorized Transaction List, as shown in Figure 7-3. The transaction you want should already be highlighted.

4. Press Enter. — Inserts the entire memorized transaction into the check. □

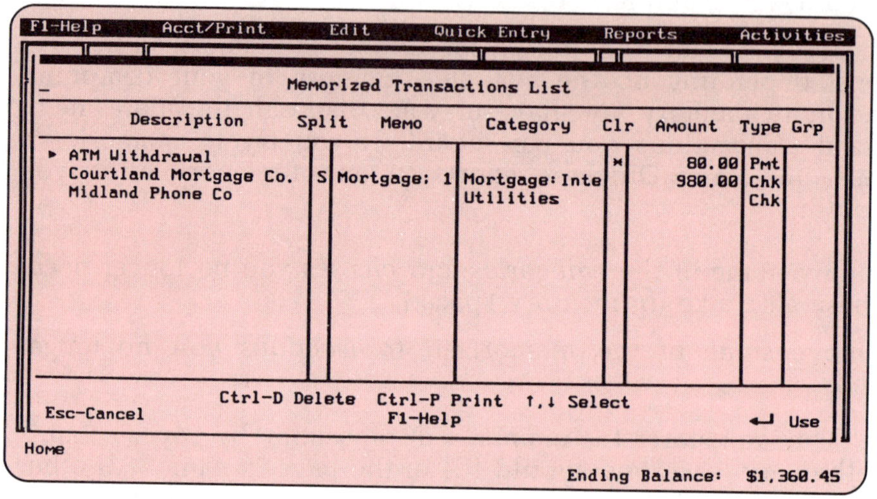

Figure 7-3. The Memorized Transaction List.

The more characters you type in the payee blank before pressing Ctrl-T, the more Quicken can differentiate between all the memorized transactions it holds. You need to type enough characters to differentiate between similar transactions, or Quicken won't be able to decide which one you want to use. If Quicken can't decide, you'll need to select the proper transaction from the list. That entails more keystrokes and a little more work on your part.

For instance, suppose you have a memorized transaction for *Acme Rental* and another for *Acme Rents*. (As we mentioned earlier, this is not a good procedure to follow, for obvious reasons.) To differentiate between the two, you'll have to type in most of the name before Quicken can discern which one you want.

Viewing the Memorized Transactions List

You don't need to type some or all of the payee's name in the payee blank to recall a memorized transaction. From anywhere within the Write Checks screen, merely press Ctrl-T, and the Memorized Transaction List will appear. Use the cursor keys in the normal fashion to scroll through the available transactions. When you find the one you want, press Enter.

Editing Memorized Transactions

Things change, and you may find that a transaction you memorized months ago has to be updated. For example, your bank may have moved, or the dollar amount of your mortgage payment may have changed (you took out a second mortgage or the payments are increasing because you have an adjustable rate mortgage). You can edit a memorized transaction at any time. When you recall the transaction and make the necessary changes, Quicken fills in the new information.

Q Editing a Memorized Transaction

1. In the Write Checks screen, recall the transaction using one of the methods described earlier.
2. Make the necessary changes.
3. Press Ctrl-M. — Asks if you want to Replace the transaction or Add the edited transaction to the list, as shown in Figure 7-4.
4. Answer Replace.

Deleting Memorized Transactions

You can (and should) delete from the list those memorized transactions you no longer need. This clears the way for other memorized transactions and gives Quicken a little more memory with which to work. Follow these steps to delete a memorized transaction:

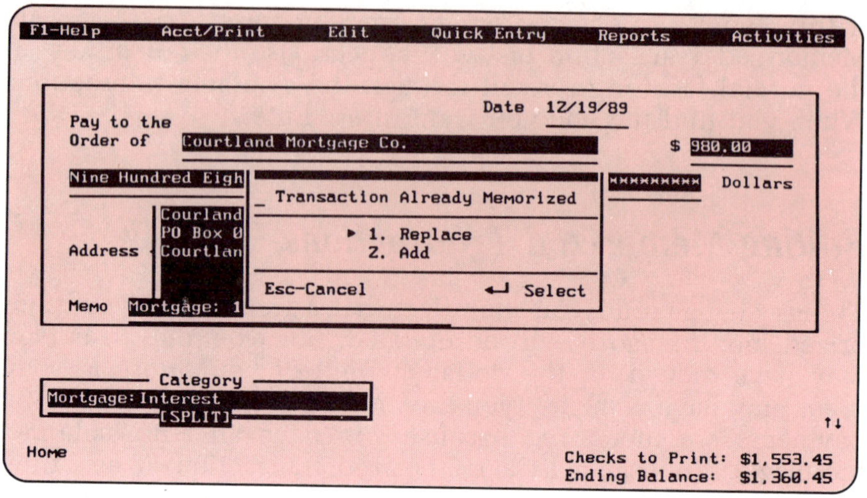

Figure 7-4. Quicken lets you Replace or Add memorized transactions.

1. From within the Write Checks screen, press Ctrl-L to view the Memorized Transactions List.
2. Scroll to the transaction you want to erase.
3. Press Ctrl-D then Return. If you decide you don't want to delete the memorized transaction after all, press the Escape key.

You can delete any number of transactions. When you're done, press the Escape key to return to the Write Checks screen.

Printing the Memorized Transactions List

If you use Quicken to pay a lot of checks, you'll probably forget which ones you've recorded as memorized transactions. To help you remember, print the Memorized Transactions List.

1. Press Ctrl-T while in the Write Checks screen to view the Memorized Transactions List.

2. Press Ctrl-P. The Print Memorized Transactions List window appears.
3. Indicate the printer you are using, and press the Enter key or Ctrl-Enter.

Memorizing Other Transactions

While the memorized transaction feature is most often used to capture recurring checks, you can use it to remember any transaction you create with Quicken. While in the check register screen (or any other register screen of any Quicken account type), fill in the desired information and press Ctrl-M. Quicken will record the transaction according to the information you provided in the register.

If you indicate $500 as a deposit of your paycheck, for example, Quicken records the transaction as "Paycheck" and puts $500 in the Amount column of the Memorized Transactions List (see Figure 7-5). Quicken codes the transaction type as "Dep" rather than "Chk," so that when you recall it, the $500 will be placed in the DEPOSIT column of the register rather than the PAYMENT column.

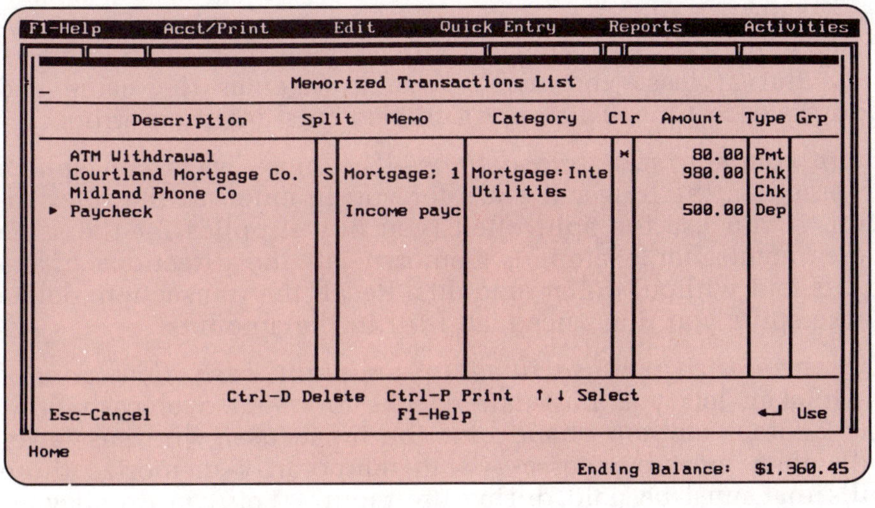

Figure 7-5. A listing of memorized transactions, includint a regular deposit.

> **Note:** While Quicken will let you memorize a check transaction from the check register screen, if you write a check and memorize it there, you can't produce a printable check at the Write Checks screen. If you want to be able to create and print a check using a memorized transaction, memorize the data at the Write Checks screen.

Some Handy Uses for Memorized Transactions

You probably don't need much prompting to figure out how you can best use the memorized transaction feature. But here are some ideas to start the creative juices flowing:

Record common ATM withdrawals—If you regularly withdraw, say, $60 from the ATM machine, enter an ATM payment in the register and memorize it. Then, whenever you have another ATM withdrawal for the same amount, you can recall the memorized transaction.

Record the names and addresses of regular payees—If you're in business and pay the same individuals and companies regularly, record their addresses as a memorized transaction. Each payment will likely be different, with varying memos and categories. But at least you won't have to re-enter the name and address each time. This approach also cuts down on errors.

Store common split transactions—The more ways you split a transaction, the longer it takes for you to enter all the information. If you use the split often (you buy supplies for the same departments, for example), memorize all the directions of the splits, but without dollar amounts. Recall the transaction, delete those splits you don't need, and fill in the amounts.

Use memorized transactions to maintain cash flow control—Quicken lets you post-date checks to watch over cash flow, but another method—handy for the home user who has fewer bills than most businesses—is to temporarily memorize those bills that must be paid during the month. You can do all your "paperwork" at once, then when it comes time to prepare and print the bills, you can quickly recall each memorized transaction in turn. Delete the memorized transactions, unless they are recurring.

Transaction Groups

An extension of memorized transactions is the transaction group. In addition to recording vital statistics about recurring transactions (e.g., checks, deposits, and ATM withdrawals), transaction groups let you consolidate those bills you pay at specific intervals or specific times of the month. When you need to pay bills, whether it's once a week, once every other week, or almost any other cycle, you can instruct Quicken to create checks for those bills. If necessary, you can fill in amounts, memos, and other variable data, then record the check for printing.

The best candidates for inclusion in a transaction group are those bills you pay every month. These include rent or mortgage payments, car payments, phone and other utilities, and cable TV bills. If the bills are due at about the same time, you can include them in one transaction group. If they are due at dissimilar times, and you don't want to record the check for the transaction ahead of time, you can enter just one bill in the group.

The transaction group feature also includes an optional reminder system, using the Billminder program included with Quicken. The Billminder program (the actual DOS name is BILLMIND.EXE) checks the scheduling of transaction groups to see if you have any bills coming due. If so, you are warned, and you can take a moment to run Quicken and print out the checks.

Even though Quicken's transaction group feature makes it easy to pay bills in chunks, you still retain control over the actual check-making process. If you decide to wait to pay a bill, that's up to you. Quicken's only interest in the matter is reminding you that the bill is due. How and when you pay it is your business.

Organizing a Transaction Group

The first step in establishing a transaction group is to gather up all the transactions you want to include. This involves memorizing each of the transactions, using the memorize transaction feature detailed in the first part of this chapter. You then select among those memorized transactions you want included in the group. Optionally, you can set a reminder frequency or date.

Q Organizing a Transaction Group

1. If they aren't already memorized, memorize those transactions you want included in the group.
2. From the Write Checks or check register screen, choose the Set Up Transaction Group command from the Quick Entry menu. — The Select Transaction Group to Set Up/Change window appears, as shown in Figure 7-6.
3. Highlight the next available <unused> group and press Enter. — Creates a new transaction group. The Describe Group ## (where ## is a number from 1 to 12) window appears, as detailed in Figure 7-7.
4. Provide a name for the group; the other settings are optional and discussed below.
5. Press Ctrl-Enter when done. — Displays a list of available memorized transactions in the Assign Transactions to Group ## window (see Figure 7-8).
6. Highlight a transaction; press the Spacebar to select or deselect it.

Running a Transaction Group

Whenever you like, you can run the transaction group and make checks or other transactions. Before you execute the group, open the register for the account you want to use. As with memorized transactions, transaction groups transcend the boundaries of accounts; you can use the same groups in any Quicken account.

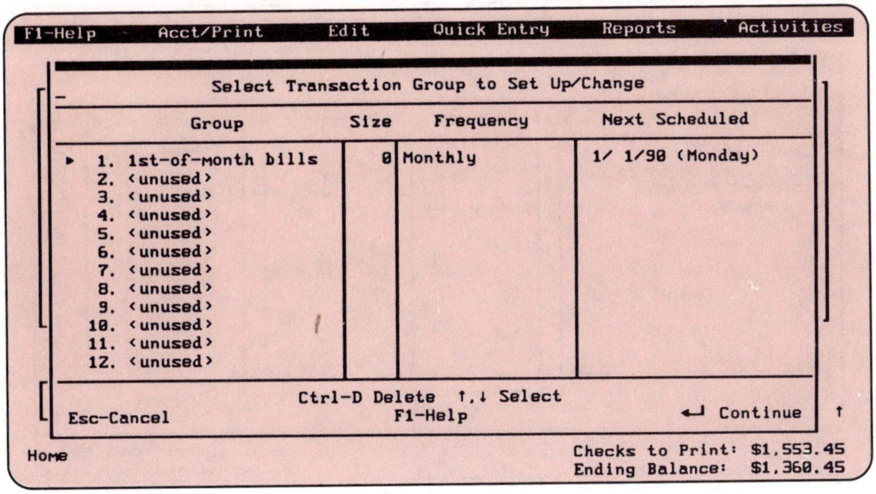

Figure 7-6. The Select Transaction Group to Set Up/ Change window.

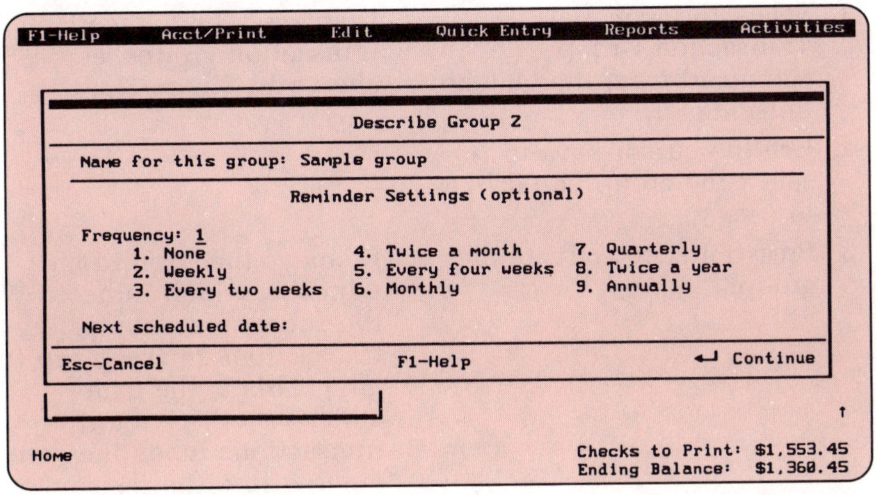

Figure 7-7. The Describe Group # window.

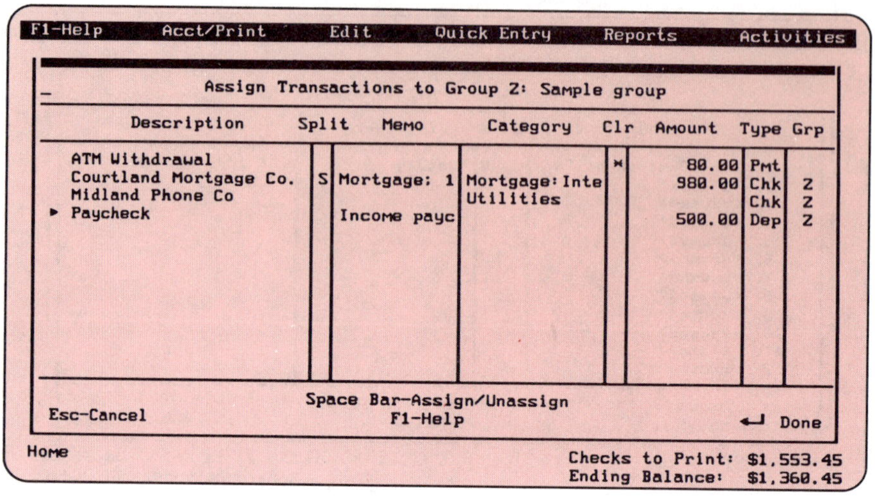

Figure 7-8. Quicken lets you assign transactions to a group in this window.

Running a Transaction Group

1. Select the Execute Transaction Group command from the Quick Entry menu. — Displays a list of available transaction groups, as shown in Figure 7-9.
2. Use the cursor keys to select the group you'd like to use.
3. Press Enter to activate the group. — Displays the Group Date window, which indicates the scheduled date for the transactions in the group (if any). This is the date Quicken will give to the transactions when they are entered into the register.
4. Press Enter to accept the date. Press Esc if you want to cancel the operation. — Announces that it is about to execute the transaction group.
5. Press Enter to execute the group.

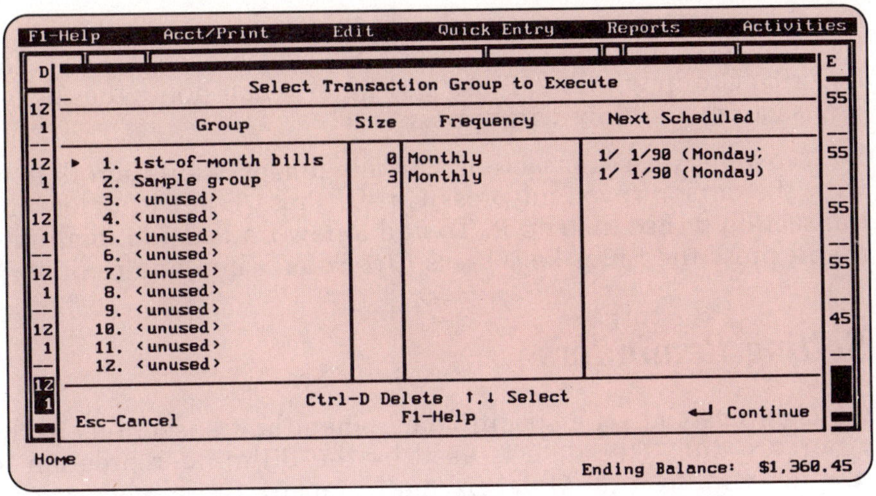

Figure 7-9. A listing of available transaction groups.

> **Tip:** If you're paying bills before or after the scheduled date, as shown in the Group Date window, you can enter a new date, if you wish, by typing it in or by pressing the + or − keys.

Once Quicken has created the new entries from the transactions in the group, you can always go back and make changes. You can delete those transactions you don't want, edit dollar amounts, post-date checks—in short, you can do anything you'd normally do in Quicken.

If the transaction group included checks, press Ctrl-W to access the Write Checks screen. You can now print the checks. (This subject is covered in Chapter 8, "Printing Checks.")

Modifying a Transaction Group

From time to time you may wish to add or remove transactions from a transaction group. To do so, follow the same basic procedures for creating the group. At the Select Transaction Group to Set Up/Change window, highlight the group you want to modify and press the Enter key. Make any desired changes in the Describe Group window. Press Ctrl-Enter when done; the Assign Transactions window will appear.

To remove a transaction you no longer want, scroll to it with the cursor keys and press Ctrl-D. Press Enter to delete the transaction or Esc to keep it. To add a new transaction, highlight it and press the Enter key. Press Ctrl-Enter when you're done.

Setting Reminders

Quicken lets you set a specific date when the transactions in the group are due. This date is used by the Billminder program to remind you to run Quicken and prepare those checks. (Of course, you're not limited to using transaction groups and Billminder for accounts payable only, although this is the mostly likely application.) You can use this date to remind you of important bills, for example, like a yearly tax bill or a quarterly insurance payment.

You can also set a frequency of payment. This indicates how often the group is scheduled to be run. You have nine choices:

- None
- Weekly
- Every two weeks
- Twice a month
- Every four weeks
- Monthly
- Quarterly
- Twice a year
- Annually

Note that Quicken makes the distinction between "every two weeks" and "twice a month," as well as "every four weeks" and "monthly." Every two weeks is every two calendar weeks —every other Monday, for example. Twice a month is two payments in any calendar month, such as the 1st and 15th. Likewise, every four weeks is four calendar weeks (such as every fourth Monday), and monthly is once a month, specifically, on a particular day of the month.

One of the most useful applications of transaction groups is its ability to produce payroll checks. The name and salary of every employee is memorized as a separate transaction, then all of the payroll transactions are combined into one group. If payday is once a week, set the frequency to weekly. If payday is every two weeks, or twice a month, set the frequency accordingly. When it comes time to create and print the paychecks, Quicken will do most of the hard work for you.

About the Billminder Program

If you have a hard disk drive, you can install Billminder on the drive and run it automatically each time the computer starts. Quicken gives you the option of including Billminder on your hard disk when you install the rest of the Quicken files. Along with the actual BILLMIND.EXE program file, Quicken adds a BILLMIND command prompt at the end of your AUTOEXEC.BAT file. The AUTOEXEC.BAT is a batch file that is executed automatically each time you start or reset your computer.

If you did not install Billminder when you installed the rest of the Quicken files, you can do so manually now. Simply copy the BILLMIND.EXE file to the root directory of your hard drive. Optionally, you can copy it into the QUICKEN3 directory. In the AUTOEXEC.BAT file, enter the line

```
BILLMIND
```

at the end. Or, if you use a shell program or DOS menu, add the command line above it. Type `/P` after the BILLMIND command to force the program to pause after it displays its message. Otherwise, your shell program or menu will execute before you have a chance to see the Billminder message.

If you've copied the BILLMIND.EXE file into the QUICKEN3 directory, you'll need to provide the full path in the AUTOEXEC.BAT file:

```
/QUICKEN3/BILLMIND
```

At any time, you can turn the Billminder program off and on with Billminder Active option in the Other Settings menu. Refer to Chapter 2, "Getting Started with Quicken" for more details on using the Other Settings menu.

What You Have Learned

This chapter discussed two of Quicken's most important time-shaving shortcuts: memorized transactions and transaction groups. Here's what you should have learned:

- Quicken remembers transactions you've made in the past with its memorized transactions feature.
- Quicken stores all memorized transactions together, regardless of the account you are using.
- The memorized transaction feature is most often used to capture recurring checks, yet you can use it to remember any transaction you create with Quicken—deposits, ATM withdrawals, transfers, and so forth.
- A transaction group is a set of recurring transactions. The best candidates for inclusion in a transaction group are those bills you pay every month.
- As an option, you can use the transaction group feature with the Billminder program (which is part of Quicken) to remind you when bills need to be paid.
- Before you can create a transaction group, the transactions you want included must be memorized.
- Hard disk users can install the Billminder program and use it to check for bills that are coming due.

Chapter 8

Printing Checks

In This Chapter

- *About Quicken checks*
- *Getting ready for printing*
- *Using a laser printer*
- *Printing checks*

Your efforts with Quicken culminate when you finally print the checks you've been entering, recording, splitting, categorizing, and memorizing. Check-printing is where Quicken shines, making the process as painless as possible. Quicken works with both line-at-a-time (daisywheel, dot matrix) printers and page-oriented (laser) printers. If you have more than one printer at home or in the office, you can select one as the reports printer and the other as the checks printer.

This chapter describes printing checks with Quicken. You'll learn how to test your printer with Quicken to make sure that the two are compatible and how to test check alignment. The Quicken package comes with several sample checks you can use for testing purposes. If you run out, you can continue your tests with plain paper. You'll need to order your own checks (Quicken comes with an order form for this purpose) when you're ready to use the program to print your real checks.

In this chapter you'll also learn how to solve common printer alignment problems, how to use a laser printer with Quicken, how to print checks selectively, and how to reprint checks that didn't come out right.

Quicken Checks

Although Quicken can be used with a variety of preprinted computer checks, the ones Intuit offers are the best choice. Checks for dot matrix or daisywheel printers come with alignment marks on the tear-off pin-feed holes. These help you to make slight adjustments in printing to make sure that the entries align with the blanks on the check.

Quicken has three basic types of checks.

Regular checks—The check area is 3-1/2 inches high by 8-1/2 inches wide, as shown in Figure 8-1.

Voucher checks—The check area is the same as for regular checks, but there is an extra 3-1/2 inches high voucher stub below the check.

Wallet checks—The check area is 2-5/6 inches high by 6 inches wide with a 2-1/2 inches wide register stub at the left.

In addition, regular checks are available in a number of formats, including single-, two-, and three-part, as well as special payroll checks. Payroll checks include a pay stub voucher.

These checks are available from Intuit in two forms: *continuous,* for use in dot matrix and daisywheel printers, and *full-sheet laser.* With the exception of voucher-style checks, laser checks come packed three to a sheet. Voucher checks come one to a sheet, with the check on top and the rest of the page for the voucher stub.

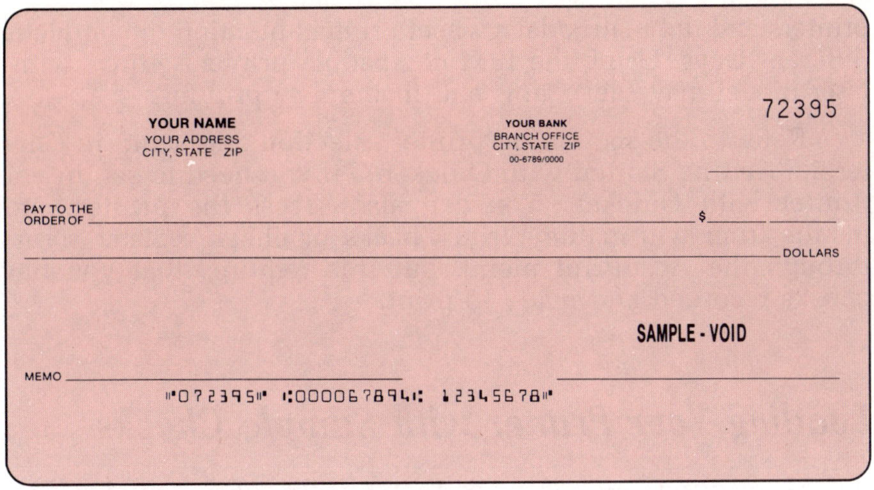

Figure 8-1. A sample check; these are provided with the Quicken package.

Quicken checks look just like the Write Checks screen. There's a place for the date, payee, dollar amount (numerals and words), and memo. Your personalized checks include:

Preprinted name and address for you and your bank.

Check number—Quicken doesn't print the check number.

Bank routing and account number digits—These digits identify you as the originator of the check and help banks locate your account.

Getting Ready to Print

Quicken comes set up for use with an IBM compatible printer set at 10 characters per inch (10 pitch). If your printer matches this description, you can use the program without further setup. Most likely though, you'll want to customize Quicken for use with your specific printer. This is especially necessary if you are using a laser printer, such as the Hewlett-Packard LaserJet I or II. Laser printers and dot matrix/daisywheel printers function in completely different ways. Using the IBM compatible printer settings with a laser model may cause jams and incomplete printing.

Refer to the section on printer selection and setup in Chapter 2, "Getting Started with Quicken," if you need to set up your printer with Quicken. You can also access the printer setup menus from within the Write Checks or check register screen, through the Acct/Print menu, but this requires that you have checks recorded and ready to print.

Loading Your Printer with Sample Checks

Before printing one of your real checks with Quicken, you should test that everything works and that the checks will be aligned properly. Quicken provides a number of helpful shortcuts to make check testing and alignment easier.

For daisywheel and dot matrix printers, load the checks in the printer as you would any continuous form paper. Make sure the holes on the sides of the checks line up properly with the platen sprockets inside the printer. Adjust the first check so that the top is flush with the print head. Then, loosen the sprocket clamps and slide the checks back and forth to center them on the platen. Most printers allow 1/2-inch or more of side-to-side play, to compensate for different paper sizes. Lock the clamps in place.

For laser printers, place one sheet of check stock in the paper tray. If you're using the sample checks that came with Quicken, tear off a set of three and remove the sprocket holes. These should feed properly through your printer. Note: For best results, keep at least 25 sheets of paper in the paper tray. This helps reduce paper jams, especially when using the fairly slick check stock.

If you don't have a check waiting to print in the register, write a dummy check.

1. From the Write Checks screen, choose the Print Checks command from the Acct/Print menu (or press Ctrl-P).
2. Indicate the number of the printer you are using. If you don't see it listed, press Esc, then choose the Change Printer

Setting command from the Acct/Print menu (the printer setup procedure is the same as outlined in Chapter 2, "Getting Started with Quicken").

3. If you're using wallet or voucher checks (as opposed to the sample regular checks that came with Quicken) or a laser printer, press the F8 key to display the select check type screen. Select the check type and press Enter.
4. Press the F9 key to make a sample check.

Assuming your printer is turned on and working properly, Quicken should print one sample check, as shown in Figure 8-2.

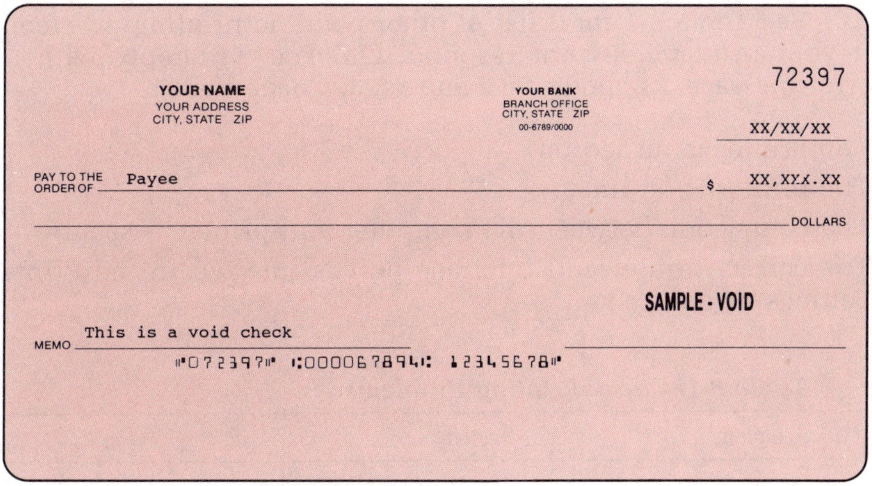

Figure 8-2. A sample printed check.

Diagnosing Alignment Problems

The first sample check you print may not be aligned properly. Don't worry; it's fairly easy to fix. If you're using a laser printer and the print is not aligned or is skewed, the most likely problem is *misfeed*—the paper went through the printer crooked. Try another sheet. Note that you can print a single check at a time if you have a manual feed tray. This feature does not work when printing sample checks. See below for more information on tips when using a laser printer.

If you're using a dot matrix or daisywheel printer, note the position of the POINTER LINE, printed about half-way down the check (in a properly printed check, the POINTER LINE should point to number 26 in the alignment marks on the side of the check). If the POINTER LINE is too low or too high, enter the number the line points to at the prompt that appears. Quicken will make the adjustments automatically so that the next check it prints will be aligned properly.

Should the check be *off-center*—the print is too far to the right or left—loosen the sprocket clamps and slide the paper over in the same direction. That is, if the print is too far to the right, slide the checks over to the right.

See Table 8-1 for a list of other possible printing problems. If your printer does not respond, Quicken will reply with an error message, as shown in Figure 8-3. Check that:

The printer is turned on.
The printer is on-line.
The connection between the computer and printer is secure.
The correct printer and interface port is selected in the Printer Settings menu.

Table 8-1. Check-Printing Problems.

Symptom	Remedy
Checks are blank	Check printer connection; check ribbon or cartridge; try printing with another program
Prints too far to the right	Slide checks over to the right
Prints too far to the left	Slide checks over to the left
Prints below lines	Indicate new POINTER LINE setting
Prints above lines	Indicate new POINTER LINE setting
First line prints OK but prints above other lines	Printer set to eight lines per inch (must be set to six lines per inch)
Prints over right or left sides	Print pitch setting too large, adjust

Continued

Prints OK on left side, but doesn't reach right side	Print pitch setting too large, adjust
Too much space between lines	Printer is sending extra line feed, adjust printer

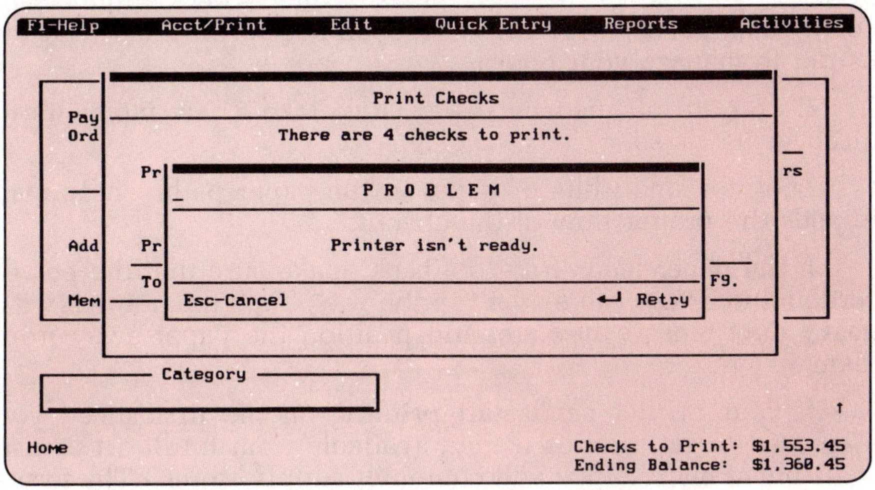

Figure 8-3. Quicken warns you when the printer is not responding.

Keep printing new samples until the checks come out right. If you're using a dot matrix or daisywheel printer, note the starting position of the checks in the printer. For example, if the top left-hand corner of the checks just reaches the left edge of the print head, make a note of that for future reference. Then, when you re-load the printer with check stock, you'll be able to return to that setting and make perfect prints.

If there doesn't seem to be a convenient alignment cue, you can make one yourself. Place a piece of masking tape or white paper tape toward the rear of the printer where the checks enter. On the tape, draw a line marking the tear-off between checks.

Handling Paper Jams

It seems that frequent jamming is the nature of some printers. Ordinarily, printer jams that occur when using regular paper are merely a frustration; the cost of the paper is minimal compared to your anger. But wasting preprinted check stock is a different matter. Not only are the checks fairly expensive (you don't pay a service charge on a check unless it goes through your bank, of course), but wasted checks throw off the counting sequence. Instead of a series of checks that starts with 1000 then counts up by ones, your check register shows printed check numbers of 1000, 1003, 1008, 1014, 1015, 1019, and so forth. That makes it harder to manage your books.

If you are plagued by paper jams, take a few moments to discover its cause.

Look for small bits of paper in the paper path. These may impede the proper flow of the checks.

If the paper feeds from the back, make sure that the power cord and interface cable aren't in the way. Tape them down with heavy duct tape if they are, and position the paper away from them.

If your printer can't start printing on the first sheet, you may need to get a forms leader, available from Intuit. (It is also available at many office and computer supply stores.) The forms leader uses a tacky surface to grab the paper so that it will feed properly. These are especially handy if your printer uses a paper bail roller that often gets in the way of the first check.

Using a Laser Printer

Laser printers aren't as prone to the same misalignment problems as daisywheel and dot matrix printers. Quicken makes it genuinely easy to print checks with a laser printer, but there are some tips and techniques you'll want to know about.

Most laser printers print on the top of the paper, as the paper is fed through the mechanism. If yours works this way, load the check stock into the paper tray face up. On Hewlett-Packard laser printers, as well as many other laser printer models, the checks should be loaded into the machine top first. That is, the top edge of the checks should feed through the machine first. If you insert the checks the other way, they'll print upside down.

You may wish to experiment with the orientation of your laser printer on a plain piece of paper. Quicken doesn't know the difference between plain paper and check stock. Make a sample print, as detailed earlier, and watch how the paper emerges.

By design, laser printers must print an entire page at a time. When using regular and wallet-size checks, you must print your checks in threes, or you'll waste those checks that are unprinted. This doesn't apply if your printer is Hewlett-Packard LaserJet compatible and is equipped with a manual paper feed tray. If your printer is so endowed, you can print one or two checks at a time. The full procedure is provided below in the "Printing Checks" section of this chapter.

Laser printers are as prone to jamming as a dot matrix or daisywheel printer, but they jam for different reasons. If your printer jams on check stock, there may not be enough "cushion" of extra pages in the paper feed tray. Even if you are printing a small bundle of checks, load the rest of the tray with regular paper. If you're using continuous feed checks that have been torn off in threes, lay the checks flat and place a heavy book on top. Keep them there, preferably for several hours—or even overnight. This helps remove the crease at the fold.

Quicken lets you print additional copies of your checks when using a laser printer. You can choose 0 (the default), 1, 2, or 3. Why would you want to print extra copies of checks? Laser printers are not capable of making an impression on multipart forms. The top pages print, but the bottom ones are blank, because they rely on impact to produce printed text.

However, you should not use the extra copies feature to make additional checks on check stock. Those checks are *negotiable,* and you probably don't want them floating around your office or home. Rather, you should order multipart laser checks, or at least, stack one or more blank sheets of plain paper under each sheet of check stock.

Printing Checks

With your sample checks now printing properly, you can use Quicken to print your real checks. Replace the sample check stock with your personalized checks. Be sure that the checks are inserted in the printer properly and that they are lined up with your previously identified alignment mark. Then, follow these simplified steps at the Write Checks screen.

Printing a Check

1. Press Ctrl-P.	Chooses Print Checks command. The window in Figure 8-4 appears.
2. Select printer and print options (see below).	
3. Press the F8 key and indicate the type of checks you want to use. This step isn't required each time.	Remembers your check selection for the next time you use the program.
4. Press Ctrl-Enter.	
5. Indicate the number of the NEXT check in the printer. Type a new number or press the + and − keys to set a higher or lower number.	Displays the check number window shown in Figure 8-5.
6. Press the F9 key or Enter.	The F9 key prints the first check only (this helps you stop the printer in case of misalignment or misfeed). Enter prints all checks.

Quicken now initiates printing. After printing is done, Quicken asks if the checks were printed correctly. Answer yes or no accordingly.

If the checks printed correctly, you are done printing and can return to the Write Checks screen.

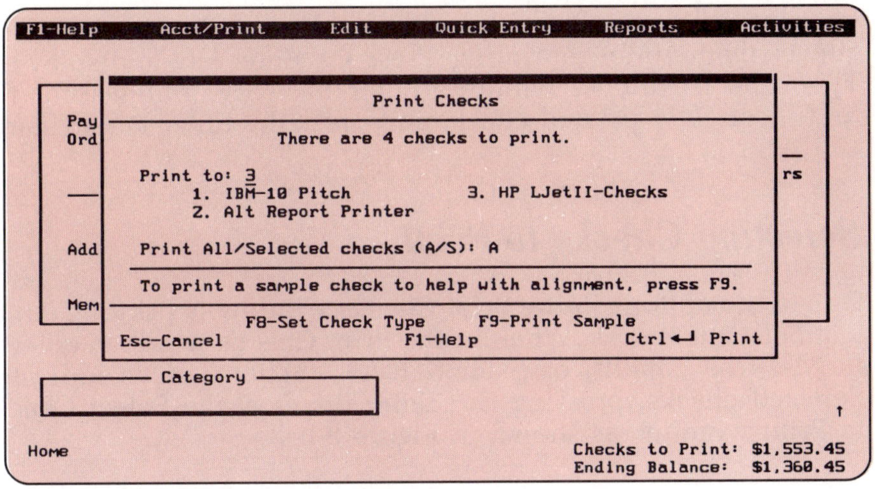

Figure 8-4. The Print Checks window.

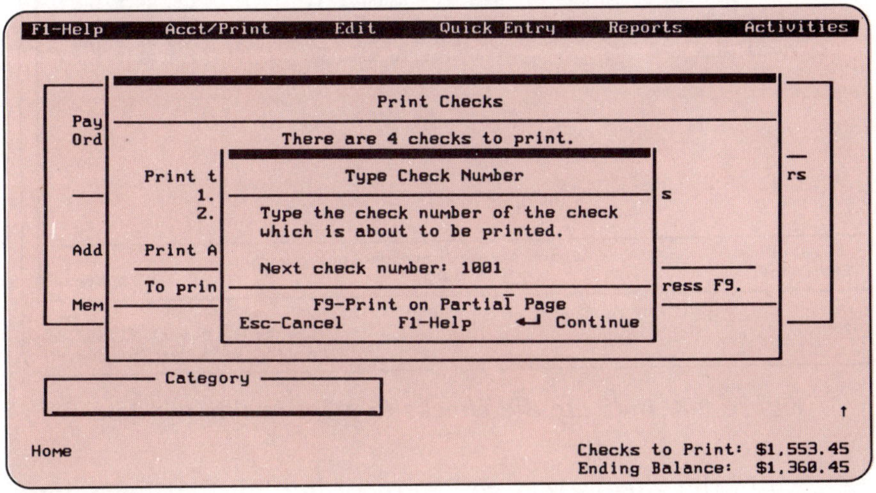

Figure 8-5. Enter the first check number to print in this window.

If one or more of the checks didn't print correctly, fix the problem (if any), then in the window that appears, type the number of the first check that didn't print correctly. Quicken assumes all remaining checks also did not print properly and queues them up for reprinting. Press the Enter key to display the Type Check Number window. Enter the NEW number for the first incorrectly printed check, and press the Enter key to start.

Selecting Checks to Print

One of the options in the Print Checks window is printing All or just Selected checks. When in the Print Checks window, enter A for All (the default) or S for Selected. When you've indicated Selected checks, pressing Ctrl-Enter displays the Select Checks to Print window, as shown in Figure 8-6.

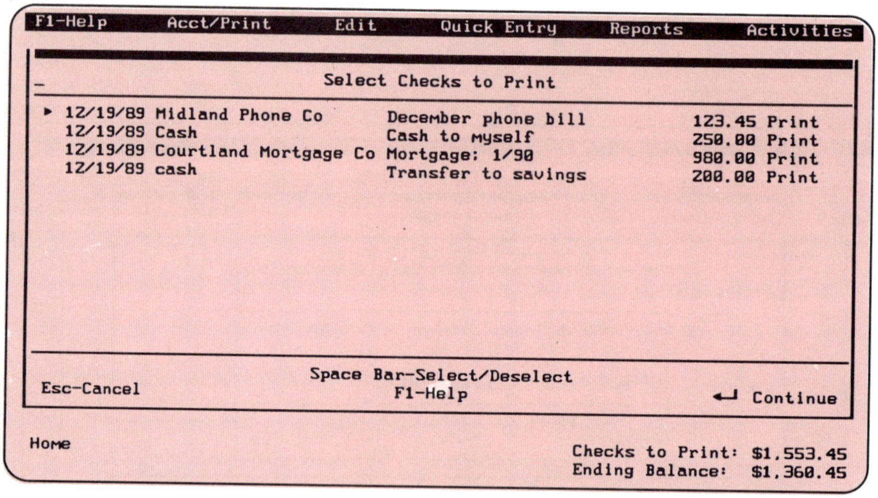

Figure 8-6. Indicate the checks to print in this window.

All of the checks that you've recorded but that have not yet been printed are listed, even checks that have been post-dated. (See the following section for more information on post-dated checks.) Quicken assumes that you want to print them all, so it initially places a Print indicator in the right-hand column. If you don't want to print a certain check, highlight it with the cursor keys and press the Spacebar to toggle the Print indicator on and off. With the Print indicator off, that check won't be printed. You can select and deselect any number of checks in this manner. Press the Enter key when you are done.

Working with Post-Dated Checks

When you have post-dated checks waiting to be printed, Quicken reminds you of this fact in the Print Checks window, as shown in Figure 8-7. The program initially displays the current date, not the date written on the post-dated checks. Alter this date if you want to print post-dated checks after today. Any check dated after the date you select will not be printed.

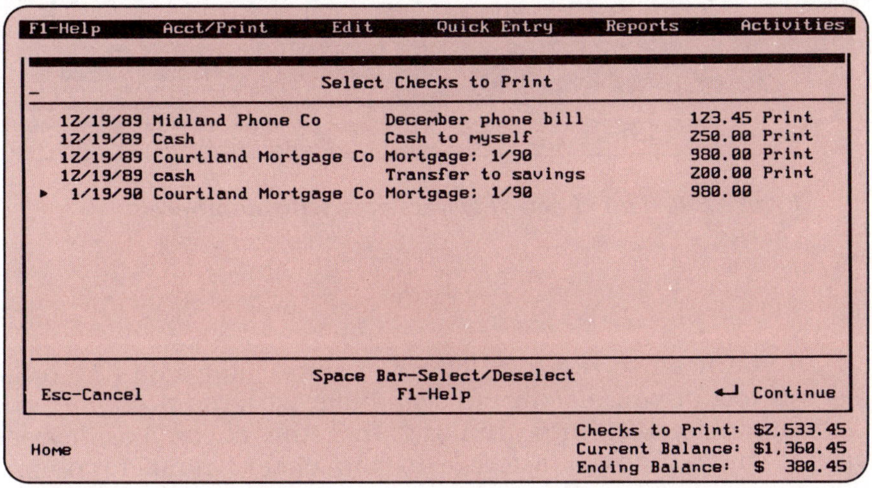

Figure 8-7. A sample list of checks, some post-dated.

Quicken also lets you select each post-dated check for printing. Using the list in the Select Checks to Print window, follow the same procedure for selecting and deselecting post-dated checks you would for any check.

Check Numbers in the Register

Once you've printed a check, Quicken appends that number next to it in the check register. You can tell that a check has been printed if there's a number beside it in the register, as shown in Figure 8-8.

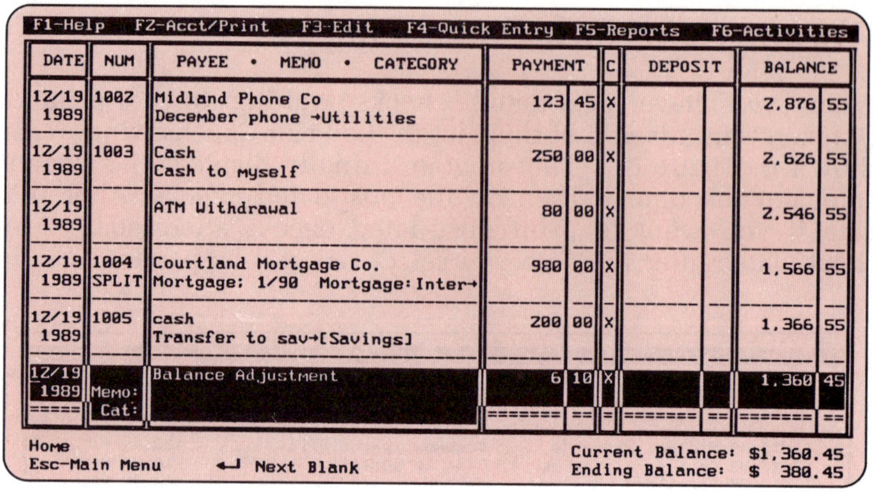

Figure 8-8. The check register, now with numbered checks.

If you need to reprint a check at some later date (the original was lost or you discovered a problem with the first one), you can force Quicken into thinking that the check hasn't been printed by typing an asterisk in the check number column. When you access the Print Checks menu, the check will be listed with all the other ones waiting to be printed.

Printing Single Checks with a Laser Printer

If you use a Hewlett-Packard LaserJet or compatible, and it is equipped with a manual feed tray, you can use it to print one or two checks at a time.

Let's assume that you have just one check to print. This check can be a regular, wallet, or voucher check. Place it sideways in the manual feed tray so that the check number and date feed into the printer first.

Follow these steps to set up Quicken to print on a partial page.

1. Choose the Print Checks command from the the Acct/Print menu.
2. Select the checks to print, as usual (or just press Ctrl-Enter if you've indicated that you want to print All checks).
3. At the Type Check Number window, press the F9 key, for Print On Partial Page. (This option appears only when using a laser printer.)
4. At the window shown in Figure 8-9, enter 1 (If you're printing two checks, enter 2.) Press the Enter key.
5. Indicate the next check number, and press Enter.

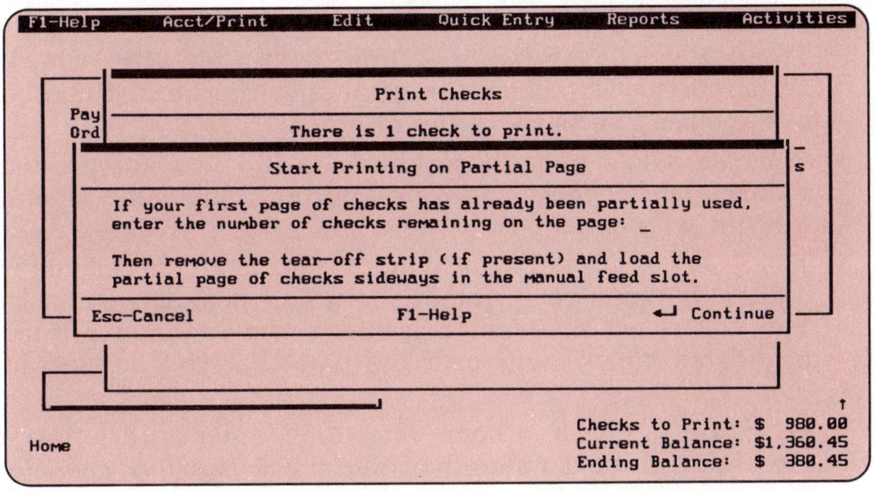

Figure 8-9. Quicken displays this message when you choose to manually feed checks using a Hewlett-Packard LaserJet printer.

What You Have Learned

This chapter concentrated on printing checks with Quicken. Here's what you should have learned:

- For best results, use the checks offered by Intuit when printing checks with Quicken.

- Quicken can be used with three basic types of checks: regular, voucher, and wallet. These checks are available in either continuous-form or full-sheet laser formats.
- Unless you're using a "plain vanilla" printer, you will need to establish the type of printer you're using prior to producing checks.
- Before actually printing your checks, you should print one or more samples to ensure alignment and operation. Quicken comes with several sample checks you can use for this purpose.
- Most problems in printing will be due to alignment. You should also be sure that your printer is set to the proper print pitch and line height.
- To print checks, press Ctrl-P (from within the Write Checks screen). Select the checks to print and indicate the number of the check currently in the printer.
- You can select only those checks that you want printed. Indicate those checks you want to print in the Select Checks to Print window.
- The Select Checks to Print window shows all checks you've written but not yet printed, including post-dated checks. You can select these for printing, as well. When printed, post-dated checks will bear the date that you entered for them.
- To reprint a check at some later date, enter an asterisk in the check number column of the check register. The next time you print checks, Quicken will include it.

Chapter 9

Working with Other Quicken Accounts

In This Chapter

- *Overview of other account types*
- *Setting up a savings account*
- *Setting up a cash account*
- *Setting up a credit card account*
- *Maintaining asset and liability accounts*
- *Building special-purpose accounts*

Throughout this book we've concentrated on using Quicken to maintain a standard personal or business checking account. While checking accounts are the type of account most often exploited by Quicken, they aren't the only kind the program can handle.

This chapter briefs you on applying Quicken to track various types of financial matters, for both home and business use. You'll learn how to maintain savings, cash, credit card, and miscellaneous asset and liability accounts, plus how to follow almost any financial situation using one of Quicken's account types.

Other Account Types

Setting up a checkbook register account is just one option when starting a new account. As shown in Figure 9-1, you can set up any of the following accounts:

Cash
Credit card
Other asset
Other liability

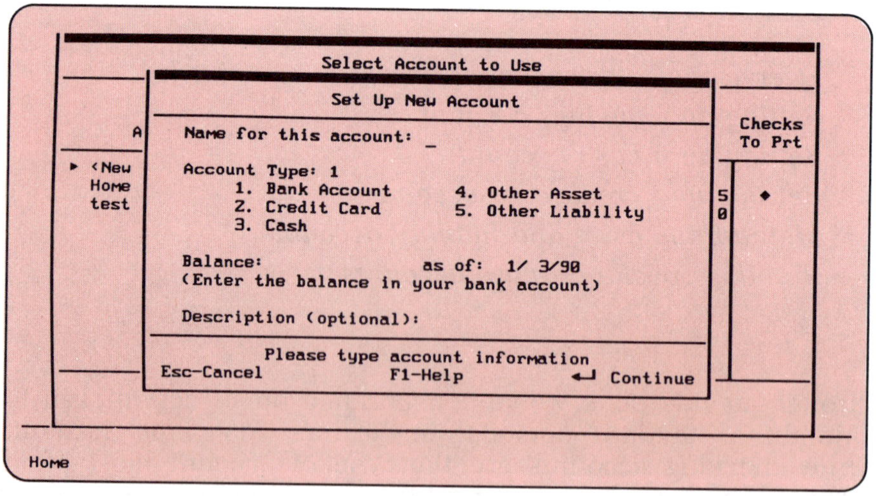

Figure 9-1. Account type options.

Quicken groups any account that deals with both credits and debits and allows you at least some free access to funds, as with a bank account. This includes, but is not limited to, checking accounts, savings accounts, money market savings accounts, IRAs, and CD accounts.

For the sake of simplicity, we'll differentiate between checking accounts and all other bank accounts, because—with few exceptions—only checking accounts allow you to write checks. With savings accounts, CD accounts, IRAs, and the like, credits and debits are entered directly into the register; no check is ever written or printed. This "rule" doesn't apply to unique checking-type accounts, like money market savings accounts that allow you to write checks to make withdrawals.

Setting Up a Savings Account

There are numerous types of savings accounts, from regular passbook savings accounts to money market accounts to CD accounts to IRAs. While these accounts vary in the interest that they pay and the regulations regarding withdrawal (especially early withdrawal), they have a similarity: you put money in for a period of time and withdraw it—generally by writing a voucher or countercheck at the bank. A checkbook is not issued, because the savings account is not designed to handle many transactions. In fact, most banks place a ceiling on withdrawals during a particular month or quarter.

Whatever type of savings account you have, you maintain it entirely from the register. The register looks exactly like the check register (in fact, it's the same), except that you don't have to worry about tracking check numbers or printing checks. When maintaining a savings account you are concerned about two types of transactions:

- *Credits*—money that goes *into* your account.
- *Debits*—money that goes *out* of your account.

Credits are typified by deposits and interest payments. Debits are typified by withdrawals, penalty fees, and service charges.

To set up a savings account, you should follow the same basic procedure outlined for checking accounts.

Setting Up a Savings Account

1. At the main menu, press 4 then Enter.	Chooses the Select Account command.
2. Highlight the <new account> option, and press Enter.	Displays the Set Up New Account window.
3. Type name, and press Enter.	Names the account (e.g., Savings).
4. Press 1 then Enter.	Indicates Bank Account as account type.
5. Enter balance, and press Enter. You can always change the balance later.	Provides starting balance.
6. Enter date if different from today's date, and press Enter.	
7. Type description, and press Enter. This is optional, but recommended since you may have more than one savings account.	Describes the account.

Select the newly created account in the Select Account window, and press Enter. Quicken drops you into the register screen. You may now enter the various credit and debit transactions.

Tip: Quicken lets you write checks for any type of bank account, whether it's a checking or savings account. If you prefer, you can enter savings account withdrawals as checks using the Write Checks screen. As usual, Quicken will record these as checks and will always prompt you that you have checks to print for the savings account. To avoid this, you can enter a transaction number instead of a check number beside each withdrawal, as shown in Figure 9-2. This will trick Quicken into thinking that the withdrawal check has been printed.

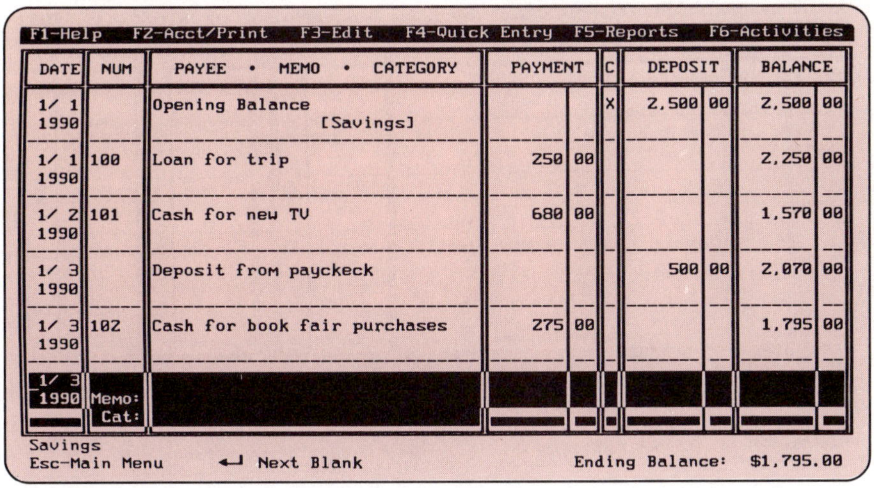

Figure 9-2. Transacation numbers for withdrawals.

Entering Deposits

You enter deposit information into the savings account register the same as you do into a checking account register. At the register screen, type the date of the transaction, a description (in the PAYEE column), and a dollar amount in the DEPOSIT column. You may furnish memo and category information if you like. When you've finished entering the information for the transaction, press Ctrl-Enter to record it.

Entering Withdrawals

Withdrawals are debits from your savings account, so instead of entering an amount in the DEPOSIT column, you enter it into the PAYMENT column. When you're done entering the information for the withdrawal, press Ctrl-Enter to record it.

Because withdrawals won't be the only type of debits you'll include in the register, as shown in Figure 9-3, you may wish to enter a transaction number or identifier in the NUM column. (You can also use this technique when entering deposits.) Make up your own codes for the transaction identifiers, such as D for deposit, I for interest payment, W for withdrawal, and S for service charge.

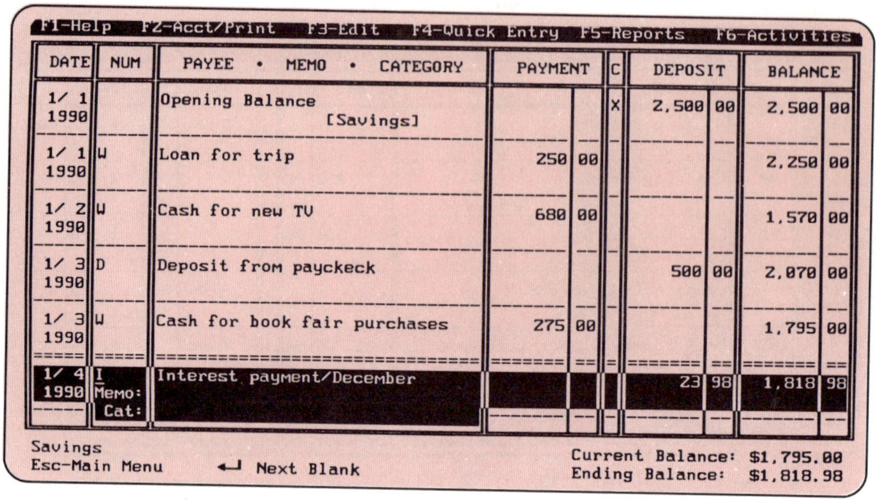

Figure 9-3. Sample transaction identifiers in the NUM column.

Entering Other Credits and Debits

All other transactions in a savings account (indeed, any type of financial account) are handled either as a payment (debit) or as a deposit (credit). In most cases, these additional transactions will be added when you reconcile your account using the bank statement. To enter interest paid by your bank, enter the amount paid for the last period as a deposit. To enter a service fee charged by your bank, enter the amount charged as a payment. To enter a penalty (e.g., an early withdrawal penalty) charged by your bank, enter the amount charged as a payment.

Certain types of savings accounts will have other forms of debits and credits. For example, credit unions may pay share dividends in addition to (or instead of) interest. Enter these into the appropriate PAYMENT or DEPOSIT column.

Setting Up a Cash Account

You remember cash: it's that green stuff that always seems to disappear once you put it in your wallet. In this age of credit cards, debit cards, and push-button financial transactions, it can be easy to forget your cash expenditures, and the importance of keeping tabs on where the money goes. You can track your cash outlay in either of two ways:

- As transactions in a checking or savings account.
- As a separate account type.

Depending on your spending habits and requirements, you may want to use both systems. Each has its special application within Quicken.

Tracking Cash in a Bank Account

Assume that you deposit your $750 paycheck into the bank, but hold back $100 for spending loot. Quicken will record the paycheck deposit as $650; the $100 you received as cash is unaccounted for. When entering the deposit into the account, you should split the transaction as shown in Figure 9-4. (See Chapter 6, "Keeping Track of Transactions," for more details on splitting transactions.)

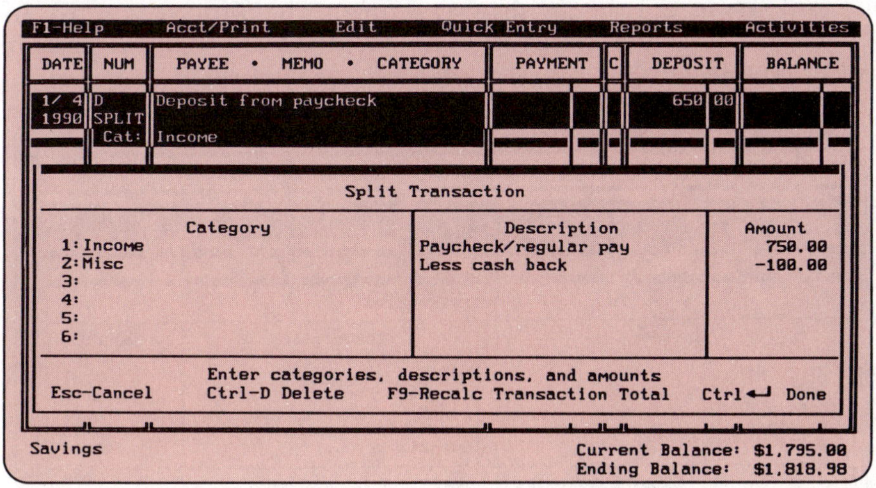

Figure 9-4. A sample split transaction—less cash back.

On the first line, enter the amount of the paycheck. On the second line, enter the amount of cash you received back at the bank. Record this as a negative number, so Quicken will know to subtract the cash, rather than add it. When the transaction is recorded, Quicken will enter a 650.00 in the DEPOSIT column.

With the split added, you will always know that your paycheck was really for $750 and that you received $100 back at the bank. The transaction reports, if you choose to print them, will also show the split.

If you need to itemize your cash expenses, enter them separately in the Split Transaction window. How you enter the dollar amounts depends on whether the main transaction is a payment or deposit.

If the main transaction is a deposit (e.g., a paycheck with cash back), enter the itemized split transactions as negative numbers, as shown in Figure 9-4.

If the main transaction is a payment (e.g., a check for cash or an ATM withdrawal), enter the itemized split transactions as positive numbers.

Figure 9-5 illustrates an example of a transaction using the payment approach. Here you write a check to cash for $500 at the bank. (This is the same as a cash withdrawal from a savings account or an ATM withdrawal from a checking account.) As shown in Figure 9-5, that $500 is distributed six ways. A portion of the money is listed as Miscellaneous Expenses.

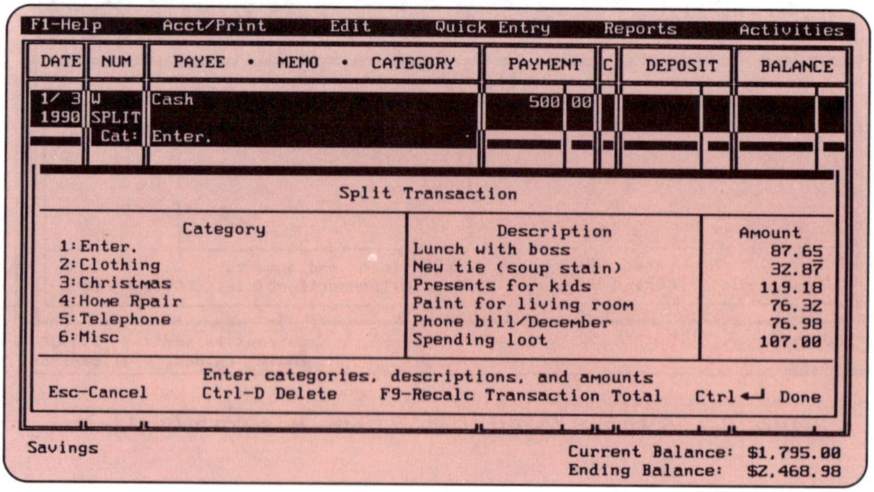

Figure 9-5. Itemizing cash transactions as payment splits.

Tracking Cash in a Cash Account

A separate cash account is ideal for those who prefer to deal with cash or who need to maintain a record of petty cash. Quicken uses a special account type for cash-only transactions. Follow these steps to create a cash account.

Setting Up a Cash Account

1. At the main menu, press 4 then Enter.	Chooses the Select Account command.
2. Highlight the <new account> option, and press Enter.	Displays the Set Up New Account window.
3. Type name, and press Enter.	Names the account (e.g., Cash).
4. Press 3 then Enter.	Indicates Cash as account type.
5. Enter starting cash amount in dollars, and press Enter.	Provides amount of cash you have to start.
6. Press Enter if date is correct.	
7. Type description, and press Enter.	Describes account (optional).

Select the newly created account in the Select Accounts window, and press Enter. Quicken drops you into the register screen, shown in Figure 9-6. Note that the Cash register is slightly different from the check or Bank Account register. However, it is used in much the same way.

Entering a Cash Transaction

1. Set cursor in first empty transaction line.
2. Enter date.
3. Enter reference (optional).
4. Enter data for payee, memo, and category.

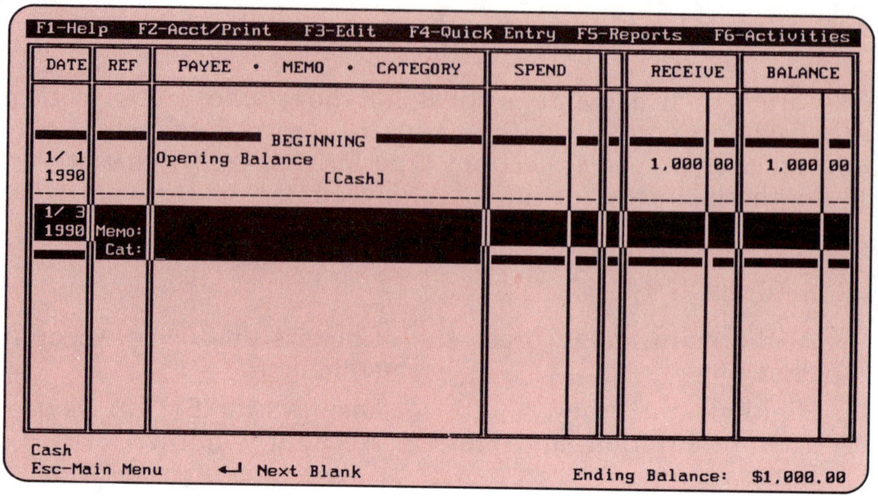

Figure 9-6. The Cash register.

5. If you are paying cash, enter the amount in the SPEND column.	Indicates a payment.
OR	
If you are receiving cash, enter the amount in the RECEIVE column.	Indicates a deposit.
6. Press Ctrl-Enter when done.	Records the cash transaction. □

The Cash register lets you split, transfer, and memorize transactions just like the check register. You use these features in the normal manner.

The level of detail you provide to your cash transactions is completely up to you. If you're interested in recording important cash transactions and leaving the rest unaccounted for, Quicken will automatically balance the remainder and consider it as Miscellaneous Expenses.

To reconcile your cash account (while in the Cash register), press F6 and choose the Update Account Balance command from the Activities menu. Quicken then displays the window shown in Figure 9-7. In the "Update this account's balance to" entry field, enter the amount of cash you currently have on hand. You can optionally indicate a category for the balance adjustment. If you have less cash than Quicken's records indicate, the program will enter a deduction in the SPENT column. If you have more cash than Quicken's records indicate, the program will enter a credit in the RECEIVE column.

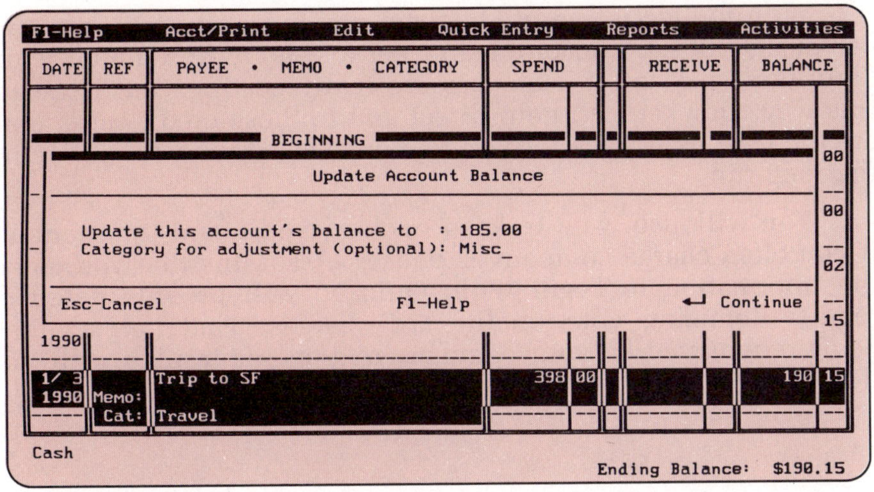

Figure 9-7. Quicken displays this window when you want to update the cash account balance.

Transferring Money to a Cash Account

Rely on Quicken's transfer feature to transfer funds quickly and easily to and from your cash account. Suppose you have a checking account and you write a check to Cash. Assuming your cash account is named Cash, enter Cash in the category blank in the Write Checks screen. Quicken will automatically deduct the amount of the check from your checking account and credit it to your cash account. Of course, you can transfer money to and from other pre-existing Quicken accounts in the same manner. (For more details on account transfers, see Chapter 6, "Keeping Track of Transfers.")

Setting Up a Credit Card Account

In an old Flintstone cartoon episode, the favorite refrain of Wilma Flintstone and Betty Rubble was "Chaaaaarge it!!" That sentiment goes far beyond animated TV shows. Each year, hundreds of billions of dollars worth of goods are charged to credit cards. These cards allow you to "buy now, pay later." Even though the cash outlay is deferred, you may still want to use Quicken to record and maintain the purchases.

With judicious use of Quicken, you have a better overview of your credit card accounts and know exactly how much your "buy now, pay later" expenses are really costing you. Used in this way, Quicken can help direct you to those credit cards that are the least expensive for you to own. That saves you money in the long run.

You will also want to keep track of credit card transactions if you often charge company expenses. Assuming that you enter the information to begin with, Quicken will provide detailed reports itemizing your credit card charges. That helps when being reimbursed by your company and avoids trouble with the IRS if you or your company are ever audited.

Types of Credit

Just because you have a credit card doesn't mean you need to set up a credit card account. Your payment schedule largely dictates whether you need to set up a credit card account. If you pay the card in full each month, there's hardly a reason to set up an account. Just treat the payment as an expense in your checking account. Cards you pay in full include American Express (certain account types), gas cards, and most open charge accounts at local businesses.

An exception to this rule can occur if you want to keep tabs on specific credit purchases. For example, suppose your small business regularly buys goods from a dozen local suppliers, all of whom have extended you credit. By using a Quicken credit card account, you can track your purchases and payments and know exactly what you bought and when you paid for it. You'd still use your checking account to write the check, but the individual credit card account would provide all the specific details. In this way, you use the credit card account as a record-keeping ledger.

Conversely, if you pay the balance of the credit over time, you'll want to keep tabs on the account with Quicken. This type of account likely represents the majority of credit cards you own and includes Visa, MasterCard, Discover, and most department store chains.

Note that some department stores (such as JCPenney) separate their credit purchases into two or more distinct categories, usually regular and major. *Major charges* are set aside for durable goods, like washing machines, TV sets, furniture, and other appliances. *Regular charges* encompass just about everything else.

As the monthly statement separates these two types of purchases—and sometimes assesses different credit limits and interest rates to them—you may wish to create two separate Quicken accounts for them. One account lists regular purchases and payments made against them, and the other account lists charges and payments for major purchases. You can, of course, group these two together and treat them as a single account.

Creating a Credit Card Account

You should set up a separate account for each credit card you, your business, or your family uses. Follow these steps to set up a new credit card account.

Setting Up a Credit Card Account

1. At the main menu, press 4 then Enter.	Chooses the Select Account command.
2. Highlight the <new account> entry, and press Enter.	Displays the Set Up New Account window.
3. Type name, and press Enter.	Names the account (e.g., Visa or Diner's Club).
4. Press 2 then Enter.	Indicates Credit Card as the account type.
5. Enter a current balance owed and press Enter.	Provides the amount you currently owe on the card or charge account.

6. Press Enter if date is correct.
7. Type description, and press Enter. You can use a textual description (e.g., George's Visa) or a credit card account number (e.g., 5555-1111-444-3333). — Describes account.
8. Type credit limit (optional), and press Enter. □

> **Note:** In a credit card account, this credit limit is best used as a warning that your balance is approaching the maximum amount of credit that is extended to you. Knowing that you're approaching the credit limit helps avoid those embarrassing moments when you try to pay your restaurant bill with your credit card, only to learn that your purchase has been declined.

Entering Transactions

The Credit Card register, shown in Figure 9-8, is similar to the register used to monitor cash expenses. The register provides blanks for:

Transaction date

Transaction reference—This is an optional coded reference (e.g., D for dining, E for entertainment, or M for motel/hotel); you can fit up to five characters in the REF column.

Description of transaction, plus optional memo and category

Amount of charge

Amount of payment

You can enter transaction information as you incur the charges, using the charge slips as receipts. Or you can wait until the credit card statement arrives and use it for entering charges

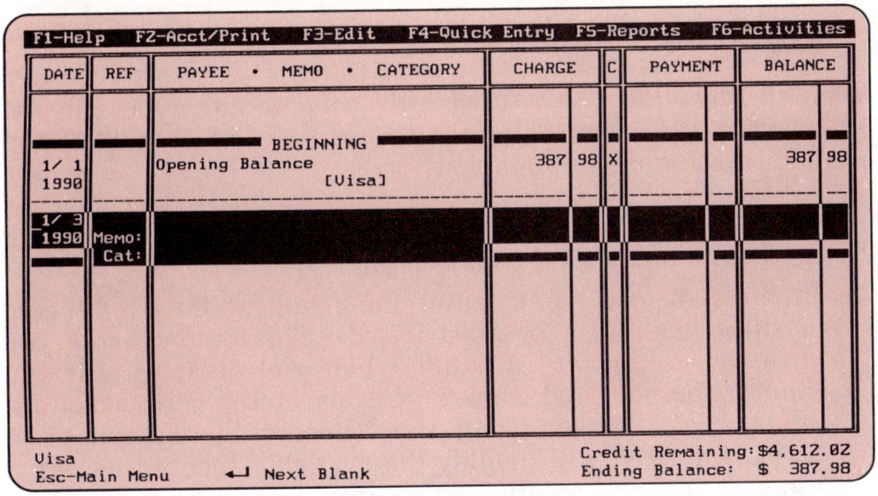

Figure 9-8. The Credit Card register.

and payments. In either case, you'll probably want to keep your own charge slips and compare them against the monthly statement. Any deviations should be reported to the credit card company immediately.

Q Entering A Credit Card Transaction

1. At the register, enter the transaction date.	
2. Enter the reference.	Identifies the transaction.
3. Enter the description in PAYEE column.	Provides description of charge or payment.
4. For a charge, enter the amount in the CHARGE column.	Indicates a charge.
OR	
For a payment, enter the amount in the PAYMENT column. In credit card accounts, the PAYMENT column is used for payments made *to* the credit card company.	Indicates a payment.
5. Press Ctrl-Enter when done.	Records the transaction. ☐

Transferring Funds

When paying your credit card bills each month, you can use Quicken's transfer feature to apply your payment to each of your credit card accounts automatically.

1. In the Write Checks screen, fill out the check to the credit card company in the usual manner.
2. In the Category blank, enter the name of the credit card account (e.g., Visa or MasterCard). This is the name you gave the credit card account when you created it. If you don't remember the names of your credit card accounts, enter a left bracket ([) in the Category blank, and press Ctrl-C. Quicken will display the available account names at the end of the Category List window.
3. Record the check (press Ctrl-Enter), and Quicken will automatically enter the amount of the check as a PAYMENT to your credit card account.

As shown in Figure 9-9, your check register will indicate those transactions that have been transferred to other Quicken accounts. Transfers are always indicated in the Cat: blank with the account name enclosed in brackets.

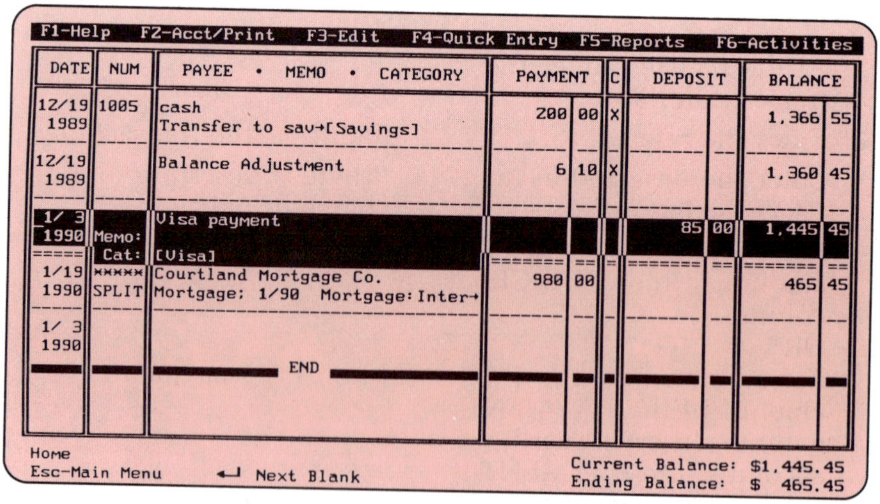

Figure 9-9. You can easily transfer deposits and payments between credit card accounts (and all other Quicken accounts, for that matter) and your checking account.

Conversely, you can transfer money from a credit card account into a checking or savings account. Use this method when you write yourself a cash advance from your credit card.

1. In the Credit Card register, enter the name of the checking or savings account (Checking, Savings, or whatever) in the Cat: blank.
2. Enter the amount of the transfer as a CHARGE.
3. Press Ctrl-Enter to record the transaction.

Quicken will deposit those funds into the appropriate account.

Reconciling Your Credit Card Accounts

Once a month you should reconcile your credit card accounts to make sure your records coincide with those of the credit card company.

Before reconciling the account, use your monthly statement to make sure all the transactions listed are included in the Credit Card register. Include previous payments, interest charges, new charges, credits, and so forth. Make sure that each transaction is posted in the proper column. For example, don't put an interest charge in the PAYMENT column or a credit in the CHARGE column. Above all, don't enter the payment you're about to make; save that for Quicken.

With all the transactions entered (while at the Credit Card register):

1. Choose the Pay Credit Card Bill from the Activities menu. The window in Figure 9-10 appears.
2. Enter the total for all charges, cash advances, and other debits, minus finance charges (if any).
3. Enter recent payments or credits listed on the statement.
4. Provide a new balance, as indicated on the credit card statement.
5. Enter the total finance charges, as indicated in the statement. You can optionally assign the finance charges to a Quicken category. The program will automatically create a separate transaction for finance charges, as a means to track them later.

6. Press the Enter key after filling in the finance charges and (optional) category. Quicken displays a window showing Uncleared Items in the Register, as illustrated in Figure 9-11.
7. If an item in the list is included on your statement, highlight it, and press the Spacebar. If you need to display the Credit Card register (e.g., to make a correction or adjustment or to add items to the register that are shown in the statement), press the F9 key. When you're done, press the F9 key again to return to the Uncleared Items window. Any difference between Quicken's register and the credit card statement are shown in the lower right-hand corner of the Uncleared Items window. After marking all cleared items and adjusting missing transactions, the difference should be 0.00.
8. When you are finished marking cleared items, press Ctrl-End.
9. If the difference between Quicken's register and the credit card statement is 0.00, you can go to step 10. If not, you'll be asked to enter an adjustment to your account. You also have the option of suspending reconciliation and looking for the difference yourself. Quicken will indicate the nature of the adjustment(s) and will tell you the amount of the disparity, as shown in Figure 9-12. If desired, enter a category for each adjustment. Press Enter when finished.
10. When Quicken is satisfied that the dollar amounts in its register and the bank statement agree, it displays the Make Credit Card Payment window, shown in Figure 9-13. If you don't want to pay the bill now, press Esc to cancel. Otherwise, enter the name of one of your checking accounts to pay the bill and indicate whether you want to make out a Quicken or hand-written check.

Electing to make a credit card payment using a Quicken checking account cuts down on a few extra steps. Not only does Quicken write the check for you, but it also pops you into the Write Checks or check register screen, where you can edit the check or print it, as desired. If you complete the check with a payee, memo, and address, Quicken will remember that information the next time.

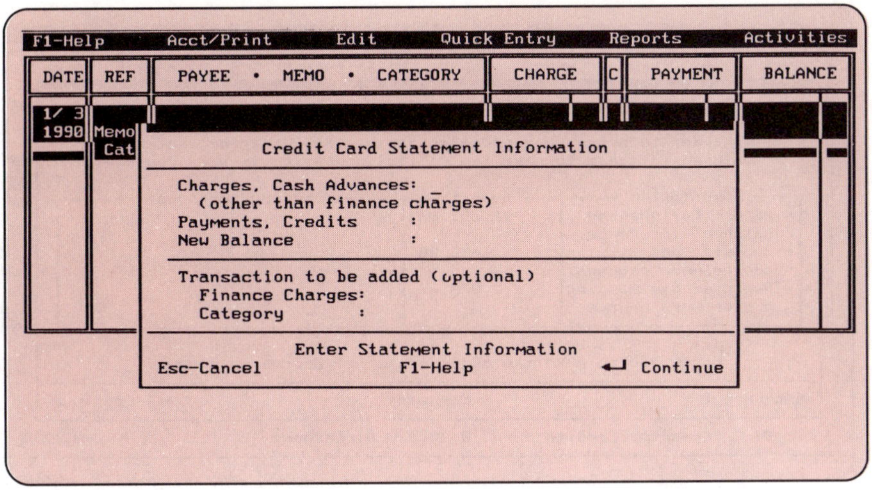

Figure 9-10. The Credit Card Statement Information window.

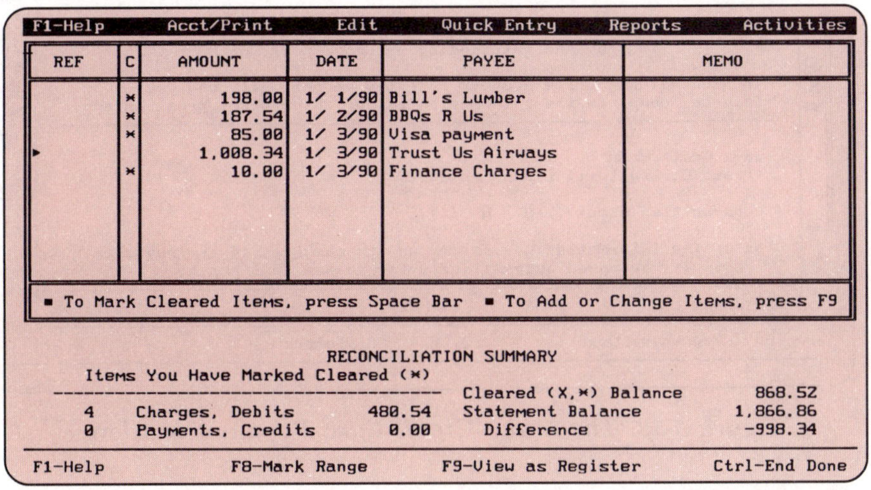

Figure 9-11. Uncleared items in the credit card register mean that the bank hasn't posted those transactions to your account.

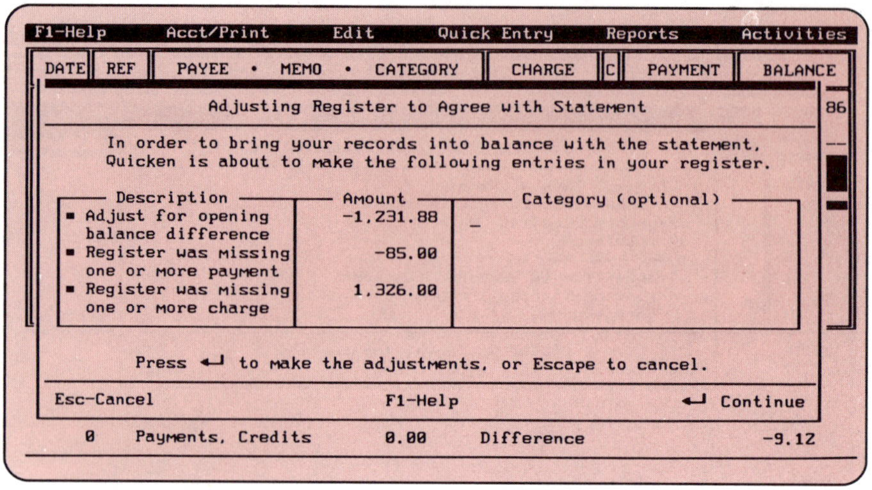

Figure 9-12. Quicken displays any disparity between the credit card register and the bank statement.

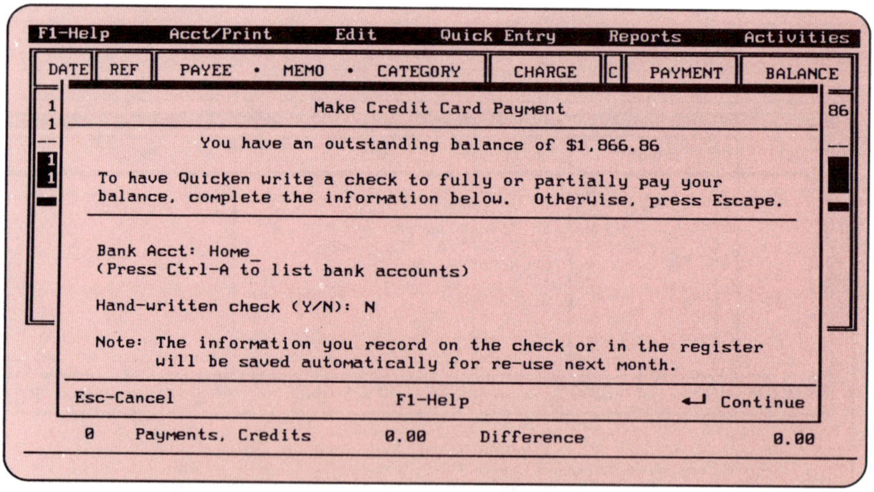

Figure 9-13. The Make Credit Card Payment window.

Maintaining Miscellaneous Asset and Liability Accounts

Financial matters that don't entail bank statements can often be maintained as an other asset or other liability account. Use an *asset account* to track something you own. You may or may not receive money for it, but if sold, you'd get some or all of the money for it.

Examples of Assets

Investments—includes stocks, bonds, IRAs, Keogh plans, and whole-life insurance policies

Your house—an equity investment

Accounts receivable—money you expect to get in the future

Personal belongings—includes jewelry, clothing, and electronic equipment, despite whether they are completely paid for

Home tax basis—includes improvements and repairs made to your home that you can deduct from your taxes when you sell the home

Use a *liability account* to track something you owe and generally make monthly or periodic payments for.

Examples of Liabilities

Your car, house, or boat payment

Debts to others

Lines of credit

Accrued business expenses—includes payroll taxes and social security for employees

Quicken tracks miscellaneous assets in an other asset account; miscellaneous liabilities are maintained in an other liability account.

You can either create individual Quicken accounts for each major asset and liability or group similar items into one account. For instance, you can group all debts into one Other Asset account, or you can separate them into separate accounts. For most individuals and businesses, a logical grouping is adequate and easier to work with.

Setting Up an Account

You set up other asset and other liability accounts the same as you do a Quicken bank account or cash account.

Q Setting Up an Other Asset or Other Liability Account

1. At the main menu, press 4 then Enter. — Chooses the Select Account command.
2. Highlight the <new account> option, and press Enter. — Displays the Set Up New Account window.
3. Type name, and press Enter. — Names the account.
4. Press 4 to create an other asset account.
   OR
   Press 5 to create an other liability account.
5. Enter the total amount of the asset or liability, and press Enter.
6. Type a description (optional), and press Enter.

The Other Asset and Other Liability registers are almost identical (the asset window is shown in Figure 9-14), and you use them in the same manner. Their design is consistent with the registers for Bank Accounts, Cash, and Credit Cards. The difference is in the DECREASE and INCREASE columns.

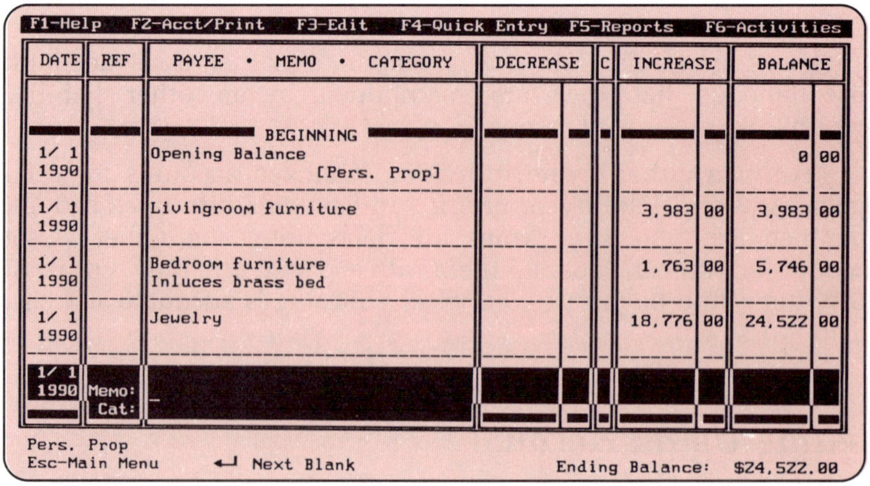

Figure 9-14. A sample Other Asset register window.

An entry in the DECREASE column decreases the balance, just as an entry in the PAYMENT column of a checkbook register decreases the amount in your checking account.

The INCREASE column functions in the same manner as the DEPOSIT column in the checkbook register. It increases the balance.

Clearing and Updating Your Account Transactions

You should use the C (CLEAR) column to mark those assets and liabilities you no longer have. For instance, if you're tracking your personal assets (e.g., antique furniture or jewelry), you'd use the C column to mark those assets you sell. To clear an item, position the cursor in the C column, and enter an asterisk.

Every once in a while, you'll want to update the value of your other assets and other liabilities. Follow these steps to ensure that Quicken has an accurate record of your financial picture:

1. From the other asset or other liabilities register, choose the Update Account Balance command from the Activities menu.
2. Enter the balance you should have (based on a brokerage statement, for instance), and press the Enter key.
3. If the balance you entered doesn't agree with the ending balance in the register, Quicken will alert you to this fact and ask if you want to make an adjustment. Provide an optional category for the adjustment transaction, and press the Enter key.

If you'd like, you can make the adjustment to the account yourself. You may prefer to review the register if the difference is great.

Creating Special-Purpose Accounts

You can apply one of Quicken's five account types to a variety of personal and business requirements. Here are some examples:

Create an other assets account—You can use this account, for example, to track your videotape or videodisc collection. Enter a retail value for each tape or disc. Quicken will maintain a running tally of the worth of the collection. You can then use this account in the event of a fire or theft, or just to brag to others that you own more movies than Ted Turner.

Create a bank account to handle employee payroll—You record and print checks from the payroll account, even though you use the same checks as your other transactions. You may want to use this technique of keeping payroll separate if you have more than a few dozen employees.

Provide a separate other liability account—You can use this account for withheld employee taxes, insurance, and social security. By maintaining these items in a separate account, you are less likely to consider the money part of the general operating fund. The IRS takes a dim view of employers spending their employee's tax withholding.

Build numerous other asset subaccounts under your main bank accounts—These subaccounts track unique personal or business financial matters (e.g., vacation and college funds). The money is all in one pool (e.g., your savings or checking account), but your subaccounts help you to remember how you want the funds divided. Using subaccounts helps you to set aside money for special purposes, to "squirrel" it away for a rainy day.

Use an other asset account to keep track of the various improvements and repairs you make to your home—Generally, these costs are for the home you live in, as opposed to a house you own as income property. Not only does this help you track the costs of home ownership, but it's also helpful when it's time to sell the house. You can apply the improvements and repairs to the tax basis of your home (and therefore reduce the income taxes you might have to pay on the capital gains on the sale of your house). You can also defend a higher selling price, apart from the value set by an appraiser.

Schools and other nonprofit organizations will want to keep track of charitable donations and their amounts—This is especially true if your school or organization is also funded with public money (grants, taxes, and whatnot).

What You Have Learned

This chapter discussed additional forms of Quicken accounts: cash, credit card, other asset, and other liability. Here's what you should have learned:

- Savings, cash, credit card, and asset/liability accounts are maintained entirely from the register. You don't use the Write Checks window to enter payment transactions.
- Savings accounts have two general types of transactions: credits (e.g., deposits and interest) and debits (e.g., withdrawals and service charges).
- Cash accounts let you track your loose change or monitor expenditures from a petty cash fund.
- You can track your cash outlay either as transactions in a checking or savings account or as a separate account type.
- As with all Quicken account types, you can split cash transactions to indicate the origin or destination of a lump sum.
- Credit card accounts let you track any financial dealings (e.g., a loan) where you owe money and must regularly pay back the loan in installments.
- You should create a separate credit card account for each credit card (or other consumer/business credit) you own. Identify the card by its name and/or account number.
- Quicken will reconcile your Credit Card registers automatically.
- You should use an other asset account to track something you own and an other liability account to track something you owe and generally make monthly or periodic payments for.

Chapter 10

Creating and Printing Reports

In This Chapter

- *About Quicken's reports*
- *Building a standard report*
- *Examples of personal and business reports*
- *Producing custom reports*
- *Transaction filtering with text matching*

Dragnet fans remember the immortal words of Sergeant Joe Friday: "Just the facts, ma'am." As a Quicken user, you can ask the program to provide you with just the facts, and it will spit out reams of digested information and reports on your spending habits, your budget, even the exact dollar amount of your financial worth. Quicken's reports feature is nearly automatic: you just select the type of report you want to review, and Quicken will build it. If needed, you can fine-tune the design of reports to include the information you want, organized as you want.

This chapter deals with creating and printing reports in Quicken. You'll learn how to print Quicken's preset personal and business reports quickly, as well as how to build customized reports that contain just the data you're interested in.

An Overview of Quicken Reports

Although Quicken can display its reports on screen, you'll probably want to print them so you can refer to them readily at a later date. After printing, place your reports in a binder or notebook for safekeeping. If you print reports often, you may want to separate them into categories. For example, Quicken offers five types of preset personal reports, including cash flow, monthly budget, and itemized categories. If you regularly print these reports, say, each month or each quarter, store them separately in your reports notebook.

Quicken divides its report-making facility into three major components: personal reports, business reports, and custom reports. You can use any report regardless of your application: just because you use Quicken for business doesn't mean that you can't produce a personal report. Personal reports are geared primarily to the needs and requirements of individuals, while business reports are specifically enhanced to take care of business accounting needs.

Personal Reports

You can choose from among the following five predesigned personal reports. If desired, you can add customizing touches to these reports; customizing options are detailed later in this chapter.

Cash flow report—shows the amount of incoming money compared to outgoing money. Quicken cash flow reports cover bank, cash, and credit card accounts.

Monthly budget report—compares what you spent during a month with what you wanted to spend. You can indicate the exact categories to compare (e.g., utilities and housing); you can also vary the budget on a month-to-month basis. Quicken gives you a monthly budget for all bank, cash, and credit card accounts.

Itemized categories report—itemizes transactions, grouped and subtotaled by category. This report covers all account types.

Tax summary report—summarizes all those transactions that have been categorized as tax related. This report covers all account types.

Account balances report—summarizes the ending balance from all your accounts, providing you with a net worth statement current up to the day it was produced.

Business Reports

You can choose from among the following seven predesigned business reports. As with personal reports, you can add customizing touches to these reports. Customizing options are detailed later in this chapter.

P&L statement report—totals your income and expenses for each category, by month. This is the standard profit and loss statement used in business. It covers all account types.

Cash flow report—shows the amount of incoming money to outgoing money. Quicken cash flow reports cover bank, cash, and credit card accounts.

A/P by vendor report—lists checks you've written but not yet printed, grouped and subtotaled by payee. This report includes transactions from bank, cash, and credit card accounts.

A/R by customer report—lists outstanding balances by customer, by each month. This report applies only to select other asset accounts.

Job/project report—totals income and expenses for each class, assuming you've classified your job and projects in this manner. This report covers all account types.

Payroll report—totals income and expenses for each employee, subtotaled by category. This report uses only those transactions categorized as Payroll (from any account type).

Balance sheet report—shows the net worth of your business, using the ending balances from all your accounts.

Custom Reports

In addition to Quicken's 12 preset personal and business reports, you can create customized reports to fit your specific needs. Quicken provides the basic framework for each custom report; you fill in the blanks by telling the program what you want included and how you want it to appear in the final report. Quicken offers the following four custom reports:

Transaction report—creates a report listing specific transactions. You indicate how the report is sorted and subtotaled.

Summary report—creates a report summarizing your transactions, but it does not include the actual transactions. You can include category, class, payee, or account information.

Budget report—creates a report itemizing selected transactions, comparing them with preset budget limits.

Account balances report—summarizes and totals the ending balance from all your accounts, at specified intervals.

Producing a Standard Report

The preset personal and business reports are the easiest to produce. You can elect to view the report on screen (using cursor keys to move around the report if it's larger than one screen) or to print it on paper.

Q Producing a Standard Report

1. From any register, choose the Personal Reports or Business Reports command from the Reports menu.	The Reports List window appears as shown in Figure 10-1. (This screen shows the available personal reports.)
2. Select the report to use.	The report window appears, such as the one in Figure 10-2. Some reports require slightly different information, but the

	contents of the report window are fairly self-explanatory.
3. Fill in the blanks in the report window; press Enter when done.	
4. View the report, using cursor keys to move around. OR Print the report by pressing the F8 key.	Displays the Print Report window, shown in Figure 10-3.
5. When printing reports, Quicken asks you to select a destination printer. Select a printer, and press Enter.	

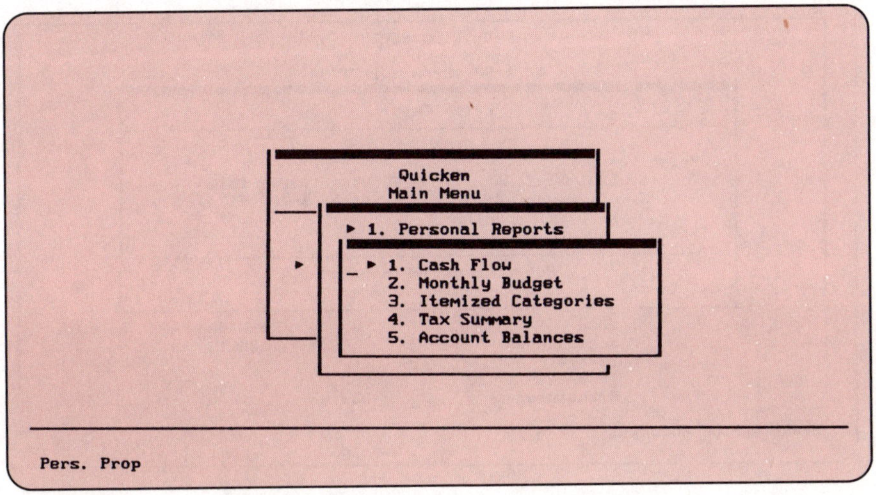

Figure 10-1. Quicken's five personal reports.

Viewing Reports on Screen

Quicken always displays its reports on screen before they are printed. You can use this feature in lieu of printing or to check

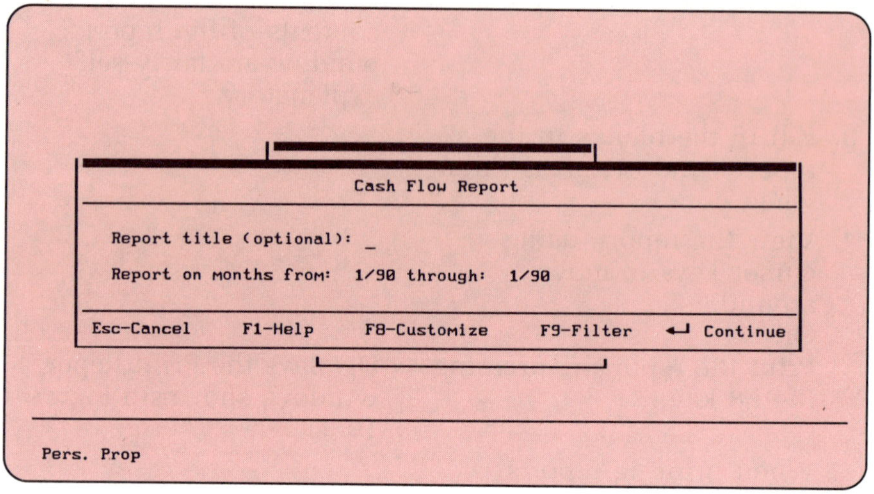

Figure 10-2. A sample report window.

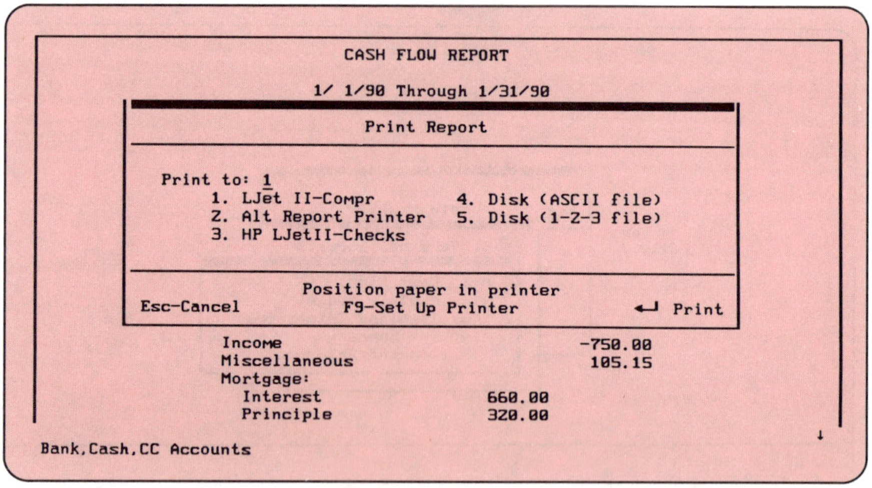

Figure 10-3. Print any report by indicating the printer (you can also change printer selections).

that the information you want to print is included in the report. Most likely, the entire report will extend beyond the boundaries of your computer screen. Use the cursor keys, as detailed in Table 10-1, to see more of the report.

Table 10-1. Moving Within the Reports on Screen.

To Move	Press
Down one screen	Page Down
Up one screen	Page Up
Right one screen	Tab or Ctrl-right arrow
Left one screen	Shift-Tab or Ctrl-left arrow
To the upper left corner of report	Home
To the bottom right corner of report	End

Note that while previewing a report, Quicken displays a border around the text. This border, shown in Figure 10-4, represents the edge of the paper and shows you the extent of the report.

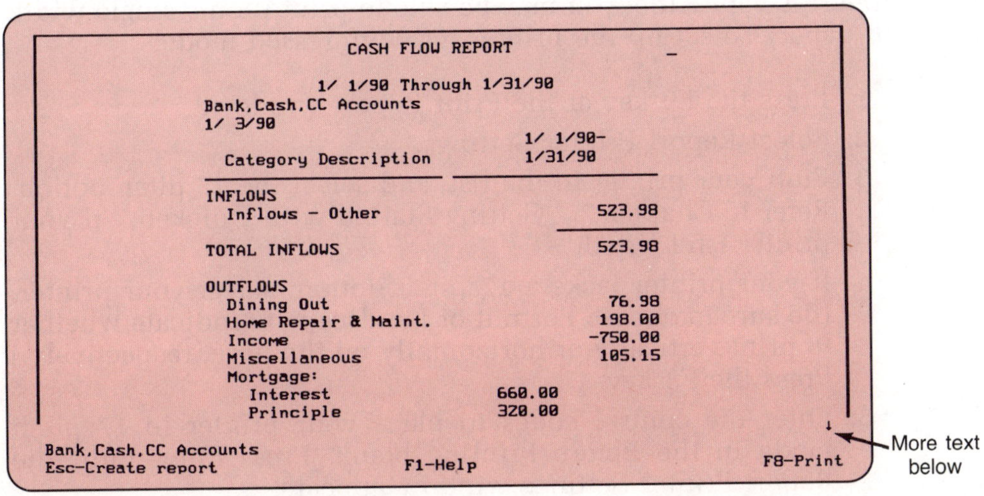

Figure 10-4. The border around the on-screen report shows the edges of the "paper."

Printing Wide Reports

Reports that are too wide to fit on a single width of paper are automatically printed in strips. After printing, you can tape the strips together to make one large report. In this fashion, Quicken

> **Tip:** Quicken attempts to cram as much information into the screen at once. If your report includes transactions, some of the columns may be set to half-width, thereby making room for more columns but cutting off some of the transaction text. To view the report in its full width, press the F9 key and increase the total width of the report from 80 to 132 characters. Likewise, you'll want to print this report in compressed mode, as detailed in the next section.

can produce a report of almost unlimited width (as well as length), although it's a rare report that's wider than about two or three pages.

If your printer can print in compressed (17 characters per inch) mode, you can cram more text on one page. Unless the report is very wide, you may be able to print it on a single width of paper. To set up the printer for compressed mode:

1. Press the F9 key at the Print Report window.
2. Select Report Printer Settings.
3. Find your printer in the list, and select the 17 pitch option. Refer to Chapter 2, "Getting Started with Quicken," if your printer isn't listed.
4. If your printer lacks a 17 pitch option, select your printer. (Be sure to choose Portrait or Landscape to indicate whether to print vertically or horizontally on the page, respectively.) Press the F8 key.
5. Enter the control codes to place your printer in 17 pitch mode in the Before Printing blank. Press Enter until the Report Printer Settings window appears.
6. Fill in the Report Printer Settings menu, as required; press Ctrl-Enter when done.
7. When you're back at the Print Report screen, press Enter to initiate printing.

Printing to Disk

In addition to sending the report data to a printer, you can capture it in a disk file. Quicken lets you save the report data as a

> **Tip:** If you seldom print wide reports, you may wish to define the Alternate Report Settings printer to compressed and leave the standard Report Printer Settings alone. In Step 2 above, merely select Alternate Report Settings. In the Print Report window (Step 7), select Alt Report Printer (option 2). When you print a normal-width report, select Report Printer (option 1) at the Print Report window.

standard ASCII text file, which you can use with almost any word processor or electronic spreadsheet program. Alternatively, you can save the report in a .PRN spreadsheet text file.

To save the report in ASCII format, choose option 4, Disk (ASCII file) at the Print Report window. Provide a name for the file. You may include an optional file extension. Indicate the maximum width of the lines and the total number of lines per page. The defaults are 80 character per line and 66 lines per page. These values include space for margins.

To use the file, start your word processor, and edit the document. You may need to adjust the margins in your word processor to accommodate the format of the report. Depending on the capabilities of your word processor, you can change such features as the type style (or font), type size, and boldfacing.

To save the report as a spreadsheet text file, choose option 5, Disk (1-2-3 file). Enter a file name, without an extension. Quicken automatically adds the .PRN extension to the file. After saving the file, Quicken displays a help message telling you how to import the file into 1-2-3.

Note that most spreadsheet programs for the PC, including Microsoft Excel and Works, can also read .PRN files. If you're using Microsoft Works, for example, select the saved .PRN file, then indicate that you want it opened as a Spreadsheet file (as opposed to a Word Processor or Database file). The program will format the text automatically to fit into the cells of the spreadsheet. Enlarge the columns of the spreadsheet so you can view and print all the text contained within them. Figure 10-5 shows an example of a cash flow report imported as a .PRN file into Microsoft Works.

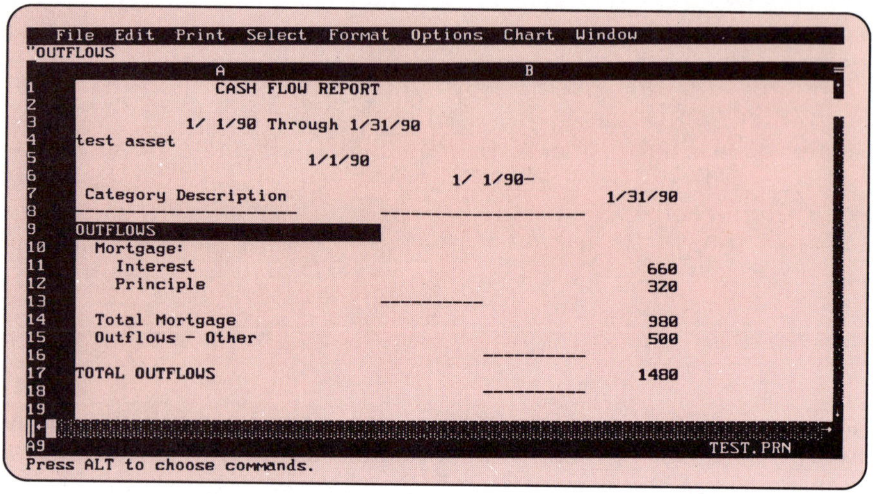

Figure 10-5. A sample imported .PRN file in Microsoft Works.

Customizing Standard Reports

You can elect to customize any of the five preset personal reports. At the Report window, press the F8 key to customize the report (e.g., determine exact report dates, subtotal formats, and sort formats) or the F9 key to indicate the transactions you want, based on text-search information. For instance, you can include only those transactions to a particular payee, restrict the reports to include only tax-related transactions, or include transactions that match certain categories, classes, or memos.

The section entitled "Producing Custom Reports," later in this chapter, details the use of these two options.

Examples of Personal Reports

The following are examples of Quicken's five preset personal reports.

Cash Flow

The cash flow report (see Figure 10-6) lists money that comes in as INFLOWS and money that goes out as OUTFLOWS. The difference, or the OVERALL total, shows whether you have a surplus or a deficit. To keep on top of your finances, obviously, you'll want to make sure you have a surplus—however small—for all or most of the months in the year.

```
                                   Cash Flow
                          12/ 1/89 Through 1/31/90
Bank,Cash,CC Accounts                                                   Page 1
1/ 3/90
                                                  12/ 1/89-
                  Category Description             1/31/90
                 ---------------------- --------------------
                 INFLOWS
                   Inflows - Other                        1,023.98
                                                        ----------
                 TOTAL INFLOWS                            1,023.98

                 OUTFLOWS
                   Dining Out                                76.98
                   Home Repair & Maint.                     198.00
                   Income                                  -750.00
                   Miscellaneous                            105.15
                   Mortgage:
                     Interest                  1,320.00
                     Principle                   640.00
                                              ----------
                   Total Mortgage                         1,960.00
                   Travel                                   398.00
                   Water, Gas, Electric                     123.45
                   Outflows - Other                       3,081.85
                                                        ----------
                 TOTAL OUTFLOWS                           5,193.43

                                                        ----------
                 OVERALL TOTAL                           -4,169.45
                                                        ==========
```

Figure 10-6. A sample personal cash flow report.

Included as entries under INFLOWS and OUTFLOWS are categories within your bank, cash, and credit card accounts. If you've used subcategories, these are itemized separately.

Monthly Budget

The monthly budget report, illustrated in Figure 10-7, compares what you've spent during a particular month with what you planned to spend. For example, if you planned to spend $100 per month for clothing for your family, and you spent $150, you know you're over budget for that category. The monthly budget report contains only those categories from bank, cash, and credit card accounts that you specify. You can set a standard monthly budget or vary the budget every month for the entire year (e.g., you're more likely to spend more money in August and September for clothes than during other times of the year).

```
                              Monthly
                                                                  _
              1/ 1/90 Through 1/31/90
          Bank,Cash,CC Accounts
          1/ 9/90
                                         1/ 1/90        -        1/31/90
            Category Description         Actual      Budget       Diff
          ________________________     __________  __________  __________
          OUTFLOWS
            Clothing                        43.98      100.00      -56.02
            Dining Out                      76.98       75.00        1.98
            Groceries                        0.00      350.00     -350.00
            Home Repair & Maint.           198.00      100.00       98.00
            Household Misc. Exp            134.05       75.00       59.05
            Housing                          0.00    1,250.00   -1,250.00
            Medical & Dental                 0.00       75.00      -75.00
            Telephone Expense                0.00       50.00      -50.00
                                       __________  __________  __________
          TOTAL OUTFLOWS                   453.01    2,075.00   -1,621.99
                                       ==========  ==========  ==========
                                                                          ↓
Bank,Cash,CC Accounts
Esc-Create report                F1-Help                          F8-Print
```

Figure 10-7. This monthly budget report helps you spot if you're spending too much in one category.

To enter or change monthly budget values when viewing the report, press the F7 key from the Monthly Budget Report window. (You must set up the monthly budgets for at least one category before you can view or print a monthly budget report.) The Specify Budget Amounts window appears, as shown in Figure 10-8.

1. Use the cursor keys to select a category to include. Those categories without a monthly budget amount are not included in the report.
2. Type the monthly budget. If you don't want to enter a budget amount, but want the category listed in the monthly budget report, enter a 0 (zero).
3. If you'd like to enter a different budget amount for each month of the year, select the desired category and press

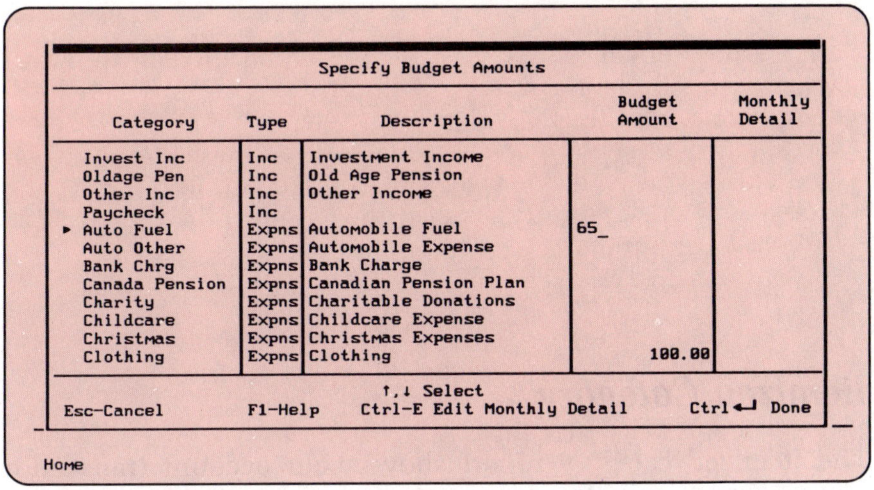

Figure 10-8. Specify budgeted amounts for each category here.

Ctrl-E. In the window that appears (shown in Figure 10-9), enter a budget amount for each month, as desired. As a shortcut, press the F9 key to copy the last entered amount to all months to the end of the year. Press Enter when done.

4. When you're done entering the budget amounts, press Ctrl-Enter. You can now view and print the monthly budget report.

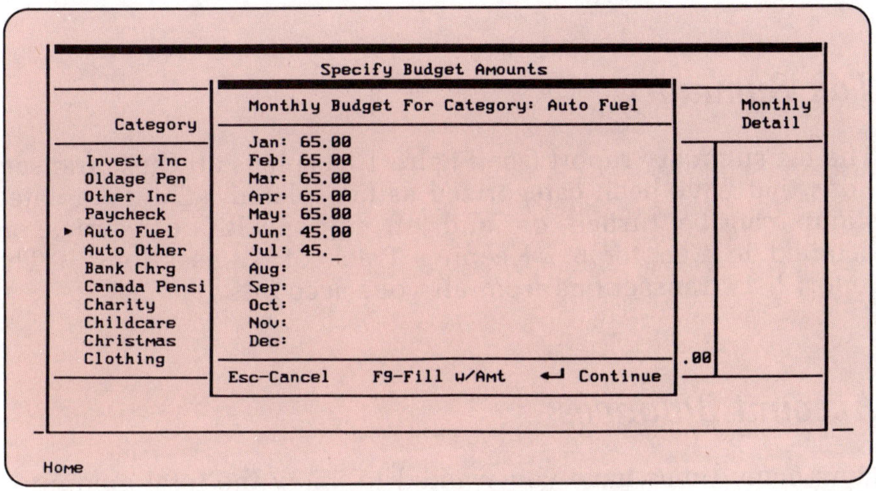

Figure 10-9. You can optionally assign a different budgeted amount for each month of the year.

> **Tip:** Quicken omits the category when there's no entry in the Budget Amount column. To delete a category from your monthly budget report, select it with the cursor keys, and press the Spacebar until the old budget amount is deleted. If you want to change the budget amount for a particular category, simply type a new number in the Budget Amount column.

Itemized Category

The itemized category report shows your account transactions grouped and subtotaled by category. The itemized category report, as depicted in Figure 10-10, lists transactions from all Quicken accounts. Included in the report is all the information provided in the account register, including payee, memo, category, and clear status.

Normally, the report shows all your transactions. Most likely, you'll want to narrow the transactions to include only those transactions that are most important to you. This requires that you "filter" the report before viewing or printing it. Filtering is more fully discussed in the section entitled "Producing Custom Reports," later in this chapter.

Tax Summary

The tax summary report (see Figure 10-11) lists all those transactions that have been categorized as tax related. (The tax-related stamp can be turned on and off for specific categories, as detailed in Chapter 6, "Keeping Track of Transactions.") The report lists transactions from all your accounts.

Account Balances

How many times have you wanted to know the total amount of cash you have in all of your bank accounts? The account bal-

```
                              Itemized
                    1/ 1/90 Through 1/31/90
All Accounts                                                   Page 1
1/ 9/90

 Date   Acct     Num       Payee          Memo       Category    Clr  Amount
----- -------- ------ --------------- ----------- -------------- - ----------

                INCOME/EXPENSE
                  INCOME
                    Income - Other
                    --------------
 1/ 3 Savings  D       Deposit from pay                                 500.00
 1/ 4 Savings  I       Interest payment                                  23.98
 1/ 1 Pers. Pr         Livingroom furni                               3,983.00
 1/ 1 Pers. Pr         Bedroom furnitur Inluces bra                   1,763.00
 1/ 1 Pers. Pr         Jewelry                                       18,776.00
                                                                    ----------
                    Total Income - Other                             25,045.98
                                                                    ----------
                  TOTAL INCOME                                       25,045.98


                  EXPENSES
                    Clothing
                    --------
 1/ 5 Home     *****   Jackets Etc.                Clothing             -43.98
                                                                    ----------
                    Total Clothing                                      -43.98

                    Dining Out
                    ----------
 1/ 2 Cash             El Taco Palance             Dining               -76.98
                                                                    ----------
                    Total Dining Out                                    -76.98

                    Home Repair & Maint.
                    --------------------
 1/ 1 Visa             Bill's Lumber               Home Rpair     X    -198.00
                                                                    ----------
                    Total Home Repair & Maint.                         -198.00

                    Household Misc. Exp
                    -------------------
 1/ 5 Home     *****   Fred's TV & Appl            Household           -134.05
                                                                    ----------
                    Total Household Misc. Exp                          -134.05

                    Income
                    ------
 1/ 4 Savings  D     S Deposit from pay Paycheck/re Income              750.00
                                                                    ----------
                    Total Income                                        750.00
```

Figure 10-10. Sample personal itemized category report.

ances report, illustrated in Figure 10-12, provides you with this information, plus the balance from your cash, credit card, other asset, and other liability accounts. In this way, the account balances report furnishes you with a statement of net worth. Money listed in bank, cash, and other asset accounts increases your net worth; debts listed in credit card and other liability accounts reduce that net worth.

```
                           Tax Summary
                   1/ 1/90 Through 1/31/90
All Accounts
1/ 9/90

 Date   Acct     Num        Payee          Memo       Category     Clr Amount
 ----   ----     ---        -----          ----       --------     --- ------
               INCOME/EXPENSE
                 EXPENSES
                   Mortgage:
                   ---------
                     Interest
                     --------
 1/19 Home     *****S Courtland Mortga Interest pa Mortgage:Interes      -660.00
                                                                       --------
                     Total Interest                                      -660.00
                                                                       --------
                   Total Mortgage                                        -660.00
                                                                       --------
                 TOTAL EXPENSES                                          -660.00
All Accounts                                                          (Filtered)
Esc-Create report                  F1-Help      F8-Print   F9-Full column width
```

Figure 10-11. Use this tax summary report at tax time.


```
                                  Balances
                               As of 1/ 9/90
All Accounts
1/ 9/90
                                                              1/ 9/90
                       Account                                Balance
          ------------------------------------   ----------------------
          ASSETS
            Cash and Bank Accounts
              Cash                                                185.00
              Home
                Ending Balance                       1,200.33
                plus: Checks Payable                   245.12
                                                  -----------
              Total Home                                        1,445.45
              Savings-Main savings account                      2,668.98
                                                              -----------
            Total Cash and Bank Accounts                        4,299.43

            Other Assets
              Pers. Prop-Personal property                     24,522.00
                                                              -----------
            Total Other Assets                                 24,522.00

                                                              -----------
          TOTAL ASSETS                                         28,821.43

          LIABILITIES
            Checks Payable                                        245.12

            Credit Cards
              Visa-11234-123-123-123                            1,876.86
                                                              -----------
            Total Credit Cards                                  1,876.86

                                                              -----------
          TOTAL LIABILITIES                                     2,121.98

                                                              -----------
          OVERALL TOTAL                                        26,699.45
                                                              ===========
```

Figure 10-12. An account balance report.

Examples of Business Reports

The following are examples of Quicken's seven preset business reports.

P&L Statement

A P&L (profit and loss) statement shows your profit and loss, by category. Income categories are grouped together at the top of the report; expenses categories follow. Figure 10-13 shows a sample P&L statement produced by Quicken.

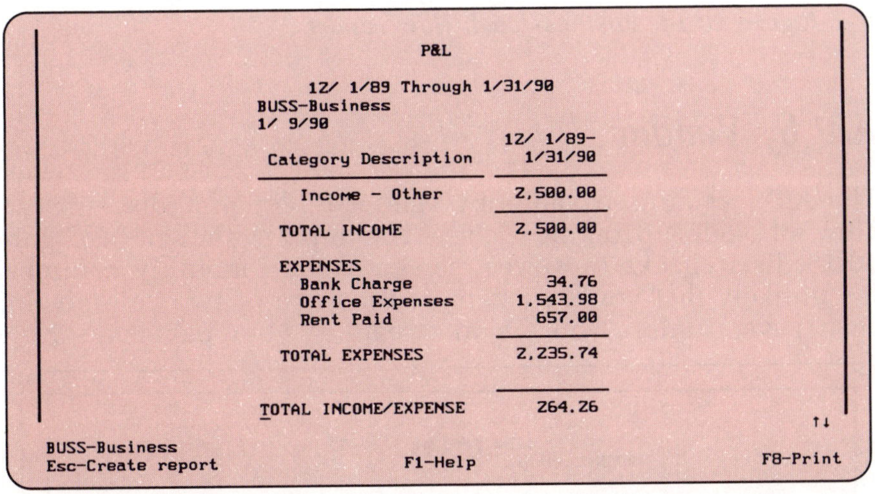

P&L

12/ 1/89 Through 1/31/90
BUSS-Business
1/ 9/90

Category Description	12/ 1/89- 1/31/90
Income - Other	2,500.00
TOTAL INCOME	2,500.00
EXPENSES	
Bank Charge	34.76
Office Expenses	1,543.98
Rent Paid	657.00
TOTAL EXPENSES	2,235.74
TOTAL INCOME/EXPENSE	264.26

BUSS-Business
Esc-Create report F1-Help F8-Print

Figure 10-13. A sample profit and loss statement, ideal for small businesses.

Cash Flow

The cash flow report (see Figure 10-14) lists money that comes in as INFLOWS and money that goes out as OUTFLOWS. The difference, stated as the OVERALL total, shows whether you have a surplus or a deficit. The business cash flow report is the same as the personal cash flow report, detailed above.

```
                          Cash
                                                          _
             12/ 1/89 Through 1/31/90
        BUSS-Business
        1/ 9/90
                                        12/ 1/89-
         Category Description            1/31/90
        ______________________       ___________
        INFLOWS
          Inflows - Other               2,500.00
                                     ___________
        TOTAL INFLOWS                   2,500.00

        OUTFLOWS
          Bank Charge                      34.76
          Office Expenses               1,543.98
          Rent Paid                       657.00
                                     ___________
        TOTAL OUTFLOWS                  2,235.74

                                     ___________
                                                                  ↓
BUSS-Business
Esc-Create report            F1-Help                        F8-Print
```

Figure 10-14. Business cash flow report.

A/P by Vendor

The A/P (accounts payable) by vendor report provides an overview of your upcoming debts. The report, shown in Figure 10-15, lists checks by payee, separated into monthly columns. It's unlikely that you'll have more than one or two columns for each payee, unless you are in arrears in your payments. Note

```
                          A/P
                                                          _
              1/ 1/90 Through 1/31/90
        BUSS-Business
        1/ 9/90

                  Payee                   1/90
        ________________________   __________
        Bill Computer Shop           -1,498.00
        Federal Express                -247.54
        Northern Stationery             -45.98
        Pacific Leasing Co.            -657.00
        Steel Market Industries        -400.98
                                   __________
        OVERALL TOTAL                -2,849.50
                                   ==========



BUSS-Business                                             (Filtered)
Esc-Create report            F1-Help                        F8-Print
```

Figure 10-15. This report itemizes accounts payable (bills you need to pay).

that the A/P by vendor report lists only those checks you've written, but not yet printed. This can include regular dated checks that you've not printed yet or post-dated checks.

A/R by Customer

The A/R (accounts receivable) by customer report (see Figure 10-16) lists money you expect to receive in the near future. In order to use this report, you must set up an other asset account where you enter your accounts receivable invoices. In the accounts receivable register, as shown in Figure 10-17, you enter the invoice date, invoice number (if any), and the payee. You can also include a category, class, and memo, if desired. The amount of the invoice is posted in the INCREASE column. As your invoices are paid, they are marked off in the DECREASE column.

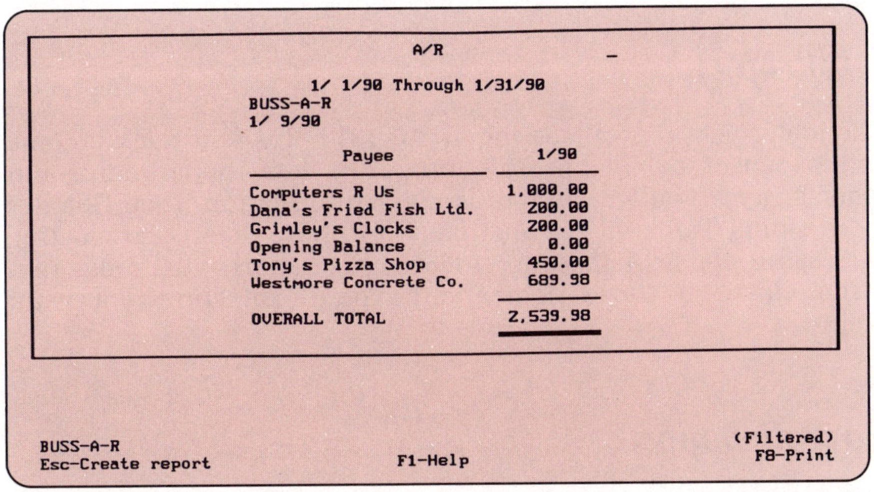

Figure 10-16. This report itemizes accounts receivable (money you're getting in).

Before printing the A/R by customer report, Quicken preselects all other asset accounts. You'll want to deselect those you don't want included in the report. (Deselect by highlighting the account and pressing the Spacebar.)

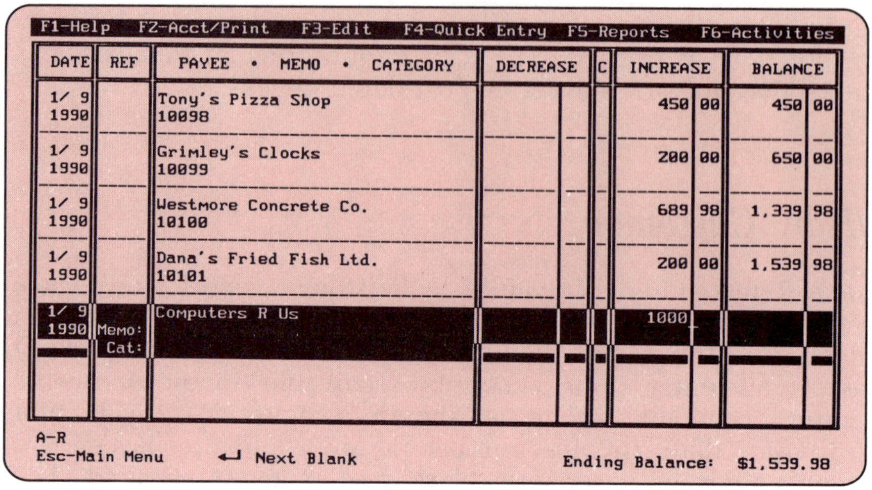

Figure 10-17. Entries in a sample accounts receivable register.

Job/Project

The job/project report (see Figure 10-18) helps you track income and expenses by job, project, property, date, department, and other criteria you've entered as class information. (See Chapter 6, "Keeping Track of Transactions," for more details on creating and using classes.) In order to use this report, you must first assign classes to those income and expense categories you want included.

Payroll Report

The payroll report, as illustrated in Figure 10-19, lists your employees and the various payroll-related expenses, during a given time period. To use the report, you must use the Payroll category in the Category blank for each payroll check you write. If you want to itemize the payroll deductions (a good idea) and have them show up in the payroll report, you must split the check as shown in Figure 10-20. Deductions will most often be posted into other liability accounts, so you can keep track of them. Therefore, when you enter the Payroll category, you'll actually be entering a transfer to another Quicken account.

Job/Project
1/ 1/90 Through 1/31/90

Category Description	Prod 100A	Prod 100B	Other	OVERALL TOTAL
INCOME/EXPENSE				
INCOME				
Income - Other	45.98	103.00	5,039.98	5,188.96
TOTAL INCOME	45.98	103.00	5,039.98	5,188.96
EXPENSES				
Bank Charge	0.00	0.00	34.76	34.76
Freight	0.00	0.00	247.54	247.54
Office Expenses	0.00	0.00	1,543.98	1,543.98
Rent Paid	0.00	0.00	657.00	657.00
Expenses - Other	601.71	819.05	400.98	1,821.74
TOTAL EXPENSES	601.71	819.05	2,884.26	4,305.02
TOTAL INCOME/EXPENSE	-555.73	-716.05	2,155.72	883.94
BALANCE FORWARD				
A-R	0.00	0.00	0.00	0.00
Business	0.00	0.00	5,000.00	5,000.00
Job	0.00	0.00	0.00	0.00
TOTAL BALANCE FORWARD	0.00	0.00	5,000.00	5,000.00
OVERALL TOTAL	-555.73	-716.05	7,155.72	5,883.94

Figure 10-18. Job/project report.

Payroll
1/ 1/90 Through 1/31/90

Payee	INC/EXP EXPENSES Payroll Gross	INC/EXP EXPENSES Payroll TOTAL	INC/EXP EXPENSES Payroll-Dues	INC/EXP EXPENSES Payroll-Fed	INC/EXP EXPENSES Payroll-FICA	INC/EXP EXPENSES Payroll-Ins	INC/EXP EXPENSES TOTAL
Arnold Gross	-676.90	-676.90	250.00	157.00	56.98	83.00	-129.92
Bill Smithers	-500.00	-500.00	25.00	128.00	45.00	-78.76	-380.76
George Stout	-750.00	-750.00	0.00	166.87	75.98	98.00	-409.15
Tony Abalone	-500.00	-500.00	25.00	128.00	45.00	-78.70	-380.70
OVERALL TOTAL	-2,426.90	-2,426.90	300.00	579.87	222.96	23.54	-1,300.53

Figure 10-19. Sample business payroll report.

Balance Sheet

The balance sheet, shown in Figure 10-21, lists the balances from all your accounts: bank, cash, credit card, other asset, and other liability. Each balance is listed separately, under the main headings of ASSETS and LIABILITIES.

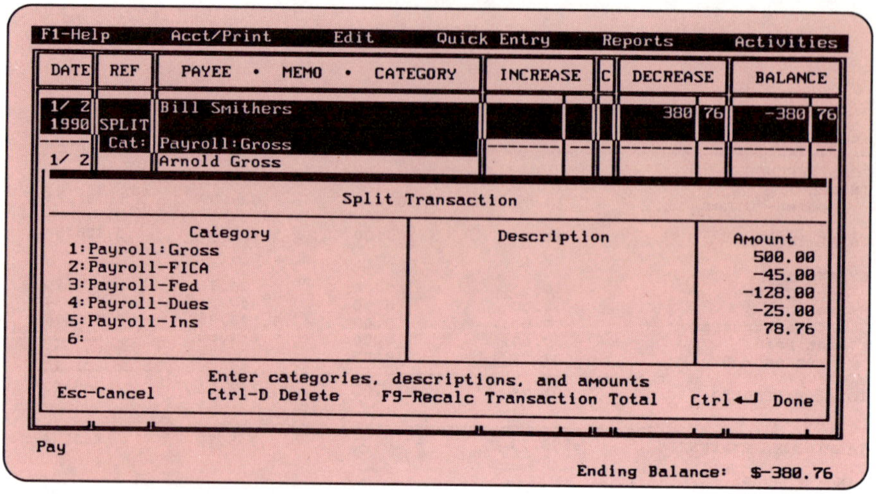

Figure 10-20. Payroll checks must often use split transactions to show the gross pay and all deductions.

Balance
As of 1/ 9/90

BUSS-All Accounts
1/ 9/90

Page 1

Account		1/ 9/90 Balance
ASSETS		
Cash and Bank Accounts		
Business-Business acct		
Ending Balance	4,615.74	
plus: Checks Payable	2,849.50	
Total Business-Business acct		7,465.24
Job-Job/project accountin		-1,271.78
Total Cash and Bank Accounts		6,193.46
Other Assets		
A-R-Accounts Receivable		2,539.98
Total Other Assets		2,539.98
TOTAL ASSETS		8,733.44
LIABILITIES		
Checks Payable		2,849.50
Other Liabilities		
Pay-Payroll account		-1,400.53
Total Other Liabilities		-1,400.53
TOTAL LIABILITIES		1,448.97
OVERALL TOTAL		7,284.47

Figure 10-21. The balance sheet for business.

Producing Custom Reports

Quicken lets you create four unique forms of custom reports—transaction, summary, budget, and account balances—as well as customize any of the 12 preset personal and business reports. The process is the same whether you are designing a custom report or customizing a preset report.

Q Creating a Custom Report

1. From the main menu, choose the Reports command.
2. Select the report you want to produce. The exact content of the window varies depending on the report type you select. Note: If you are currently at a register or a Write Checks screen, choose one of the report types from the Reports pull-down menu.

   If you selected a custom report, the Create Transaction Report window appears. A transaction is shown in Figure 10-22.
3. Press the F8 key, if you selected a preset personal or business report.

   The Create Report window appears.

The exact contents of the window varies depending on the exact report type you selected.

> **Important Note:** All of Quicken's preset personal and business reports are really custom reports that have already been defined for you. That's why you can further customize them, if you desired. The 12 preset personal and business reports belong to one of Quicken's four custom report types, as shown in Table 10-2.

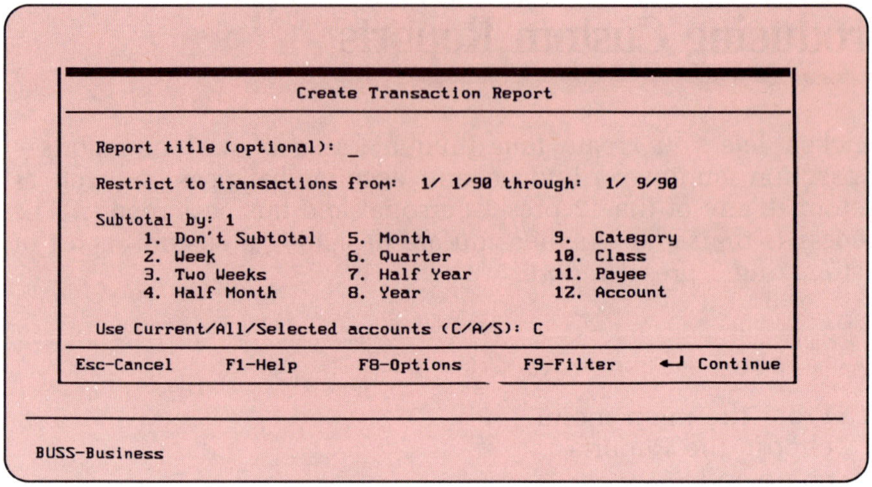

Figure 10-22. The Create Transaction Report window.

Table 10-2. Preset Report Types.

Personal Report	Custom Form
Cash flow	Summary
Monthly budget	Budget
Itemized category	Transaction
Tax summary	Transaction
Account balances	Account balances
Business Report	**Custom Form**
P&L statement	Summary
Cash flow	Summary
A/P by vendor	Summary
A/R by customer	Summary
Job/project summary	Summary
Payroll	Summary
Balance sheet	Account balances

Filling in the Create Report Window

At a minimum, the Create Report window allows you to enter:

A name for the report—Enter a name for the report. If you leave this blank, Quicken will provide a name for you, using a descriptive title based on the criteria you've set.

The range of dates included in the report—Enter the start and stop dates for transactions you want to include. You can provide whole months, or indicate specific days.

How transactions are subtotaled—Indicate whether they are subtotaled by week, year, class, category, and so forth. Enter a selection, or press 1 for Don't subtotal.

The transactions you want included—Indicate either Current, All, or Selected. Current transactions are those only in the currently selected account. All transactions are from accounts. (Note: Many reports are restricted to bank, cash, and credit card accounts.) When using selected accounts, you specify the accounts that contain the transaction you want in your reports, as shown in Figure 10-23. Press the Spacebar to include the account in the report; press it again to exclude it.

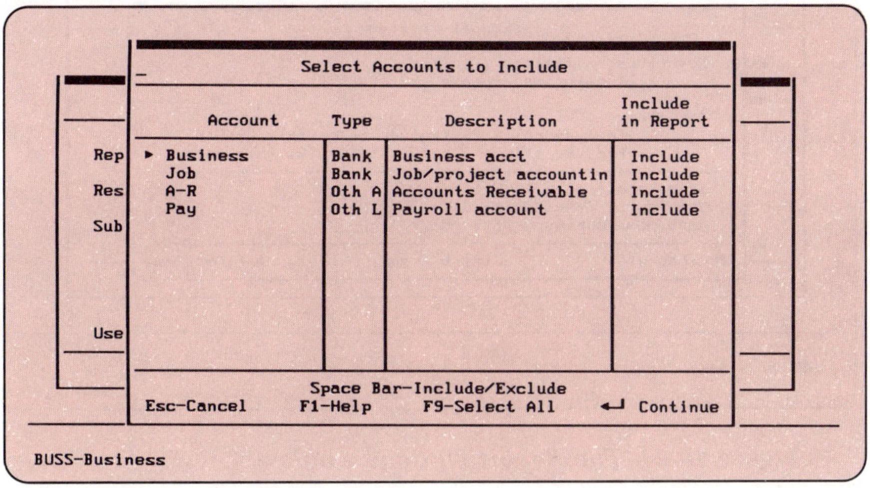

Figure 10-23. Select accounts to include in the report in this window.

In addition, certain Create Report windows expect you to provide other information.

Summary reports allow you to indicate row headings for categories, classes, payees, or accounts. Enter the number of the type of row headings you want.

Summary and budget reports allow you to indicate column headings. Type the number that corresponds to the type or column heading you want.

Account balances reports allow you to specify the intervals at which you want the ending balances to be calculated. The available choices are: one week, two weeks, a half month, a month, a quarter, a half year, or a year.

Setting Report Options

Pressing the F8 key from any Create Report window displays the Report Options window, shown in Figure 10-24. For all report types, you can select an organization for the report (by income/expense or cash flow basis) and how transfers are to be handled.

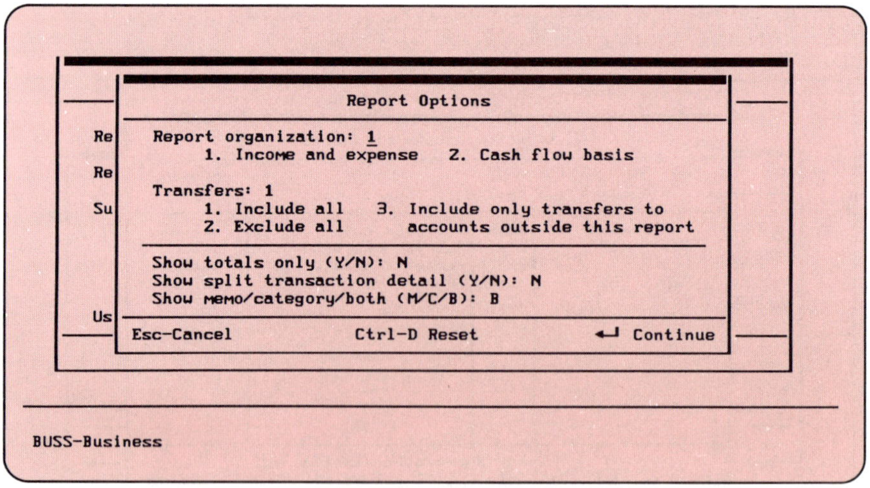

Figure 10-24. The Report Options window.

When the report is organized by income/expense, transactions are grouped by income first, then by expense. When the report is organized by cash flow basis, Quicken groups transactions and transfers by INFLOWS and OUTFLOWS, respectively.

Transaction reports offer three additional selections:

- *Show totals only*—Type `Yes` when you want the report to show only the total income and expenses for selected transactions.
- *Show split transaction detail*—Type `Yes` to include a rundown of split transactions.
- *Show memo/category/both*—Press M or C to include just the memo or category in transaction reports; press B to include them both.

When you're finished with the Report Options window, press the Enter key to go back to the Create Report window.

Filtering Transactions

Pressing the F9 key at any Create Report window displays the Filter Report Transaction window, illustrated in Figure 10-25. Using the options in this window, you can specify the kinds of transactions you want included in the report. Only those transactions that meet *all* of the criteria you have indicated will be processed into the report. You have the following options.

Restrict report to transactions meeting these criteria—Enter a text string for matching with Payee name, memo, category, or class. You can use an exact text match or find text that includes or excludes the text you've indicated. See the section entitled "Transaction Filter Text Matching," below, for more information.

Select categories to include—Type `Yes` if you want to select categories to include in the report. The window in Figure 10-26 appears. Initially, all categories are Included; to exclude a category, highlight it with the up and down arrow keys, then press the Spacebar.

Select classes to include—Type `Yes` if you want to select classes to include in the report. You include/exclude classes the same as you do categories (see above).

Tax-related categories only—Type `Yes` if you want to include only tax-related categories in the report.

Below/Equal/Above the amount—Press B if you want to include transactions that are below a specified amount, or press E or A if you to want to include transactions that are equal to or greater than the specified amount. Indicate the amount, in dollars and cents.

Payments/Deposits/Unprinted checks/All—This option specifies the type of transactions. Press A if you want to include all transactions, press P to include only payments, press D to include only deposits, and press U to include only unprinted checks.

Cleared status is blank—Type Yes or No beside both or either of the cleared status symbols to include these transactions in the report. The * clear symbol is for transactions that have been marked clear, but haven't been reconciled with the bank statement. The X clear symbol is for transactions that are both marked clear and reconciled.

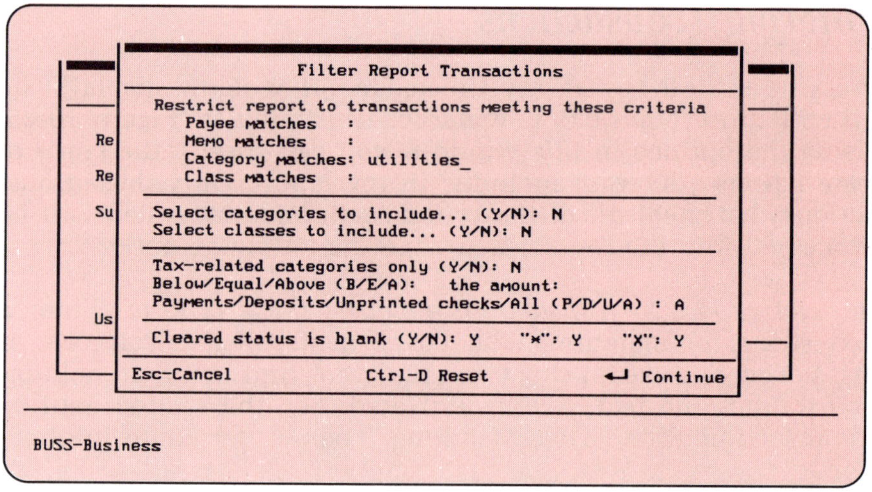

Figure 10-25. Specify the information you want to include in your reports in the Filter Report Transactions window.

When you are finished entering the filter information, press the Enter key to continue. Quicken takes you back to the Create Report window. Alternatively, you can press F8 then Ctrl-D to reset all the entries to their default settings. You can now return to the Create Report window, or re-enter your custom settings.

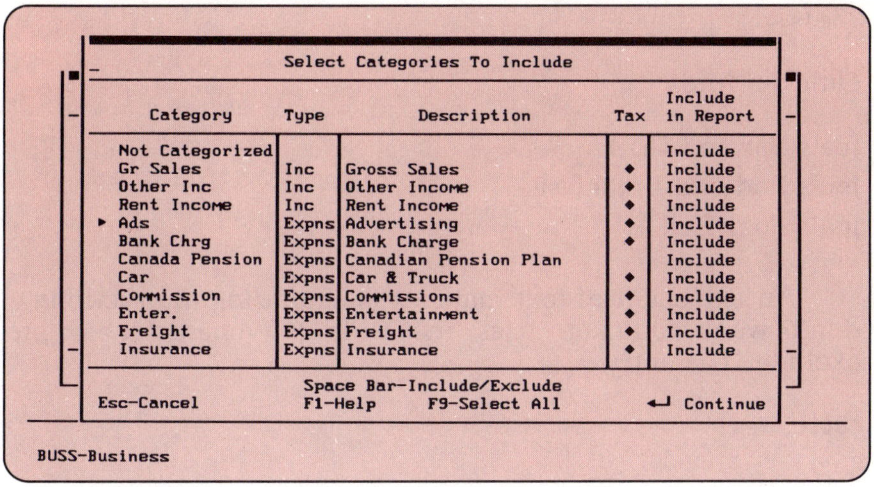

Figure 10-26. The Select Categories to Include window.

Transaction Filter Text Matching

Having Quicken find those transactions that meet certain criteria is the fastest and most accurate way to produce reports. When using the transaction filter options listed above, you can find those transactions that meet only the criteria you specify. That criteria is in the form of a text match. You can locate transactions by payee, memo, category, or class, or a combination of all four.

The most straightforward use of the transaction filter text matching is exact text searches. For example, if you want to include only those transactions that list "Joe's Bar and Grill" as the payee, enter "Joe's Bar and Grill" in the Payee blank within the Filter Report Transactions window. Quicken will search through your accounts and list in its report only the transactions with the text you specify. You can do the same for memos, categories, and classes.

You can also use text matching to find approximate entries. Quicken uses double periods as a "wildcard"; the double periods match up to any text. For example, to find checks written to any of Joe's businesses (Bar and Grill, Bed and Breakfast, and Pool Hall), enter

```
Joe's..
```

Quicken finds

Joe's Bar and Grill
Joe's Bed and Breakfast
Joe's Pool Hall

An extension of text matches is *excluding* transactions you don't want. Quicken uses the tilde (~) character to mean exclude. The entry

```
~Utilities
```

will *not* include any transactions with the utilities category. You can combine the double periods and tilde character to build elaborate text-matching schemes. The entry


```
~Joe's..
```

will *not* include

Joe's Bar and Grill
Joe's Bed and Breakfast
Joe's Pool Hall

Examples of Custom Reports

Figures 10-27 through 10-30 illustrate some examples of custom Quicken reports. Because these reports were defined using the customizing options detailed earlier in this chapter, their format and content should only be considered as representative of the types of reports you can produce. You are free to design your own reports any way you desire.

Sample Custom Transaction
1/ 1/90 Through 1/ 9/90

BUSS-All Accounts
1/ 9/90

Page 1

Date	Acct	Num	Payee	Memo	Category	Clr	Amount
1/ 1	Business		Opening Balance		[Business]	X	5,000.00
1/ 5	Business	*****	Pacific Leasing		Rent Paid		-657.00
1/ 6	Business	*****	Bill Computer Sh		Office		-1,498.00
1/ 6	Business	*****	Northern Station		Office		-45.98
1/ 6	Business	*****	Steel Market Ind				-400.98
1/ 6	Business	*****	Federal Express		Freight		-247.54
1/ 1	Job		Opening Balance		[Job]	X	0.00
1/ 2	Job		Parts In		/Prod 100A		-354.98
1/ 2	Job		Parts In		/Prod 100B		-498.33
1/ 4	Job		Labor		/Prod 100A		-100.98
1/ 4	Job		Labor		/Prod 100B		-123.09
1/ 5	Job		Shipping		/Prod 100A		-45.12
1/ 5	Job		Shipping		/Prod 100B		-10.29
1/ 6	Job		Misc. Expenses		/Prod 100A		-100.63
1/ 6	Job		Misc Expenses		/Prod 100B		-187.34
1/ 1	Pay		Opening Balance		[Pay]		0.00
1/ 2	Pay	S	Bill Smithers		Payroll:Gross		500.00
					Payroll-FICA		-45.00
					Payroll-Fed		-128.00
					Payroll-Dues		-25.00
					Payroll-Ins		78.76
1/ 2	Pay	S	Arnold Gross		Payroll:Gross		676.90
					Payroll-FICA		-56.98
					Payroll-Fed		-157.00
					Payroll-Dues		-250.00
					Payroll-Ins		-83.00
1/ 2	Pay	S	Tony Abalone		Payroll:Gross		500.00
					Payroll-FICA		-45.00
					Payroll-Fed		-128.00
					Payroll-Dues		-25.00
					Payroll-Ins		78.70
							100.00
1/ 2	Pay	S	George Stout		Payroll:Gross		750.00
					Payroll-FICA		-75.98
					Payroll-Fed		-166.87
					Payroll-Dues		0.00
					Payroll-Ins		-98.00
			TOTAL 1/ 1/90 - 1/ 6/90				2,130.27
1/ 7	Business		Gorshon Developm				2,500.00
1/ 8	Business		Bank charges		Bank Chrg		-34.76
1/ 7	Job	S	Permits		/Prod 100A		45.98
					/Prod 100B		103.00
1/ 9	A-R		Opening Balance		[A-R]		0.00
1/ 9	A-R		Tony's Pizza Sho 10098				450.00
1/ 9	A-R		Grimley's Clocks 10099				200.00
1/ 9	A-R		Westmore Concret 10100				689.98
1/ 9	A-R		Dana's Fried Fis 10101				200.00
1/ 9	A-R		Computers R Us				1,000.00

Sample Custom Transaction
1/ 1/90 Through 1/ 9/90

BUSS-All Accounts
1/ 9/90

Page 2

Date	Acct	Num	Payee	Memo	Category	Clr	Amount
			TOTAL 1/ 7/90 - 1/ 9/90				5,154.20
			OVERALL TOTAL				7,284.47
			TOTAL INFLOWS				12,873.32
			TOTAL OUTFLOWS				-5,588.85
			NET TOTAL				7,284.47

Figure 10-27. A sample custom transaction report.

Sample Summary Report
1/ 1/90 Through 1/ 9/90

Payee	A-R	Business	Job	Pay	OVERALL TOTAL
Arnold Gross	0.00	0.00	0.00	129.92	129.92
Bank charges	0.00	-34.76	0.00	0.00	-34.76
Bill Computer Shop	0.00	-1,498.00	0.00	0.00	-1,498.00
Bill Smithers	0.00	0.00	0.00	380.76	380.76
Computers R Us	1,000.00	0.00	0.00	0.00	1,000.00
Dana's Fried Fish Ltd.	200.00	0.00	0.00	0.00	200.00
Federal Express	0.00	-247.54	0.00	0.00	-247.54
George Stout	0.00	0.00	0.00	409.15	409.15
Gorshon Development	0.00	2,500.00	0.00	0.00	2,500.00
Grimley's Clocks	200.00	0.00	0.00	0.00	200.00
Labor	0.00	0.00	-224.07	0.00	-224.07
Misc Expenses	0.00	0.00	-187.34	0.00	-187.34
Misc. Expenses	0.00	0.00	-100.63	0.00	-100.63
Northern Stationery	0.00	-45.98	0.00	0.00	-45.98
Opening Balance	0.00	5,000.00	0.00	0.00	5,000.00
Pacific Leasing Co.	0.00	-657.00	0.00	0.00	-657.00
Parts In	0.00	0.00	-853.31	0.00	-853.31
Permits	0.00	0.00	148.98	0.00	148.98
Shipping	0.00	0.00	-55.41	0.00	-55.41
Steel Market Industries	0.00	-400.98	0.00	0.00	-400.98
Tony Abalone	0.00	0.00	0.00	480.70	480.70
Tony's Pizza Shop	450.00	0.00	0.00	0.00	450.00
Westmore Concrete Co.	689.98	0.00	0.00	0.00	689.98
OVERALL TOTAL	2,539.98	4,615.74	-1,271.78	1,400.53	7,284.47

Figure 10-28. A custom summary report.

Custom Budget Report
1/ 1/90 Through 1/ 9/90

Category Description	1/ 1/90 Actual	- Budget	1/ 6/90 Diff	1/ 7/90 Actual	- Budget	1/ 9/90 Diff	1/ 1/90 Actual	- Budget	1/ 9/90 Diff
INCOME/EXPENSE									
EXPENSES									
Automobile Fuel	0.00	8.70	-8.70	0.00	4.35	-4.35	0.00	13.06	-13.06
Clothing	43.98	19.35	24.63	0.00	9.67	-9.67	43.98	29.03	14.95
Dining Out	76.98	14.51	62.47	0.00	7.25	-7.25	76.98	21.77	55.21
Groceries	0.00	67.74	-67.74	0.00	33.87	-33.87	0.00	101.61	-101.61
Home Repair & Maint.	198.00	19.35	178.65	0.00	9.67	-9.67	198.00	29.03	168.97
Household Misc. Exp	134.05	14.51	119.54	0.00	7.25	-7.25	134.05	21.77	112.28
Housing	0.00	241.93	-241.93	0.00	120.96	-120.96	0.00	362.90	-362.90
Medical & Dental	0.00	14.51	-14.51	0.00	7.25	-7.25	0.00	21.77	-21.77
Telephone Expense	0.00	9.67	-9.67	0.00	4.83	-4.83	0.00	14.51	-14.51
TOTAL EXPENSES	453.01	410.27	42.74	0.00	205.10	-205.10	453.01	615.45	-162.44
TOTAL INCOME/EXPENSE	-453.01	-410.27	-42.74	0.00	-205.10	205.10	-453.01	-615.45	162.44

Figure 10-29. A custom budget report.

```
                    ACCOUNT BALANCES REPORT BY MONTH
                             As of 1/ 9/90
BUSS-All Accounts                                                    Page 1
1/ 9/90
                                                1/ 1/90        1/ 9/90
              Account                           Balance        Balance
       ----------------------------------  --------------  --------------
       ASSETS
         Cash and Bank Accounts
           Business-Business acct
             Ending Balance                   5,000.00        4,615.74
             plus: Checks Payable                 0.00        2,849.50
                                             ----------      ----------
           Total Business-Business acct           5,000.00        7,465.24
           Job-Job/project accountin                  0.00       -1,271.78
                                                 ----------      ----------
         Total Cash and Bank Accounts             5,000.00        6,193.46

         Other Assets
           A-R-Accounts Receivable                    0.00        2,539.98
                                                 ----------      ----------
         Total Other Assets                           0.00        2,539.98

                                                 ----------      ----------
       TOTAL ASSETS                               5,000.00        8,733.44

       LIABILITIES
         Checks Payable                               0.00        2,849.50

         Other Liabilities
           Pay-Payroll account                        0.00       -1,400.53
                                                 ----------      ----------
         Total Other Liabilities                      0.00       -1,400.53

                                                 ----------      ----------
       TOTAL LIABILITIES                              0.00        1,448.97

                                                 ----------      ----------
       OVERALL TOTAL                              5,000.00        7,284.47
                                                 ==========      ==========
```

Figure 10-30. A custom account balances report.

What You Have Learned

This chapter detailed Quicken's numerous reports and how to make them. Here's what you should have learned:

- You can view reports on screen or print them out.
- Quicken offers five preset personal reports: cash flow, monthly budget, itemized categories, tax summary, and account balances.
- Quicken offers seven preset business reports: P&L statement, cash flow, A/P by vendor, A/R by customer, job/project, payroll, and balance sheet.
- You can customize any preset personal or business report.

- All reports (including preset personal and business) are based on one of Quicken's main report types: transaction, summary, budget, or account balances.
- You can view and print wide reports by changing the number of characters per line from 80 to 132.
- Reports saved as a disk file can be opened by word processor and electronic spreadsheet programs.
- Filtering allows you to include in your reports only those transactions you specify.

Chapter 11

Quicken Applications

In This Chapter

- *Home inventory*
- *Tracking home repairs and improvements*
- *Tracking investments*
- *Budgeting expenses*
- *Managing rental properties*
- *Business accounting*
- *Managing payroll*
- *Non-account applications of Quicken*

There's practically no limit to the ways you can use Quicken. Although Quicken is primarily a check register program for the home and small business, it's versatility lets you use it to track all kinds of financial records. You can even apply Quicken as a recordkeeper for inventory, stocks, bonds, personal collections (like stamps and coins), and more.

In this chapter you'll discover some interesting uses for Quicken and how to use the program in ways you may not have considered. You'll learn how to use Quicken to inventory your personal belongings (for estate and insurance purposes), how to track investments (including stocks and bonds), how to budget expenses, how to maintain payroll records, and more.

Home Inventory

Take a mental journey through your home, and catalog your personal belongings. Even if you spend hours on this exercise, you'd probably miss thousands of dollars in personal property—a camera that's stuffed away in a closet somewhere, a large record collection that you simply take for granted, summer and fall clothes stashed away in a cedar closet.

In the event of a fire, flood, burglary, or other catastrophe, would you remember about all your belongings and recall their worth? More importantly, would your insurance company reimburse you for personal belongings you say you had, but have no record of?

You can use Quicken to maintain an inventory of everything you own. You can catalog all of your personal belongings in one account, or create several accounts—one for furniture, one for jewelry, one for clothes, and so forth. Figure 11-1 shows an example of a Quicken Other Assets register used to record entries of a video movie collection.

The register lets you record a lot of details about your personal belongings. As shown in the example, you can use the date column to indicate the date of acquisition. If you don't care about when you bought an item—or can't remember—use the current date. The reference column can be used to code each item. If you're creating one large register, for example, you can use the REF column to indicate the type of item being cataloged—JEWEL for jewelry, CLOTH for clothes, COIN for coins in a coin collection, and ELEC for electronic items like keyboards, TVs, radios, and stereos.

The PAYEE/MEMO/CATEGORY column is used to describe the item. Enter a description (e.g., Microwave Oven or Fur Coat) in the top line of the PAYEE/MEMO/CATEGORY column. You can enter an additional description in the second (memo) line.

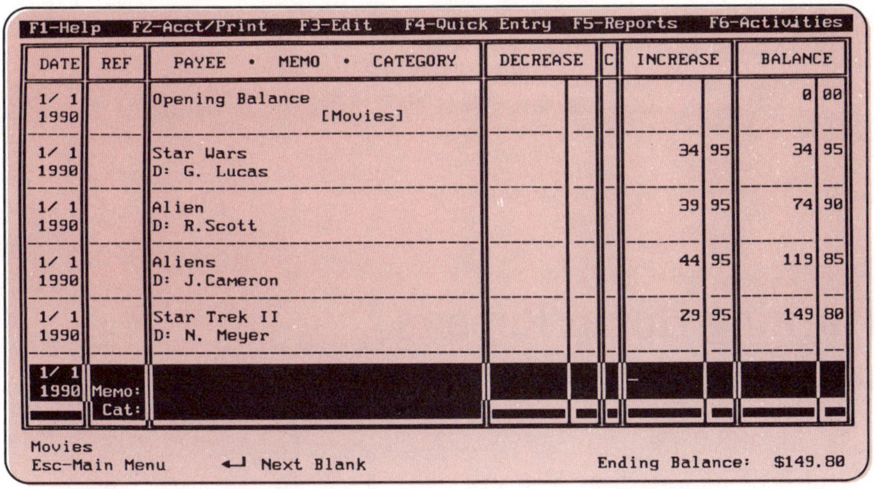

Figure 11-1. This example shows how you can use Quicken to manage personal property, like a collection of science fiction movies on video disc.

The use of categories is up to you. You probably don't need to use categories if you're separating your belongings into individual accounts. If you're compiling one large account that lists all your personal property, you may wish to identify them by using categories and subcategories.

Your personal belongings add to your worth, so enter a value (if appropriate) into the INCREASE column of the register. Use the most accurate value you can; however, you should avoid estimating the value of your property whenever possible. With each major purpose, record the item in the register and enter the price you paid. You should probably keep the receipt, especially if the item is covered by a warranty. If you're cataloging jewelry or collectibles, you may need to consult with an appraiser or obtain current market values from collector's price books. These price books are available at most book stores, antique shops, and public libraries.

If you don't care about the value of the item, but rather just want to catalog it, leave the INCREASE column blank. Quicken will allow you to record a transaction with the INCREASE and DECREASE columns blank.

When you sell or give away a piece of personal property, you should not delete the entry in the register. If you posted a value for the item, replace it with "0.00" so that it won't show up in the Ending Balance for the inventory.

For reference, you can print the register or produce reports, as desired.

Tracking Home Repairs and Improvements

For most of us, our home is our single most important investment. When you bought your house, you knew it would most likely appreciate in value. Depending on where you live and when you bought your property, your house may earn back enough money that your monthly payments are reimbursed. The net result: you lived in your house rent free.

But appreciation doesn't always come swiftly or surely. And taxes often take a big chunk out of any capital gains you may realize on the sale of your home.

One of the best ways to increase the value of your home, while decreasing your taxes when you sell it, is to keep faithful records of your home improvements. Let's say you installed ceiling fans in all three bedrooms, skylights in the living room and entry hall, and new carpeting throughout the house. These items increase the value of your home (beyond the immediate living comfort you enjoy).

By recording them—and keeping receipts as backups—you can deduct their cost from the tax basis when the house is sold. If your profit on the house is $10,000, for example, and these improvements cost $3,500, then you're only taxed on $6,500.

Maintaining accurate records of home improvements also helps in increasing the appraised value of your home. An independent appraiser may tack on just $1,500 for the spa you added, even though it's a deluxe $6,000 model with a $2,000 redwood gazebo. Certain types of home improvements may be tax deductible or offer tax rebates. This includes city or state rebates for solar energy panels, water savers, and so forth. Be sure to catalog these as well.

To track home improvements, create an other assets account and enter each improvement as a separate transaction (see Figure 11-2). Enter the date of the improvement (e.g., the date of completion or the purchase date), a description, and actual cost. If you're adding a substantial upgrade to your house—putting in a family room, for example—use the split transaction feature to catalog the individual costs of the addition. For instance, if the total cost of the addition was $10,000, you might enter $8,700 for labor and materials, $350 for permits, $500 for plumbing hookups, and $450 paint and materials you bought to finish the inside.

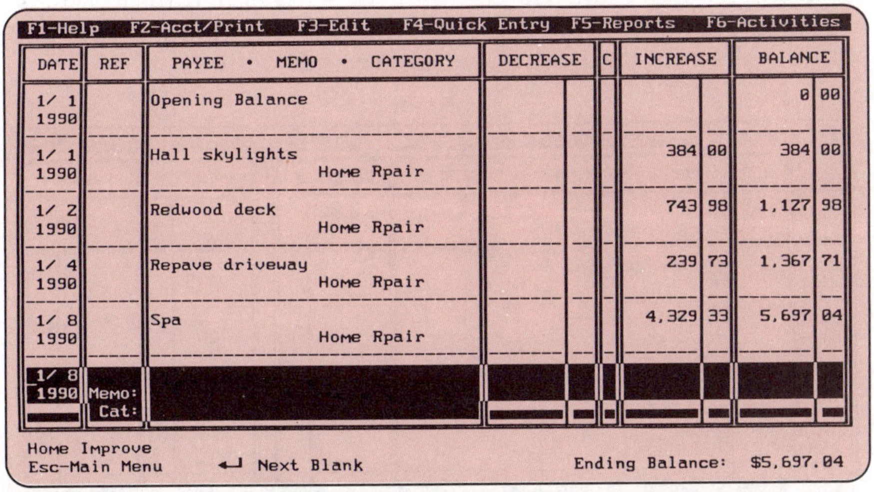

Figure 11-2. A sample register of home improvements.

Repairs you make to your home don't affect its tax basis when you sell it, but major repairs should be recorded. This helps when selling your home and also provides you with an accurate accounting of the cost of maintaining your home. You may find, for example, that the fixer-upper you thought you could affordably turn into a cozy cottage is costing you thousands of dollars more each year to repair and maintain. That information could help you decide if you want to keep the house or look for another that doesn't need so much attention.

Tracking Investments

Your investments can be maintained with Quicken. While Quicken won't tell you when to buy and sell, it will provide an easy and convenient method of managing your personal investment portfolio. The program is ideal for the occasional investor or for someone who invests in long-maturity stocks and bonds.

All investments are managed in a separate other assets account. You should not combine investments, unless they are of a similar nature. For example, if you own stock in 20 different firms, you can get by with cataloging all of them in a single other assets register, as shown in Figure 11-3. Each transaction is a buy or sell order. You can also include dividends, payments, splits, write-offs, and other necessary transactions.

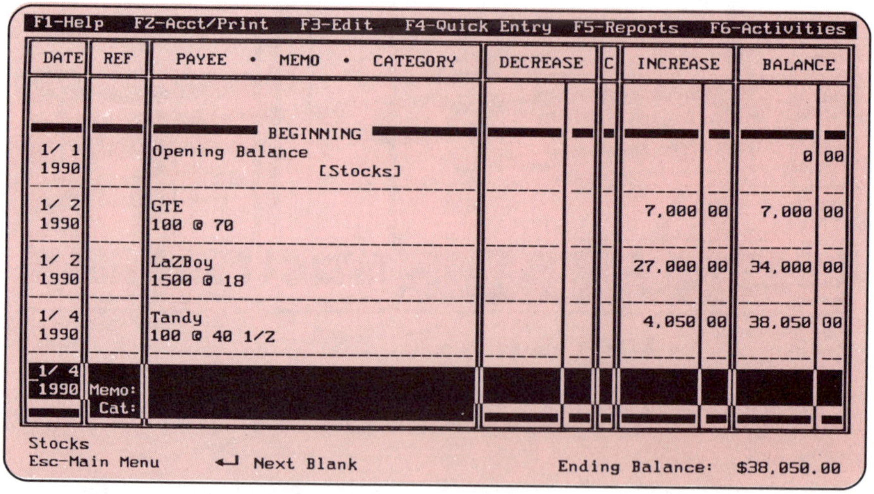

Figure 11-3. Sample stocks, tracked with the help of Quicken.

You should not mix dissimilar investments in one account—stocks, bonds, and CDs, for example. These investments operate differently. They also pay at different times and under different circumstances. For instance, you can usually cash your portfolio of stocks at any time; you may not receive full value for your bonds until maturity, and that may take years. Certificates of deposits, IRAs, Keogh plans, and other investments have different interest structures and repayments schedules. When in doubt, create a separate account for the investment. It's always easier to add an investment to a group than to remove it.

At a minimum, each transaction in the Other Assets register should include the transaction date (when you bought or sold the investment), a description of the investment, and its value. If you've just bought 100 shares of Tandy stock, for example, enter the purchase as shown in Figure 11-4 by providing the date, the description (you may wish to include the per share price in the Memo blank, as shown), and the amount of the transaction.

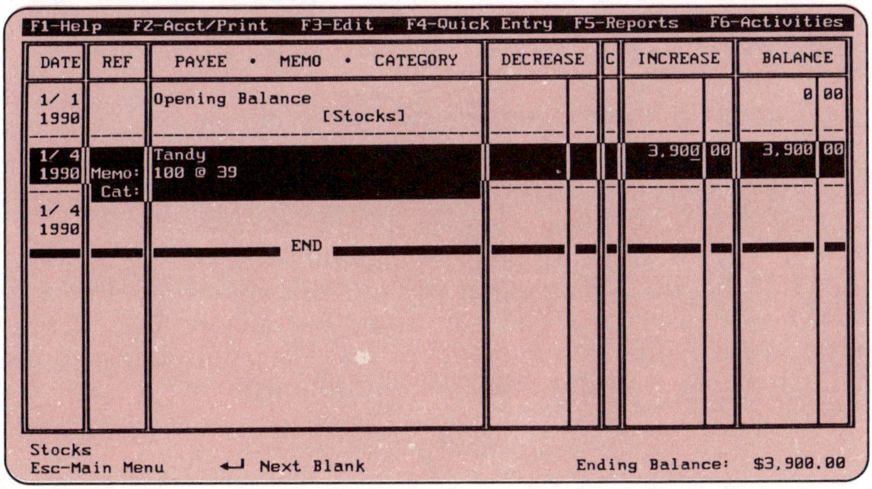

Figure 11-4. Entering a sample stock transaction into the register.

Generally, stock purchases are made in the INCREASE column, and stock sales are made in the DECREASE column. To keep the ending balance correct (showing a positive amount for a profit and a negative amount for a loss), you may wish to enter the same value for the purchase and sale price of a stock, and enter, on a separate line, the realized profit or loss. For instance, as shown in Figure 11-5, you purchased 100 shares of Tandy stock on January 2, then sold it 6 months later. Use the same value for both transactions; the INCREASE and DECREASE amounts cancel each other out. In a separate transaction, enter the amount of money you lost or gained, in the appropriate column.

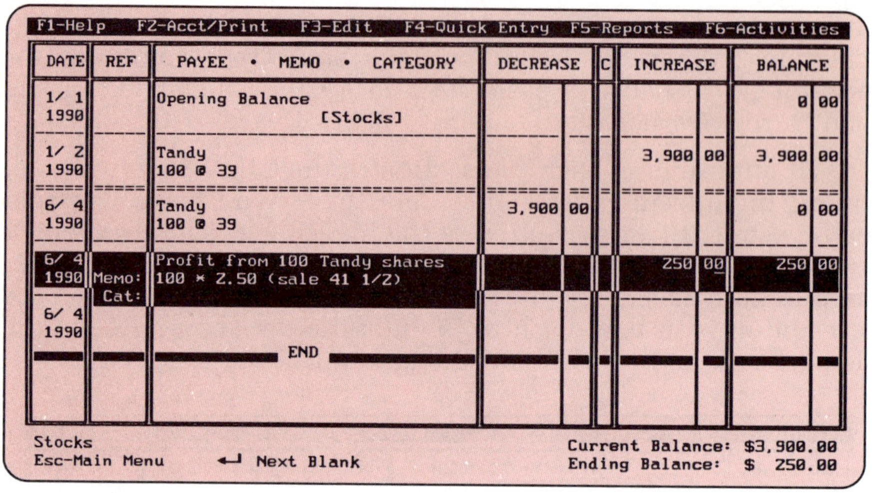

Figure 11-5. Enter separately sale and profit (or loss) transactions for all stocks (and other investments) you sell.

Other types of investments are handled in a similar manner. When tracking investments that pay interest, enter the interest as a separate transaction. You can enter just the interest if you receive regular interest payments or make separate transactions for the repayment of the principal and interest.

Budgeting Expenses

One of the most useful applications of Quicken is using the program as a "watchdog." If you're on a budget (and who isn't?), you can budget your spending and use Quicken's registers and reports to spot over- and under-spending.

The key to budgeting your expenses is to make sure your transactions are categorized (at least the transactions you want budgeted, like food, clothing, and entertainment). Without the categories, Quicken has no way of knowing how you're spending your money.

The monthly budget, one of the five preset personal report types Quicken offers, lets you assign budget amounts to the categories you are using. Before actually printing the report, indicate a monthly budget for those categories (expenses) you want to track. If needed, you can assign a different budgeted amount for each month of the year, as explained in more detail in Chapter 10, "Creating and Printing Reports."

Only those categories that you budgeted will appear in the report. You can have as many or as few budgeted expense categories as you wish. Typical budgeted categories include auto fuel, utilities, dining out, groceries, and home repair and maintenance. Unless you need to keep tabs on them, there's little need to budget for those expenses that are the same every month. This includes rent, mortgage payment, and car payment.

Quicken's budget reports also include income. This is helpful if you supplement your income from other sources or don't get a regular paycheck. In a given month (or other period of time), you can view your total income and note significant peaks and dips.

If desired, you can create custom monthly budgets. To create a custom budget report, choose Budget Reports at the Report menu, and fill in the Create Budget Report window, as shown in Figure 11-6. Indicate the report title and date range for transactions. Also, indicate how you want the columns organized—by week, two weeks, month, year, or none. You can print a report just on currently selected account, on all accounts, or just on accounts that you identify.

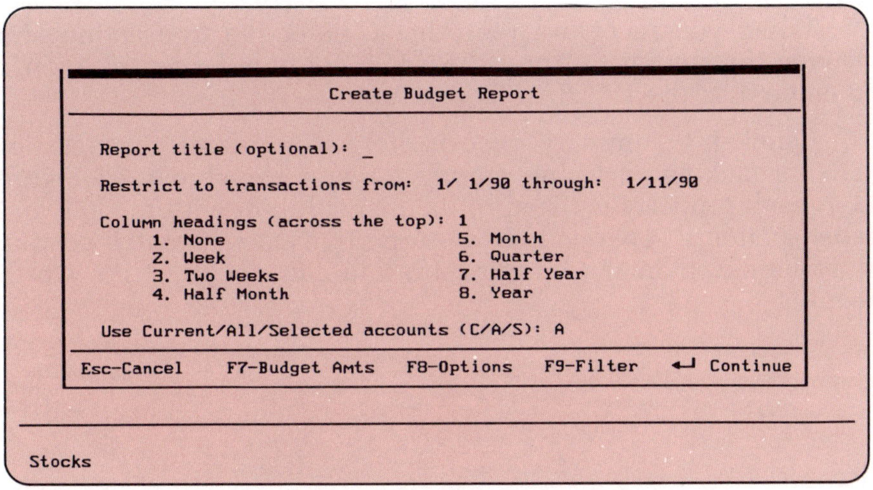

Figure 11-6. The Create Budget Report window.

Managing Rental Properties

If you own real estate that you rent to others, you can use Quicken to keep track of your income and expenses. Each property you own should be maintained in a separate other assets account. If you own an apartment building, one account can track all the units. You'll need to develop a system whereby you can identify each of the apartments, for rental and expense purposes.

You *can* use a single other assets account to manage all your rental property, but you should use classes to readily identify the income or expense of a specific property. For example, suppose you own two office spaces, one on Hyde Street and the other on Jekyll Ave. When entering income and expense transactions, you can refer to these properties as classes:

Rent payment/Jekyll Ave.	Rental income, Jekyll Ave.
Repairs/Hyde St.	Repairs expenses, Hyde St.
Utilities/Jekyll Ave.	Utilities expenses, Jekyll Ave.

As always, you must create classes before assigning them to transactions. You can create classes directly in the Class List window, or when recording the transaction. When recording the transaction, Quicken will note that the class name you've provided doesn't exist; you can add the class to the list or select another from from the list.

When you receive a rent check, enter the transaction and provide the amount in the INCREASE column. Expenses should be entered in the DECREASE column.

Quicken's summary reports help you identify properties that are making or losing money for you. As shown in Figure 11-7, each property is listed in its own column, with income and expense items separated. If a property is consistently costing more money than it's bringing in, you can decide if it's worth keeping.

Income & Expense
1/ 1/90 Through 1/11/90

Rental — Page 1
1/11/90

Category Description	Hyde St	Jekyll Ave	Other	OVERALL TOTAL
INCOME/EXPENSE				
INCOME				
Painting	0.00	245.80	0.00	245.80
Repairs	98.73	233.93	0.00	332.66
TOTAL INCOME	98.73	479.73	0.00	578.46
EXPENSES				
Rent Income	-900.00	-750.00	0.00	-1,650.00
Water, Gas, Electric	-10.98	-9.33	0.00	-20.31
TOTAL EXPENSES	-910.98	-759.33	0.00	-1,670.31
TOTAL INCOME/EXPENSE	1,009.71	1,239.06	0.00	2,248.77
BALANCE FORWARD				
Rental	0.00	0.00	0.00	0.00
TOTAL BALANCE FORWARD	0.00	0.00	0.00	0.00
OVERALL TOTAL	1,009.71	1,239.06	0.00	2,248.77

Figure 11-7. A summary report showing details about rental property.

Business Accounting

In most businesses, accounting is a full-time job. At the very least, it consumes the better part of the day of at least one employee. This time is taken up by preparing invoices, paying bills, and tracking the inflow and outflow of money. Quicken can help speed up the process by automating many of the tasks. You can use the program to set up accounts receivable and accounts payable ledgers, maintain payroll books, and forecast cash flow and cash position.

Accounts payable is money you have to spend, generally to vendors who have extended you credit or provided goods or services. You handle business accounts payable the same as you would a personal checking account, except that Quicken also offers a convenient means to monitor cash flow.

By post-dating checks (entering a date later than the current date), Quicken understands that you want to pay the bill, but may not have the cash to do so right now. The program will tally the amount of money you need to pay the post-dated checks and indicate when you need to have that money (that date is the date posted on the checks).

To get an accurate picture of your accounts payable, you'll want to print frequent reports using the A/P by vendor report selection. This report is preset by Quicken, letting you prepare and print it in seconds. Or, you can customize it, as desired. Chapter 10, "Creating and Printing Reports," provides the details.

Quicken generates A/P by vendor report from information you provide in the Date, Payee, and Amount blanks. You can optionally group the transactions in the report into weeks, every two weeks, and by month (as well as other, less useful settings). Quicken provides a subtotal for each group, as shown in Figure 11-8, as well as a grand total, of all accounts payable due.

Accounts receivable is money you receive from your customers. You can use Quicken to record when you actually get the cash, as well as to monitor cash you have invoiced and expect to receive in the near future. For meaningful accounts receivable management, enter your invoices in a dedicated other assets account. Enter each invoice as a separate transaction.

A/P by Week

1/ 1/90 Through 1/20/90

BUSS-Business
1/11/90

Payee	Week of 1/ 1	Week of 1/ 7	Week of 1/14	OVERALL TOTAL
Bank charges	0.00	-34.76	0.00	-34.76
Bill Computer Shop	-1,498.00	0.00	0.00	-1,498.00
Federal Express	-247.54	0.00	0.00	-247.54
Gorshon Development	0.00	2,500.00	0.00	2,500.00
Northern Stationery	0.00	-45.98	0.00	-45.98
Opening Balance	5,000.00	0.00	0.00	5,000.00
Pacific Leasing Co.	-657.00	0.00	0.00	-657.00
Steel Market Industries	-400.98	-110.83	0.00	-511.81
OVERALL TOTAL	2,196.48	2,308.43	0.00	4,504.91

BUSS-Business
Esc-Create report F1-Help F8-Print

Figure 11-8. Custom accounts payable by week report.

Enter the invoice number in the REF column, or use the Memo blank. The amount of the invoice is entered in the INCREASE column.

As your customers pay their bills and you receive your money, enter the transactions in the receivables account. Payments are posted in the DECREASE column. Use the Category blank to enter the name of the account you're transferring the received money to. For example, if you receive cash and enter it into an account called Bus Checking, enter `Bus Checking` in the Category blank. Quicken will automatically transfer the money as a deposit into the Bus Checking account, as shown in Figure 11-9.

The ending balance in the receivables account indicates the money you have invoiced and is still outstanding. You can use this figure for general cash flow monitoring, but you may desire more accurate cash forecasting. You can use Quicken's A/R by customer report to provide you with a run-down of expected cash, listed by customer. You can group receivables by week, every two weeks, month, and so forth, so you can quickly see how much money is due and when it should come in.

The A/R by customer report shows you how much money you're expecting, but it doesn't tally that money against the money you're spending. You can use Quicken's cash flow reports for a more detailed view.

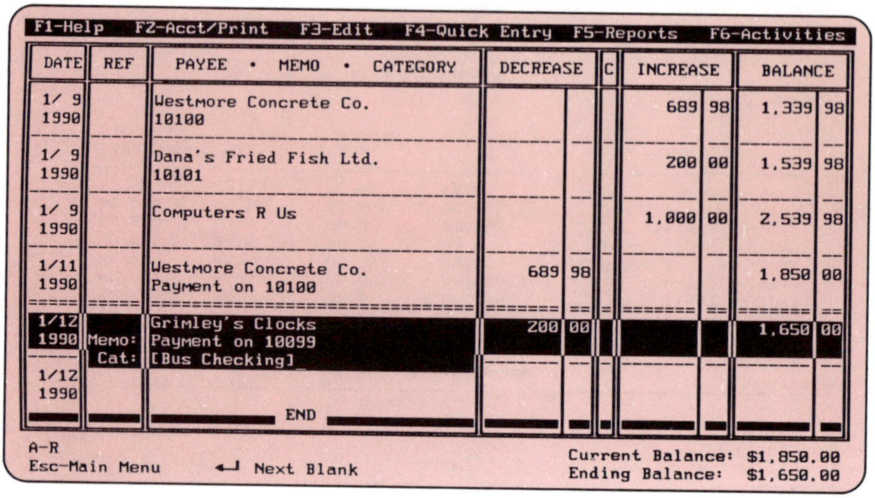

Figure 11-9. You can enter accounts receivable payments and transfer the money to your checking account in one step, by providing a transfer account in the category blank.

Managing Payroll

Payroll is a difficult task for most companies. The task of maintaining accurate payroll records can become so difficult that many firms have outside accounting companies track payroll records; some even prepare the paychecks, using a cash fund established by the employer.

Quicken paves the way to simplifying the payroll task. The journey starts with the creation of a special other liability account, created specifically to contain payroll information. Each transaction is a separate paycheck. Deductions, including federal withholding tax, state tax, social security, union dues, and so forth, are handled as separate categories or additional other liability accounts.

The other liability accounts are used to maintain a record of employee-paid social security (FICA), federal tax withholding, state tax withholding, local tax withholding, union dues, insurance, and so forth. These monies should be kept separately, because they are not part of the general business operating fund and need to be paid to the respective state and federal agencies, insurance groups, and unions.

Paychecks include a number of these categories, so they should be included as a split transaction. For each paycheck, enter the gross pay and any withholding, as shown in Figure 11-10. In a separate transaction, include company-paid payroll expenses, such as employer FICA contribution and medical. These should be listed separately from the split transaction of the payroll check, because they are not deductions from the employee's gross pay. Also, if you're using voucher checks, or checks with a pay stub, the first 16 lines of the split transactions will appear on the paycheck. If you can't avoid entering a split transaction with the paycheck, enter it after line 16 in the split transaction window.

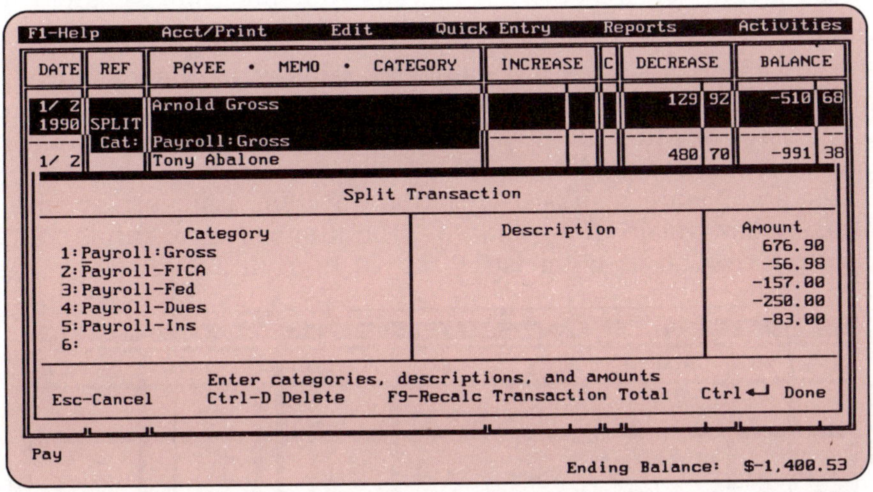

Figure 11-10. A paycheck, split several ways.

The summary, transaction, and payroll reports furnished by Quicken can be an aid in completing W-2 forms at the start of the next calendar year. Quicken will not print the required information in the W-2 forms; you must either do that manually or enter the data Quicken provides into a tax preparation program. Many such programs accept imported data either in the Lotus 1-2-3 PRN or DOS ASCII formats. If the tax preparation program accepts imported data, save your payroll reports as a disk file. If you only have a few W-2 forms to complete, the conversion from

Quicken to the tax program probably won't be worth the effort. But the more employees you have, the more time and energy you will save.

Non-Account Applications of Quicken

While Quicken is expressly designed to be used to manage financial matters, you can also use it as a form of a simplified computer database. You are limited to entering data in the column and row format Quicken imposes on financial transactions, but for many applications, this restriction is of no consequence. Armed with the program's text search features, you can locate specific data records, or groups of data records, in a flash; you can even list them in custom reports.

Inventories (where no value is assigned to the items) is a popular use of Quicken as a database. You can use either an other asset or other liability account; it doesn't matter which if you won't be using the account to tally monetary worth. Use the Payee and Memo blanks to describe the item. Categories can be used, when desired, to classify the item. An example of a Quicken register as database is shown in Figure 11-11.

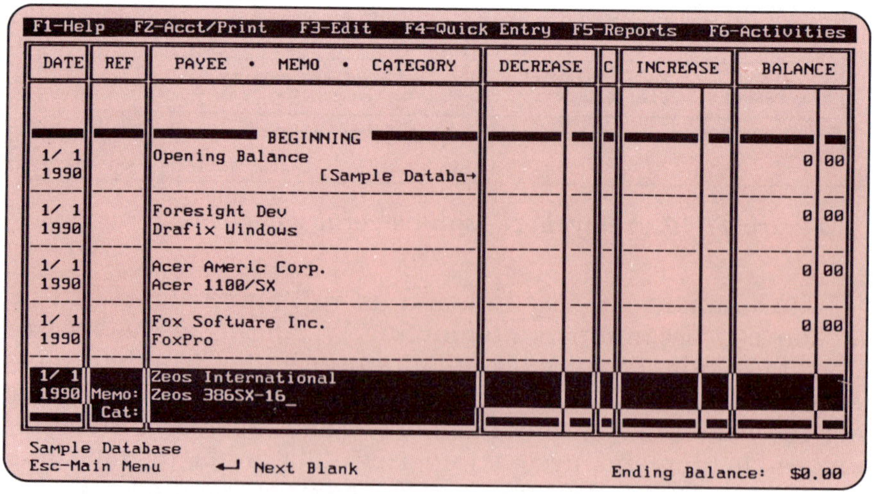

Figure 11-11. An example of using Quicken as a database.

At any time, you can print the database (choose the Print Register command from the Acct/Print menu) or prepare one of the many reports Quicken offers. If you've assigned each transaction to a particular category, you can use the itemized category report to obtain a bird's eye view of the database.

What You Have Learned

This chapter discussed numerous home and business applications for Quicken. Here's what you should have learned:

- You can use Quicken to monitor the inventory in your home, including clothes, jewelry, and electronic items.
- Personal property should be recorded in an other asset account.
- Enter the value of your personal belongings in the INCREASE column of the register. When you sell a belonging, delete the value in the INCREASE column or replace it with a "0.00."
- Recording improvements you make to your home helps decrease its tax basis, which can help you save money when you sell your home.
- Maintaining accurate records of home improvements also helps in increasing the appraised value of your home.
- Investments (e.g., stocks and bonds.) can be maintained in an other assets account.
- At a minimum, each transaction in the other assets register should include the transaction date, a description of the investment, and its value.
- To use Quicken for budgeting expenses, record transactions using categories and identify those categories as budgeted items in the monthly budget report.
- Quicken's checking, other asset, and other liability accounts can be used to maintain accounts receivable and accounts payable registers for business.
- Quicken uses a system of post-dating checks to track future accounts payable cash flow needs.

Appendix A

Standard Quicken Account Categories

This appendix lists the standard categories provided by Quicken. Home and business categories are separated. You can use these categories as is or create your own to fit your needs. You can also edit the standard categories—change the category name, type, description, or tax-time notation.

Standard Home Categories

Category	Type	Description	Tax
Bonus	Income	Bonus income	X
Canada Pen	Income	Canadian pension	X
Div Income	Income	Dividend Income	X
Family Allow	Income	Family allowance	X
Inc Sal	Income	Salary income	X
Int Inc	Income	Interest income	X
Invest Inc	Income	Investment income	X

Category	Type	Description	Tax
Oldage Pen	Income	Old age pension	X
Other Inc	Income	Other Income	X
Auto Fuel	Expense	Automobile fuel	
Auto Other	Expense	Automobile expense	
Auto Repair	Expense	Automobile repair	
Bank Chrg	Expense	Bank charge	
Canada Pension	Expense	Canadian pension plan	
Charity	Expense	Charitable donations	X
Childcare	Expense	Childcare expense	
Christmas	Expense	Christmas expenses	
Clothing	Expense	Clothing	
Dining	Expense	Dining out	
Dues	Expense	Dues	
Education	Expense	Education	
Enter.	Expense	Entertainment	
FICA	Expense	Social security tax	X
Gifts	Expense	Gift expenses	
Groceries	Expense	Groceries	
Home Repair	Expense	Home repair/ maintenance	
Household	Expense	Household misc. expense	
Housing	Expense	Housing	
Insurance	Expense	Insurance	
Int Exp	Expense	Interest expense	X
Invest Exp	Expense	Investment expense	X
Medical	Expense	Medical/dental	X
Misc	Expense	Miscellaneous expense	
Mort Int	Expense	Mortgage interest	X
Mort Prin	Expense	Mortgage principal	
Other Exp	Expense	Other expenses	
Recreation	Expense	Recreation	
RRSP	Expense	Reg Retirement savings	
Subscriptions	Expense	Subscriptions	

Category	Type	Description	Tax
Tax Fed	Expense	Federal tax withholding	X
Tax Other	Expense	Miscellaneous taxes	X
Tax Prop	Expense	Property tax	X
Tax State	Expense	State withholding tax	X
Telephone	Expense	Telephone expense	
Utilities	Expense	Water, gas, electric	

Standard Business Categories

Category	Type	Description	Tax
Gr Sales	Income	Gross sales	X
Other Inc	Income	Other income	X
Rent Income	Income	Rent income	X
Ads	Expense	Advertising	X
Bank Chrg	Expense	Bank charges	X
Canada Pension	Expense	Canadian pension plan	
Car	Expense	Car/truck	X
Commission	Expense	Commissions	X
Enter.	Expense	Entertainment	X
Freight	Expense	Freight	X
Insurance	Expense	Insurance	X
Int Paid	Expense	Interest paid	X
L&P Fees	Expense	Legal/professional fees	X
Late Fees	Expense	Late payment fees	X
Misc	Expense	Miscellaneous expenses	
Mort Int	Expense	Mortgage interest	X
Office	Expense	Office expenses	X
Other Exp	Expense	Other expenses	X
Rent Paid	Expense	Rent paid	X
Repairs	Expense	Repairs	X
Returns	Expense	Returns & allowances	X
Supplies	Expense	Supplies	X

Category	Type	Description	Tax
Taxes	Expense	Taxes	X
Travel	Expense	Travel expenses	X
Utilities	Expense	Utilities/phone	X
Wages	Expense	Wages & job credits	X

Suggested Additional Home Categories (as needed)

Category	Type	Description	Tax
Alimony Inc	Income	Alimony income	X
Alimony Exp	Expense	Alimony expense	X
Cas&Theft	Expense	Casualty & theft	X
Emp Bus	Expense	Employee business exp.	X
Legal	Expense	Legal/professional fees	X
Moving	Expense	Moving expenses	X
Penalty	Expense	Penalty/early withdrawal	X
Tax Prep	Expense	Prof. tax preparation	X
Union	Expense	Union/professional dues	X

Suggested Additional Business Categories (as needed)

Category	Type	Description	Tax
Benefit	Expense	Employee benefit	X
Copy	Expense	Copy/repro expenses	X
Dep	Expense	Depreciable expense	X
Dep Exp	Expense	Depreciation expense	X
Bad Debt	Expense	Bad debt (write-off)	X
Postage	Expense	Postage	X

Index

A

B

C

D

N–O

P

Q

R

S

T

U–V--W

Reader Feedback Card

Thank you for purchasing this book from Howard W. Sams & Company's FIRST BOOK series. Our intent with this series is to bring you timely, authoritative information that you can reference quickly and easily. You can help us by taking a minute to complete and return this card. We appreciate your comments and will use the information to better serve your needs.

1. Where did you purchase this book?

☐ Chain bookstore (Walden, B. Dalton)
☐ Independent bookstore
☐ Computer/Software store
☐ Other ______________________________
☐ Direct mail
☐ Book club
☐ School bookstore

2. Why did you choose this book? (Check as many as apply.)

☐ Price
☐ Author's reputation
☐ Quick and easy treatment of subject
☐ Appearance of book
☐ Howard W. Sam's reputation
☐ Only book available on subject

3. How do you use this book? (Check as many as apply.)

☐ As a supplement to the product manual
☐ In place of the product manual
☐ For self-instruction
☐ As a reference
☐ At home
☐ At work

4. Please rate this book in the categories below. G = Good; N = Needs improvement; U = Category is unimportant.

☐ Price
☐ Amount of information
☐ Examples
☐ Inside cover reference
☐ Table of contents
☐ Tips and cautions
☐ Length of book
☐ How can we improve this book? ______________________________
☐ Appearance
☐ Accuracy
☐ Quick Steps
☐ Second color
☐ Index
☐ Illustrations

5. How many computer books do you normally buy in a year?

☐ 1–5 ☐ 5–10 ☐ More than 10
☐ I rarely purchase more than one book on a subject.
☐ I may purchase a beginning and an advanced book on the same subject.
☐ I may purchase several books on particular subjects.
(such as ______________________________)

6. Have you purchased other Howard W. Sams or Hayden books in the past year? ____
If yes, how many? ______________________________

7. Would you purchase another book in the FIRST BOOK series? ______________

8. What are your primary areas of interest in business software?
   - ☐ Word processing (particularly ______________)
   - ☐ Spreadsheet (particularly ______________)
   - ☐ Database (particularly ______________)
   - ☐ Graphics (particularly ______________)
   - ☐ Personal finance/accounting (particularly ______________)
   - ☐ Other (please specify ______________)

Other comments on this book or the Howard W. Sams book line: ______________

____

Name ______________
Company ______________
Address ______________
City ______________ State ______________ Zip ______________
Daytime telephone number ______________
Title of this book ______________

Fold here

NO POSTAGE
NECESSARY
IF MAILED
IN THE
UNITED STATES

BUSINESS REPLY MAIL
FIRST CLASS PERMIT NO. 336 CARMEL, IN

POSTAGE WILL BE PAID BY ADDRESSEE

HOWARD W. SAMS & COMPANY
11711 N. College Ave.
Suite 141
Carmel, IN 46032-9839